AF618503

Exploring the Organizational Impact of Software-as-a-Service on Software Vendors

INFORMATIONSTECHNOLOGIE UND ÖKONOMIE

Herausgegeben von Christian Becker, Wolfgang Gaul, Armin Heinzl, Alexander Mädche und Martin Schader

Band 55

Sebastian Stuckenberg

Exploring the Organizational Impact of Software-as-a-Service on Software Vendors

The Role of Organizational Integration in Software-as-a-Service Development and Operation

Bibliographic Information published by the Deutsche Nationalbibliothek
The Deutsche Nationalbibliothek lists this publication in the Deutsche Nationalbibliografie; detailed bibliographic data is available in the internet at http://dnb.d-nb.de.

Zugl.: Mannheim, Univ., Diss., 2013

Library of Congress Cataloging-in-Publication Data

Stuckenberg, Sebastian, 1981-

Exploring the organizational impact of software-as-a-service on software vendors : the role of organizational integration in software-as-a-service development and operation / Sebastian Stuckenberg.

page cm

Includes bibliographical references.

ISBN 978-3-631-65153-7

1. Software engineering—Management. 2. Agile software development. I. Title.

QA76.758.S78 2014

005.1068—dc23

2014008879

D 180
ISSN 1616-086X
ISBN 978-3-631-65153-7 (Print)
E-ISBN 978-3-653-04380-8 (E-Book)
DOI 10.3726/978-3-653-04380-8

© Peter Lang GmbH
Internationaler Verlag der Wissenschaften
Frankfurt am Main 2014
All rights reserved.
PL Academic Research is an Imprint of Peter Lang GmbH.

Peter Lang – Frankfurt am Main · Bern · Bruxelles · New York · Oxford · Warszawa · Wien

All parts of this publication are protected by copyright. Any utilisation outside the strict limits of the copyright law, without the permission of the publisher, is forbidden and liable to prosecution. This applies in particular to reproductions, translations, microfilming, and storage and processing in electronic retrieval systems.

This book is part of an editor's series of PL Academic Research and was peer reviewed prior to publication.

www.peterlang.com

Acknowledgements

The process of developing and writing this dissertation was a very challenging endeavor but at the same time an extremely worthwhile and life-enhancing experience. Finishing this research project would not have been possible without the support of a long list of people whom I would like to thank for their individual contribution to this work.

I would like to express my deepest gratitude to Professor Dr. Armin Heinzl, who gave me the opportunity to conduct this research at his Chair of General Management and Information Systems at the University of Mannheim. Professor Heinzl provided me with valuable feedback and guidance not only with regard to my research but also beyond. I am thankful for his encouragement to present my research at national and international conferences and his exceptional support in accounting for life's special circumstances.

For their commitment in serving as members of my dissertation committee, I thank Professor Dr. Irene Bertscheck, Professor Dr. Moritz Fleischmann, Professor Dr. Alexander Mädche and Professor Dr. Martin Schader.

I am indebted to my PACIS Doctoral Consortium advisers Professor Dr. Guy Gable, Professor Dr. Kai-Lung Hui and Professor Dr. Detmar Straub for their valuable feedback on my research and Professor Dr. James Thong for going the extra mile in enabling my participation. I am grateful for the support of the Julius Paul Stiegler Memorial Foundation, the Forschungsförderung of the University of Mannheim and the Federal Ministry of Education and Research in making it possible for me to present my research to an international audience during conferences and research stays. Furthermore, a special thank-you goes to Professor Dr. Christoph Schneider, who invited and welcomed me to a research stay at the City University of Hong Kong.

As this dissertation is based on qualitative data analysis, it relies heavily on the support and insights of experts from industry. I would like to thank every single interview partner for sharing their individual perspective and knowledge with me. My thanks also go to Stefan Beiermeister, Theresa Best, Timm Loser and Patrick Schapfel who made important contributions to collecting, analyzing and discussing the qualitative data of this research. Furthermore, I would like to thank Dr. Erwin Fielt and Dr. Thomas Kude for the valuable discussions and their close collaboration on publishing excerpts of this work.

I am grateful for the fortunate situation that I was able to conduct my dissertation research while being surrounded by close friends. I would like to thank David Geiger, Erik Hemmer, Lars Klimpke, and Sven Scheibmayr for their enduring support and the unforgettable time. My thanks also go to Simon Hubert, Jens Förderer, Tommi Kramer, Tillmann Neben, Marko Nöhren, Christoph Schmidt, Alexander Scheerer, Kai Spohrer and Aliona von der Trenck. Furthermore I want to thank my former colleagues Jessica

Winkler, Miroslav Lazic and Boris Quaing. You all contributed to the great atmosphere in the office and helped to make good times memorable and bad times bearable.

For their administrative support, I want to thank Luise Bühler and Ingrid Distelrath and the student assistants Stefan Eckhardt, Nina Jaeger, Melanie Marnet, Olga Oster, Lea Offermann, Santana Overrath and Kathrin Teupe.

I would also like to thank all of my friends who supported me in writing this dissertation. Thank you for the many wonderful distractions.

I would like to express my sincere gratitude to my family, especially my parents Susanne and Johannes as well as to my sister Katharina and my brother Christian. Thank you for your unconditional support and for providing me with the opportunity and encouraging me to follow my dreams.

Finally and above all, I thank my Louise for her patience, her continuous and loving support and for enriching my life in all respects.

Mannheim, January 2014

Sebastian Stuckenberg

Contents

List of Figures

List of Tables

List of Abbreviations

API	Application Programming Interfaces
ASP	Application Software Provisioning
BI	Business Intelligence
CRM	Customer Relationship Management
ERP	Enterprise Resource Planning
IT	Information Technology
PLM	Product Lifecycle Management
SCM	Supply Chain Management
SDK	Standard Development Kits
TCO	Total Cost of Ownership

1. Introduction

1.1. Problem Statement

Software-as-a-Service describes a software distribution and payment concept that is characterized by a responsibility shift of operations and maintenance activities of software solutions from the customer to the software vendor, together with the introduction of a continuous usage-based pricing scheme (Choudhary, 2007b; Ma, 2007; Xin & Levina, 2008). Software vendors do not only focus on the development of software, but also take care of its delivery to the customer. Customers access the vendor-managed solutions via the Internet by using web browsers (Saaksjarvi et al., 2005). Software-as-a-Service can be classified as the software layer of the overarching Cloud-Computing stack model above the related models of Platform-as-a-Service and Infrastructure-as-a-Service (Weinhardt et al., 2009).

The adoption of Software-as-a-Service solutions by the customer, as well as the number of software vendors offering their solutions in a service mode, has gained significant growth rates over the last years (Merz et al., 2011). Surveys indicate that 71% of the questioned organizations have used Software-as-a-Service solution within the last three years and three-quarter of these organizations plan on increasing their Software-as-a-Service spending (Correia et al., 2012). Software-as-a-Service revenue is expected to grow by 18% in 2012, reaching US-$ 14.5 billion (Mertz et al., 2012). Although certain aspects of the concept are not entirely new and have already surfaced in preceding concepts like Application Software Provisioning (ASP), the recent technological and infrastructure advances have fueled the dissemination of solutions and helped to overcome the pitfalls of previous concepts, for instance, in terms technological capabilities to reach economies of scale (Mäkilä et al., 2010). This positive trend is expected to last and forecasts estimate that two-thirds of all new business applications in enterprises will be cloud-based or deployed in a hybrid model by 2015 (West et al., 2010). The share of organizations that chose the traditional on-premises deployment model for new applications as preferred deployment model shrinks from 50% in 2012 to an expected 13% by 2016 (Guptill, 2012). The Software-as-a-Service concept is therefore considered to sustain high relevance for research and practice.

Despite this promising development, the potential challenges for software vendors are still not yet fully understood. As business models are defined as "the rational of how an organization creates, delivers and captures value" (Osterwalder & Pigneur, 2010), a modification to the business model directly implies a change within the organization and its value creating activities. Hence, a change from the traditional on-premises to the

Software-as-a-Service business model is likely to challenge existing processes and practices of software vendors. These implications may be rather obvious consequences of the changed pricing model of software, like continuous revenues instead of up-front payments (Choudhary, 2007b). But potential implications may also be less evident, for instance, the consequences of the changed cash flow on internal resource allocation. The software product is now embedded in a service offering, with the consequence that the activities of the development and delivery process and the stakeholders involved are different from those of traditional software companies. Software-as-a-Service providers are not only required to develop solutions that satisfy customer requirements, but also need to operate the solution reliably for the customer at a moderate cost level in order to stay profitable, despite the smaller but recurring monthly subscription revenues (Choudhary, 2007b). Vendors are challenged by an additional success dimension, as they need to compete with traditional on-premises offerings not only in terms of functional quality, but also in terms of operational quality (Fan et al., 2009). At the same time, the customer relationship is changing as a consequence of operating the solutions, and vendors now maintain direct relationships to the end-users (Saeed & Jaffar-Ur-Rehmann, 2005). The mentioned aspects alone already provide proof of the potential disruptive character of the Software-as-a-Service concept and stress the importance that software vendors develop an awareness and understanding of the potential implications of the concept.

Previous studies have a focus on providing a definition of the Software-as-a-Service concept (e.g. Luoma & Rönkkö, 2012; Mäkilä et al., 2010; Saaksjarvi et al., 2005) or on discussing its advantages and disadvantages (e.g. Grohmann, 2009; Ma, 2007). Furthermore, the adoption of Software-as-a-Service solutions by customers (e.g. Benlian & Hess, 2010; Xin & Levina, 2008) and a selection of rather technical aspects (e.g. Aulbach et al., 2008; Bennett et al., 2000; Brereton et al., 1999; Turner et al., 2003) are well discussed. Recent studies suggest multiple implications for Software-as-a-Service vendors (e.g. Hao et al., 2012; Joha & Janssen, 2012; Juell-Skielse & Enquist, 2012; Saeed & Jaffar-Ur-Rehmann, 2005). However, both theory and practice are still lacking a clear understanding regarding the nature of these implications. As such, previous findings suggest that Software-as-a-Service providers tend to underestimate these implications and consider minor adjustments to be appropriate to adapt to the new context (Heart et al., 2010).

1.2. Research Objectives

In face of this critical lack of research, the goal of this study is to add to previous literature by providing an in-depth understanding of the organizational implications of Software-as-a-Service for software vendors. This study addresses the following research question:

- *How does the Software-as-a-Service concept impact software vendors?*

The objective is, however, not limited to a pure identification of potential implications, but instead aims on exploring implications in detail to create an in-depth understanding of the Software-as-a-Service context from a software vendor perspective. The knowledge will eventually enable the formation of well-founded suggestions for software vendors developing and operating Software-as-a-Service solutions. Consequently, the outcome of the study shall offer explanatory and predictive value, as classified by Gregor (2006). The research question can therefore be more specifically phrased as:

- *How do software vendors need to adapt existing organizational structures and processes to develop and operate Software-as-a-Service solutions?*

Pursuing the outlined research agenda is expected to contribute to theory and practice. Investigating the Software-as-a-Service concept and its implication for software vendors will benefit not only the body of knowledge on service-based business models, but also on software development in general. It will clarify on the concept and its characteristics and detail direct and indirect consequences for software development and operation. By including a service perspective, the analysis will complement the previous rather technical or software development-driven perspectives and link the extent literature of both fields.

The analysis will provide additional explanation as for why traditional vendors, in particular, are often struggling with Software-as-a-Service and will present empirical observations. This study will furthermore explore the influence of Software-as-a-Service on the value creation of software vendors. It will evaluate the inherent characteristics and causes that account for potential change. Software product and service characteristics will be modeled to the specific context and allow a thorough study of the phenomenon. The result of this study will provide a well-grounded foundation for the development of further theoretical advancement surrounding the Software-as-a-Service concept.

Since this study draws on knowledge that originates in neighboring disciplines, like marketing and product development, and applies it within the software development context, its findings also have implications for the theoretical developments of their original context.

Finally, answering the raised research question will not only benefit the academic discussion, but also provide companies in the field clear guidelines for offering solutions as Software-as-a-Service. The results will help software vendors to establish appropriate structures and processes to respond to arising challenges and capitalize on the given opportunities that come with the concept. Studying the outlined topic is expected to be especially fruitful for vendors that switch or complement their business models with Software-as-a-Service. The analysis of the organizational implications of the Software-as-a-Service concept will increase the awareness of software vendors about crucial aspects within the development and operation of Software-as-a-Service solutions and will enable them to take appropriate measures.

1.3. Research Design

To answer the outlined research objective, the study follows a qualitative research approach with multiple-case studies. This approach is deemed promising in the given setting and to match the raised research question of how the Software-as-a-Service concept influences software vendors (Yin, 2009). Case study research is considered to assist the creation of an in-depth understanding of a phenomena and, thus, matches the objectives of this study (Stone, 1978). The software vendors represent the unit of analysis within the study, putting the focus on an organizational level.

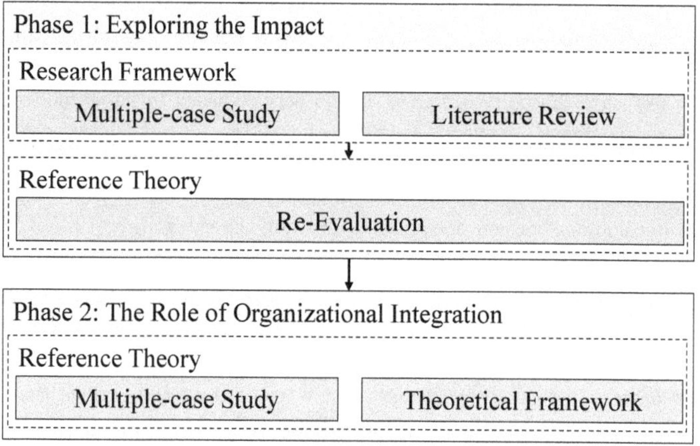

Figure 1.1.: Research approach

The research is organized in two phases that are shown in Figure 1.1. The initial phase aims at exploring the implications of the Software-as-a-Service on software vendors. An explorative multiple-case study, as well as a literature review, are conducted, guided by and structured according to two research frameworks that are taken from the literature. The first phase explores and describes the current practices and issues of Software-as-a-Service vendors. Following Eisenhardt (1989)'s suggestions, the initial phase is taking a broad view on the context with only minimal preconceptions and no specific theory in mind. After a thorough analysis of the collected data and a discussion of the related extant literature, the cases are re-evaluated by using the perspective of an indicated reference theory to support and enrich the findings. The gained knowledge of the Software-as-a-Service context is expected to allow the selection of a more focused aspect of Software-as-a-Service vendors that requires further investigation.

The second phase's objective is to substantiate the knowledge with regard to the focused context. It consists of a second multiple-case study that is guided by reference theory. Drawing on relevant extant theory, the phase aims on developing an in-depth understanding that will ultimately lead to deriving solid suggestions for software vendors developing and operating Software-as-a-Service solutions.

1.4. Study Organization

The structure of this study is following the previously outlined research design and is divided into seven chapters. After this introduction chapter, Chapter 2 lays down the terminological and conceptual foundations of the study. By introducing the key concepts and the context of the study, a shared understanding is created that enables the discussion of the research findings in the main part of the study. The chapter includes an introduction to the software industry, as well as its core offerings of software and accompanying services. The Software-as-a-Service concept is defined and differentiated from related Cloud Computing concepts and earlier variants. The second chapter is closed with a presentation and discussion of extant literature related to the research question.

Thereafter, Chapter 3 introduces the study's research method. The selection of the research strategy is discussed and justified and afterwards specified in detail. The two-staged research approach is described and objectives and procedures of both phases of empirical research are outlined. Lastly, the general data collection and analysis procedure is sketched.

Chapter 4 focuses on the presentation of the findings of the first multiple-case study. Following an introduction of the phase's research framework and case study sample, the findings are introduced. The presentation is structured and guided by the two selected research frameworks and enriched by matching contributions from extant literature. The findings are discussed and conclusions for the second phase of empirical research are deduced.

Within the fifth chapter, the findings of the second multiple-case study are showcased. In congruence with the structure of the presentation of the first case study, the chapter first provides the applied research framework and case study sample, followed by the key findings and their discussion.

Chapter 6 provides an in-depth discussion of the findings. The results from both empirical phases are combined and discussed to draw a holistic picture on the organizational implications of the Software-as-a-Service concept. The contributions to theory and practice are outlined and limitations of the research are provided. The study ends with an outlook and suggestions for future research.

2. Terminological and Conceptual Foundations

Within this chapter, the basic concepts of this study are introduced in order to lay down a shared foundation for discussing the research design and the findings from the empirical phases in the subsequent chapters.

In order to investigate the implications of the Software-as-a-Service concept on the software industry and software vendors in particular, it is required to have a shared understanding of the Software-as-a-Service concept itself and the context of software vendors. Therefore, this chapter provides an introduction to the enterprise software industry and its common principals and stakeholders. Moreover, a definition of the Software-as-a-Service concept is given and previous work on the implications of the Software-as-a-Service concept on the software industry and software vendors in particular are outlined.

2.1. The Software Industry

In order to develop a basic understanding of an industry and, thus, be able to evaluate changing trends of innovations on the industry, Messerschmitt & Szyperski (2003) suggest that it is required to be aware of the main stakeholders, their products and offering, and their interconnections. This section will, therefore, first discuss the key products of the software industry and their characteristics. Afterwards, the main stakeholders of the software industry are introduced before selected specifics of the software industry, which are frequently discussed in the relevant literature are presented.

2.1.1. Characteristics of Software and Services

The major offering of stakeholders of the software industry are based on software products or accompanying services. The following section will provide a brief introduction to the key characteristics of first software followed by services.

Software

Software subsumes programs and other operating information that are used by computers (Hansen & Neumann, 2007, p. 361). According to Heinrich et al. (2004), two different perspectives of software maybe taken. Software can be regarded as code that can be processed by machines as well as source code that can be understood by individuals (Heinrich et al., 2004, p. 603). Various classifications exist to differentiate types of software. Common once are for example the separation by license model into commercial or open-source software, by level of standardization into standardized and customized software, by target group into horizontal and vertical software or by architecture level (Heinrich et al., 2004; Stickel, 1997). A classification by architectural level, for instance classifies software solutions into different groups based on the architectural layer of software systems they provide functions to. Figure 2.1 shows a stack model for enterprise application software that is based on Grove (1996). A distinction can, for instance, be made between system

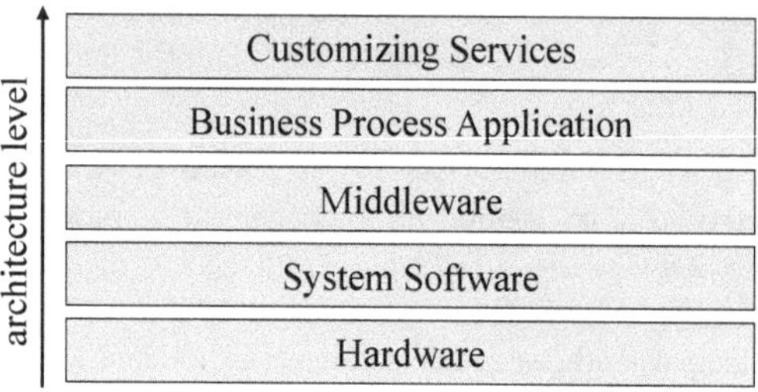

Figure 2.1.: Stack model of enterprise application software by Grove (1996)

software that is a prerequisite for the operation of a computer and application software or more specifically business process application software that aims on solving or supporting a specific task or business process. The latter can be further decomposed into standard and individual software. Standard application software aims on fulfilling the requirements of a large and mostly anonymous group of users while individual software is developed for the specific requirements of a single customer (Heinrich et al., 2004, p. 603). The further focus is on standard software, as Software-as-a-Service is considered to belong to this category (Buxmann et al., 2008). The requirements that are satisfied by standard application software are considered to represent the shared requirements of a large user group. The basis for their elicitation are often surveys and market studies but also discussions with key customers (Heinrich et al., 2004, p. 625). The objective is to develop a standard application software solution that satisfies a broad set of different requirements and thus allows targeting a large customer segment.

The main advantage of standard application software for software vendors is the possibility to spread development costs among different customers. This is not possible with individual software, as the resulting solution of an individual development is often so closely linked to the specific requirements of that specific customer that it has only little value to other organizations (Messerschmitt & Szyperski, 2003). The development cost for individual application software, therefore, has to be covered by this client. In addition, standard application software solutions are readily available, often of a higher maturity level and of higher quality. Due to the further development of the software vendor, they are also considered more future proof than individual software (Hansen & Neumann, 2007, p. 376).

The main disadvantages of standard application software for the customer are the limitations with regard to the ability to adjust the solutions to satisfy individual requirements

(Stickel, 1997, p. 670). Adjustments to the solutions are called *customizing* (Heinrich et al., 2004, p. 161). Different forms can be distinguished that mainly differ in the degree of change to the original solution (Brehm et al., 2001). Solutions often provide the ability to change different sets of parameters to allow for a different behavior of the solution without the requirement to make changes to the actual source code (Mertens, 2001, p. 435). This basic form of tailoring a solution to satisfy individual customer requirements is termed *configuration*. Compared to the alteration of source code, it ensures the solution to remain maintainable without running into conflict when executing solution updates (Brehm et al., 2001). Although different forms of customization may be executed by customers, the adjustment is often very time and cost intensive (Stickel, 1997, p. 670).

This study specifically looks at business application software which is commercial standard application software that allows integrating transaction-oriented data and business processes throughout an organization (Markus & Tanis, 2000). Examples are enterprise resource planning (ERP) systems that consolidate information, for instance with regard to inventories, that is spread across different units of an organization into an integrated information system (Chellappa & Saraf, 2010; Heinrich et al., 2011; Mertens, 2007). ERP systems assist organizations, for instance, with material management, production management, finance and accounting, or human resources (Buck-Emden & Galimow, 1996). Other business application software that is extending the core functionality of ERP systems are for instance, business intelligence (BI), customer relationship management (CRM), product lifecycle management (PLM), and supply chain management (SCM) solutions (Buck-Emden & Galimow, 1996; Heinrich et al., 2011).

Across the different classifications, software commonly shares a set of key characteristics. First of all, software is of immaterial nature and is not subject to any form of abrasion (Heinrich et al., 2004, p. 603). Using a software solution does not result in wearing it out. Instead, abrasion-like effects are based on the underlying infrastructure not being appropriate for changing demands, an insufficient data management or changing customer requirements for the solution (Messerschmitt & Szyperski, 2003). Due to software's immaterial nature as a digital commodity, software can easily be reproduced. The reproduction costs are low and the reproduction process does not result in a loss of quality of the reproduced unit compared to its original (Buxmann et al., 2008, p. 1). To reproduce the software, a digital copy of the source code is created that represents an exact copy of the original. As this process mainly requires a storage media and some processing power, the reproduction of software is not subject to quantity limitations (Buxmann et al., 2008). Therefore, software can be sold to multiple customers. The reproduction costs can be neglected and the development costs for a software solution being distributed on all customers (Messerschmitt & Szyperski, 2003). This easy reproduction procedure, however, bears the risk of unauthorized copies that are distributed outside of the software vendors' control and without reimbursing the vendor for the development costs (Reavis Conner & Rumelt, 1991).

The digital nature of software allows vendors to offer different variations and packages to different customer segments. These may, for instance, differ in feature scope. Software packages with fewer features may be sold to a different customer segment with less sophisticated requirements at a lower price, while packages with the complete feature set or specific key functions can be sold to customers with higher willingness to pay for the related benefits (Buxmann et al., 2013).

Services

Representing the highest layer in the software stack model introduced within the previous section, services have been an elementary component of the software industry even before service models like Cloud Computing and Software-as-a-Service emerged. Therefore, the following section will provide a definition of services and briefly discuss their role in the software industry.

With regard to services, the literature suggests different types of definitions. Corsten (2001) mentions the enumerative definition that defines services by providing examples, the negative definitions by providing examples of offers that are not considered to be services, and the definition by using constitutive criteria. Research mainly relies on definitions that use criteria to describe services, as only these are able to create common ground for an evaluation and discussion (Bullinger & Schreiner, 2006). Constitutive criteria that are frequently cited are intangibility, inseparability of production and consumption (simultaneity) or the existence of an external factor in the fulfillment phase. Derived from these, the literature discusses further aspects like an uncertain outcome in terms of quality or value before consumption, the often longer and more continuous relationship of providers and customers, the heterogeneity of services as they often require human interaction, or their perishability (Bodendorf, 1999; Jaw et al., 2010; Zeithaml et al., 1985).

Intangibility refers to services not being able to be perceived by senses and presents one of the most commonly attributed characteristics of services, but at the same time also one that is well criticized (Lovelock & Grummesson, 2004; Sampson & Froehle, 2006; Vargo & Lusch, 2004). Critics refer to the fact that service may well have a tangible aspect as they may be executed on a physical object of the customer (Sampson & Froehle, 2006), e.g., the service of washing a car. However, this object is not a necessity and services may as well rely on skills or know-how that cannot be perceived and the quality of which are difficult to estimate by a customer prior to the service consumption (Cloninger & Oviatt, 2006; Zeithaml et al., 1985).

Simultaneity describes the service characteristic that the production and consumption of services happen at the same time and, thus, is very often used interchangeably with inseparability (Zeithaml et al., 1985). Production in the service context covers all activities of the service provider required to offer the specified service. Though this may exclude a pre-production of some components, the capabilities required to provide the service need to be generated in the moment the customer is consuming the service. Consumption stands for the satisfaction of the value proposition linked to a service. From a customer perspective, the value of a service therefore is not created when the underlying components and pre-products are created, but in the moment the provided service capabilities are used.

Perishability refers to the situation that excess capacity and idle capacity that is not used by service requests but still generated by the vendor are wasted. The involved service capabilities cannot be stored for later use. An empty seat in an airplane, for instance, cannot be sold anymore once the airplane commenced on its journey. Heterogeneity refers to the characteristic that services differ and are adjusted to the requirements and participation of the customer.

Services may fulfill these criteria to different degrees (Cloninger, 2004; Cloninger & Oviatt, 2006). Cloninger & Oviatt (2006) suggest that organizations' offerings may be placed on a continuum for the different criteria to determine the offering's service content. Table 2.1 provides a questionnaire that organizations may use to measure the service content of their offers. The "+" and "-" in the table indicate whether a positive response to a question is increasing or decreasing the service content.

Other used criteria of the literature, like the existence of an external factor or uno-actu principle, are connected with the previous described criteria. The existence of an external factor within the service process may, for instance, also be described by the simultaneity criteria, it is partly responsible for the heterogeneity, and the missing of an external factor results ultimately in the perishability. The use of different criteria to describe service may result in a varying emphasis on specific aspects. For instance, referring to the existence of an external factor may emphasize an outcome perspective as it highlights the importance of integration capabilities of the service customer to take advantage of the service (Büttgen, 2002; Corsten, 2001).

Similarly, Bullinger & Schreiner (2006) move away from relying on a selected number of criteria and introduce four dimensions to describe and define services. These dimensions describe the capacity, the process, the outcome, and the market of a service. The capacity dimension focuses on the provider's ability to provide the service in terms of the required service infrastructure. The process dimension describes the actual service process and how the interaction with the customer is realized. The outcome dimension describes the changes performed on an object or the customer as a result of the service execution. The market dimension addresses aspects with regard to the commercial viability of a service (Bullinger & Schreiner, 2006). The earlier presented constitutive criteria continue to play a role in the different dimensions. The capacity dimension, for instance, is closely linked to the service characteristics of heterogeneity and perishability, as the service providers infrastructure needs to be capable of handling demand fluctuation and the limited ability to store services for later use (Bullinger & Schreiner, 2006). Therefore, the dimension can be utilized to ease and structure the description of services but they cannot act as a discrete and exhaustive definition.

Next to the definition by constitutive criteria and the breakdown into different service dimensions, a third stream of literature is discussing a Unified Service Theory to eliminate the definition problems. Sampson & Froehle (2006) argue the presence of customer input as a necessary and sufficient condition to define a production process as a service process. Three types of customer inputs are identified in the literature: the customer's self, a tangible object of his, or information (Wemmerlöv, 1990). Similar to the discussion about

Table 2.1.: Service content measure of Cloninger & Oviatt (2006)

	Measure	+/-	Source
Intangibility	Your firm's products or services consist of:		
	Manufactured products or assembled goods	-	Definition of manufacturing
	Specialized skills, tasks, efforts, or performances	+	Definition of services
	Mechanical skills, installation, repair, or maintenance	+	Hirsch (1993)
	Professional skills, know-how, or design tasks	+	Erramilli & Rao (1993): asset specificity
	Reports, audits, manuals, or documents	+	not specified
	Videos, software, or technical or industrial films	+	not specified
Simultaneity	Your firm's products or services are produced:		
	Through face-to-face communication with the customer	+	Clark et al. (1996): interaction coefficient
	Working without contract or communication with the customer	-	Hartman & Lindgren (1993)
	For export at a location removed from the customer	-	Erramilli & Rao (1993)
Perishability	Your firm's products or services can:		
	Be stored for later use without becoming outdated	-	Hartman & Lindgren (1993)
	Have delivery be delayed without being replaced or reproduced	-	Hartman & Lindgren (1993)
	Require a customer to wait for delivery	+	Definition of perishability
Heterogeneity	Your firm's products or services are:		
	Customized for the individual customer	+	Hartman & Lindgren (1993), Erramilli & Rao (1993)
	Standardized for all customers	-	Hartman & Lindgren (1993), Erramilli & Rao (1993)
	Independent of differences in individual skills, firm facilities, or equipment	-	Definition of heterogeneity
	Variable due to differences in individual skills, firm facilities, or equipment	+	Definition of heterogeneity

the external factor, a customer may take a central part in the co-production of the service and a service may require the customer's physical presence to be performed. The service of a hair-cut can be seen as an example. A service may also take a customer's physical object as an input. A logistics service, for instance, takes an object of the customer's belonging and changes its location based on the customer's requests. Lastly, a customer's input can be based on information that is provided by the customer. A consulting service, for example, relies on the information of the customer to provide context specific assistance. Based on this, the Unified Service Theory is defined as: *"With service processes, the customer provides significant inputs into the production process. With manufacturing processes, groups of customers may contribute ideas to the design of the product, but individual customers' only participation is to select and consume the output. All managerial themes unique to services are founded in this distinction"* (Sampson, 2001, p. 16). The latter statement is referring to this service definition approach being able to describe other service management concepts and frameworks of the literature, including the previously discussed constitutive criteria. Heterogeneity is, therefore, based on variations within the customer input and simultaneity as a result of the necessity of customer's just-in-time input (Sampson, 2001). The perishability of services capacity is induced by significant elements of production not able to begin before the customer's input is present. Sampson (2001) clarifies that the perishability is limited to the service capacity that cannot be stored, but he points out that the customer's input can well be stored, for instance, in the form of waiting queues. Sampson & Froehle regard the common constitutive criteria as symptoms of customer input and see the Unified Service Theory as generalization of existing knowledge (Sampson & Froehle, 2006). Even though Sampson & Froehle use the term "theory", the missing explanatory character of their core idea limits the concept to a service definition approach. This service definition is consolidating existing views and refines the approaches for a precise service definition. For an evaluation of the implications of a shift from products to services, a look at the symptoms may, however, yield more detailed aspects and should therefore not be neglected.

Within the software industry, three types of services can be distinguished: IT supported services, IT complementing services, and integrated hybrid products (Böttcher & Meyer, 2004). For IT supported services, IT in general and software in specific marks a necessary component of the service delivery (Meyer & Van Hussen, 2008). Examples are telecommunication services that rely on information technology to be executed. Consulting and maintenance services are examples of the second type, the IT complementing services. These services increase the value of the IT solution, for instance, by assisting the user of an IT solution. They are not directly based on IT but on knowledge about a specific IT artifact. The last type of service includes solutions that consist to equal parts of IT and services (Böttcher & Meyer, 2004). Cloud Computing and Software-as-a-Service are examples of this type and, thus, this type of IT service is a central part of this study.

2.1.2. Characteristics of the Software Industry

After gaining a basic understanding of the characteristics of the products and services of the software industry, the following section will introduce key participants of the industry and will provide an overview of economic principles of software and its surrounding industry. Different organizations with various business models can be counted as stakeholders in the software industry. Figure 2.2 provides a partition of different groups of stakeholders based on the software value chain (Messerschmitt & Szyperski, 2003, p. 174). Following

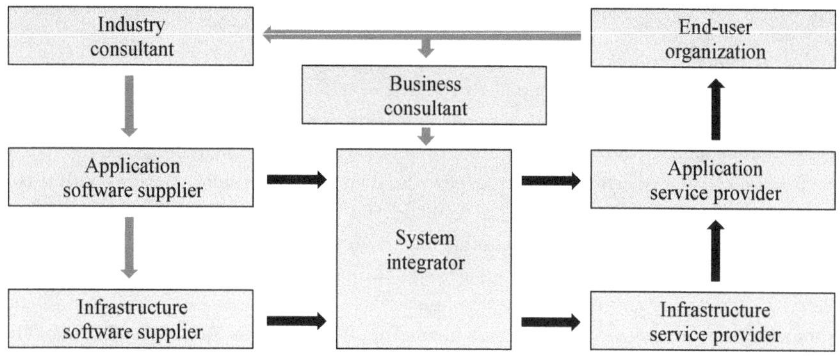

Figure 2.2.: Partition of the software industry by Messerschmitt & Szyperski (2003)

the distinction into different architectural layers of software, Messerschmitt & Szyperski (2003) distinguish between organizations focusing on services, application software, or infrastructure. A second determination is made between organizations focusing on development, integration, or operation. Organizations may have business units concerned with multiple of these segments but especially smaller organizations are often focused on a single segment (Messerschmitt & Szyperski, 2003). As shown in Figure 2.2, both, the infrastructure as well as the application software layer includes organizations that are focused on the development as well as on the operation of software and infrastructure. System integrators specialize in the provisioning of integrated solutions that may consist of multiple application software and the required infrastructure to operate them. The emergent capability is based on the proper integration of the different components into a tested package (Messerschmitt & Szyperski, 2003). On the service layer, industry and business consultants are active. The first are concerned with the needs of all firms, the latter are offering assistance in implementing application in the specific context of an end-user organization. The required knowledge is based on past experience from similar projects. While system integrators are focused on technological aspects, business consultants address organizational issues and customer needs (Messerschmitt & Szyperski, 2003).

As this study aims on investigating the implications of Software-as-a-Service, in particular on software vendors, it is focused on the application software suppliers. Buxmann et al. (2013) distinguish software vendors in a broader and narrower sense as illustrated in Figure 2.3. The latter concentrates on the development of software while the software vendor in the broader sense also addresses later phases of the software life-cycle, for instance the implementation of a software solution at a customer side or the operation of a software solution for the customer (Buxmann et al., 2013, p. 8). In Buxmann et al.'s classification, infrastructure and application software supplier can be considered software vendors in a narrower sense, while the remaining participants depicted in Figure 2.2, except of the end-user organization, are software vendors in the broader sense.

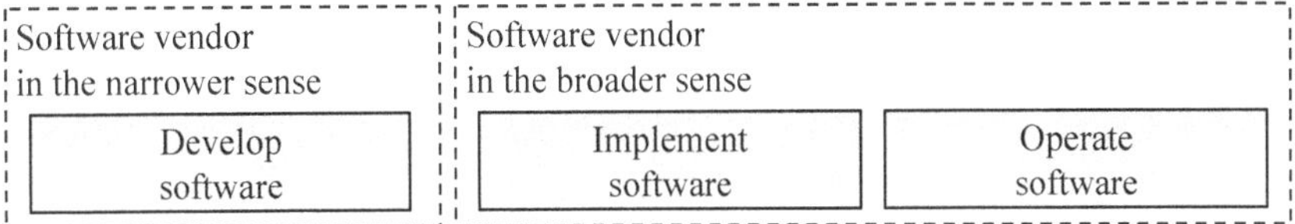

Figure 2.3.: Two types of software vendors based on Buxmann et al. (2013)

Regardless of the form of classification, all participants of the software industry are exposed to different economics of software. Comprehensive overviews of such economic principles may also be found in Buxmann et al. (2013), Engelhardt (2008), Messerschmitt & Szyperski (2003), and Stelzer (2004). Two frequently discussed economic principles of the software industry are network effects and lock-in costs. Both of these economic principles are briefly introduced in the following sections, since they highlight the complexity of the connected and interdependent value creation within the software industry.

Network Effects

The software industry is influenced by network effects that lead to the value of a software solution to be dependent on the actions of other organizations (Buxmann et al., 2013; Messerschmitt & Szyperski, 2003). Next to the stand-alone value, e.g. the usefulness of the offered software functions, value may be induced by other users using the same solution. For instance, a word processing solution may generate value by allowing an organization to create letters that are later printed and sent, but value may also be generated by the ability to save documents in a digital format and exchange these with other users that use the same solution and are, therefore, able to open the saved documents. The literature distinguishes between direct and indirect network effects (Bansler & Havn, 2002). Direct network effect refers to the effects of more users using a specific solution, while indirect network effect is based on the interdependence with complementary offerings (Buxmann et al., 2013). A broad adoption of a specific solution in the market may lead to the emergence of other organizations offering complementary service for this specific solution. The value of a solution for the customer may benefit as, for instance, a customer can take advantage of complementing consulting services that ease the implementation of the complemented solution. In the business application software market, this aspect has led to the emergence of large partner networks around business application software vendors (Baldwin & Clark, 1997; Evans et al., 2006; Messerschmitt & Szyperski, 2003).

Lock-in and Switching Costs

Not entirely unrelated to the described network effects, lock-in phenomena and switching costs play a role in the relation between customers and software vendors. A lock-in into a vendor's offering can be based on the described network effects, as data stored within software solutions may only be accessed by compatible solutions. If a customer's business partner relies on a specific solution, a customer may be required to use the same solution and cannot switch except to a compatible solution. A lock-in may also be based on a customer's data being stored in a specific format that may only be read by a selected vendor's solution. Customer may therefore be force to stick to a compatible solution or try to transform the data at potentially high cost. These effects are even greater in the case when the software vendor applies proprietary instead of open standards (Messerschmitt & Szyperski, 2003).

Replacing a software solution can result in substantial switching costs that exceed the costs of licensing and implementing the new software solution (Messerschmitt & Szyperski, 2003). These additional costs are based on required changes on other architectural layers induced by the new solution. Software may, for example, require different hardware and servers to be operated or may require additional user training and consulting services to prepare the end-users for the new solution. Also, as different standard applications may be based on different business processes, a replacement may lead to business process re-engineering or reorganization (Messerschmitt & Szyperski, 2003).

The previous section provided a brief overview of selected economic factors of the software industry and introduced its main stakeholders. The description indicates potential problems and challenges that firms entering this industry are likely to be faced with. The industry is affected by network structures and common solutions typically have various interconnections with other products and services as well as with their respective vendors and providers. Similar to new solutions, it can be expected that the Software-as-a-Service concept and its emerging offerings face similar challenges. In addition to these adoption related aspects, the question whether the Software-as-a-Service concept is influencing and changing the existing structures and business models has to be answered.

2.1.3. Software Delivery and Payment Models

The subsequent sections provides more detailed information with regard to the different delivery and payment models used within the software industry to distribute, operate, and charge for the offered software solutions.

Software Delivery and Operation Models

Software can be distributed to the customer and be operated in different ways. Dimensions to differentiate between different models are, for example, the management responsibility or location of an application. Software can be operated internally at the side of the customer or externally in the data center of a third-party. For the internal operation, the distribution of software is either done using a physical storage media or via a network-based download (Messerschmitt & Szyperski, 2003). While the first requires traditional inventory, warehousing and transportation, the latter relies on a network connection. For initial setup, a physical installation media, like a DVD, may avoid large downloads, but network-based distribution can provide updates easier and in a shorter time-frame with lower distribution costs (Messerschmitt & Szyperski, 2003). External operation generally requires the delivery of the software via a communication network from the external data center to the customer side.

A second dimension is the management responsibility that varies between the customer/ end-user organization being responsible for the operation of a software solution and the operation responsibility being transferred to a third-party. In the first case, the IT department of the client organization is operating the software solution internally on its own server infrastructure or externally on third-party servers. In the latter case, the responsibility to operate a software solution is outsourced to an external provider that takes care of the operation on the premises of the customer or in its data center.

External operation responsibility can be further broken down based on the type of software operated and the operating party. General outsourcing, application software provisioning, and Software-as-a-Service are examples of delivery and operation models that can be distinguished this way. While outsourcing in general describes the use of external agents to perform one or more organizational activities (Dibbern et al., 2004), the other two concepts can be regarded as special forms of operation responsibility outsourcing. Key differentiators are the mode of licensing and the underlying software architecture. Application software provisioning is concerned with the provision of standard application software over the internet to a customer. The software, however, does not necessarily need to be designed for a network-based delivery model and generally applies a one-to-one approach (Gupta & Herath, 2005; Tamm & Günther, 2005). In a one-to-one approach, one software solution and its underlying infrastructure is operated by a provider for one customer (Dimitrakos et al., 2003; Riedl, 2005). Software-as-a-Service solutions on the other hand are operated by the respective software vendor and specifically designed for online delivery in a one-to-many approach. The software solution and its underlying infrastructure may serve multiple customers simultaneously.

Software Pricing

Revenues of traditional software vendors come from mainly two streams: licenses and services (Buxmann et al., 2008). Maintenance and consulting services take up a major share of the service revenues. Customers who have bought a software license normally pay a monthly service fee for the provision of support, updates and small enhancements. These maintenance services are priced at typically around 20% of the license value and constitute a continuous and predictable source of revenue for software vendors (Buxmann et al., 2013). These maintenance service revenues may over the long term exceed the revenues from licenses and, therefore, represent an important source of revenue for software vendors (Choudhary, 2007b). A second group of service revenues results from consulting services that are often offered by software vendors, for instance, to advise the customer in implementing its software solutions or to train end-users and IT staff. The pricing of these services are typically based on flat-fees or the time used, for instance by the number of consulting days (Buxmann et al., 2008).

The second stream of revenues is license revenue and the price paid by a customer to obtain the rights to use a software vendor's software solution. Different models for software pricing exist in the market (Table 2.2). Bontis & Chung (2000) and Ferrante (2006) provide a comprehensive overview of different models applied. Due to the discussed low reproduction costs of software, pricing models are based on demand and value rather than costs (Buxmann et al., 2013; Shapiro & Varian, 1998). The traditional models cover the packaged, perpetual, or trial model. These are often linked to a single user or machine and may require the user to purchase additional technical support, patches, and version updates for a predefined period of time (Ferrante, 2006). Trial models generally allow a customer to test a solution for a limited time of typically 30 to 60 days and do not require the purchase of a license (Buxmann et al., 2008; Ferrante, 2006). The newer models are based on subscriptions or usage and are gaining popularity in recent years (Ferrante, 2006). With subscription-based licensing, the customer purchases a license for a fixed term and is normally provided with updates to the licensed software. The model was originally implemented by anti-virus software vendors. Usage or utility-based licensing models take the actual usage of the customer as a basis for the pricing of the solution (Ferrante, 2006).

In comparison to these general models of software licensing, Lehmann & Buxmann (2009) have collected a much more detailed list of various parameters of pricing models for software products. As shown in Table 2.3, these parameters can be divided into six perspectives providing variations in terms of the way the prices are formed, the frequency of payment, the billed unit, forms of price discrimination, types of bundles, and dynamic strategies.

With regard to the billing unit, Lehmann & Buxmann (2009), e.g., list usage-based, and usage-independent billing units. Transactions, storage and time belong to the usage-based billing units, while named user, concurrent user, server/ machine, CPU, master data, sites, production volume, and key performance indicator are considered usage-independent billing units. Table 2.3 demonstrates the numerous possibilities of software vendors to differentiate software pricing. The discussed software characteristics of low reproduction and variation costs open up additional opportunities to differentiate prices not

Table 2.2.: Common software licensing models (Ferrante, 2006)

Model	How it works
Packaged	Single license purchased for a single user or machine. Traditionally sold as out-of-the-box software.
Perpetual	Permanent licenses purchased upfront. Examples include node-locked, user-locked, or unlocked.
Trial	Users able to try software before purchasing.
Server (per CPU)	Number of processors running determines number of licenses purchased.
Network-based	Uses a centralized system to distribute licenses to network users.
Subscription-based	License purchased for some time period.
Utility-based	Customer charged according to time product used (pay per use).

only between different software solutions but also between bundles, variants or different customers' willingness to pay (Buxmann et al., 2013).

The low reproduction cost, in addition, leads to a much higher profitability of the license revenue model compared to the revenues from services. The reproduction costs can be neglected and result in a profitability of up to 100%. Services on the other hand require a much higher level of individual work and interaction that reduces the profitability (Buxmann et al., 2013).

The previously introduced variations of delivery and pricing models already provide a first indication of specific characteristics of the Software-as-a-Service concept. For a comprehensive evaluation of the implications of the concepts on the software industry and software vendors in particular, however, a much more detailed understanding is required. Thus, the subsequent section will provide a detailed definition of the Software-as-a-Service concept.

2.2. Software-as-a-Service

The common understanding of the Software-as-a-Service concept has matured over the last years. There are still varying definitions used (Table 2.4), but the key criteria of the concept are shared. Mäkilä et al. (2010) empirically tested seven criteria and showed that although even Software-as-a-Service vendors apply different configurations, the core idea can be found in all companies.

In general, Software-as-a-Service can be seen as a software delivery and pricing model of software vendors. The delivery model is characterized by the software solution being operated and maintained by the software vendor itself (Heart et al., 2010; Xin & Levina, 2008). The vendor takes over activities that previously resided within the responsibility

Table 2.3.: Parameters of pricing models for software products (Lehmann & Buxmann, 2009)

Price formation	Price determination	- *Cost-based* - *Demand-oriented* - *Competition-oriented*
	Degree of interaction	- *Unilateral, not interactive* - *Interactive*
Payment flow	Single payment	
	Recurring payments	- *Frequency* - *Duration*
	Hybrid forms	
Billing unit	Number of price components	
	Usage-based	- *Transactions* - *Storage* - *Time* ...
	Usage-independent	- *Named users* - *Concurrent users* - *No. of servers or machines* - *CPU* - *Financial KPIs* ...
Price discrimination	First-degree	
	Second-degree	- *Quality* - *Time* - *Versioning*
	Third-degree	- *Based on buyer category* - *Based on region*
	Multi-dimensional	
Price bundling	Offer	- *Pure bundling* - *Mixed bundling* - *Unbundling*
	Product type	- *Software* - *Maintenance* - *Service/support*
	Degree of integration	- *Complementary* - *Substitutive* - *Independent*
	Price level	- *Additive* - *Superadditive* - *Subadditive*
Dynamic pricing strategy	Penetration strategy Follow-the-free strategy Skimming strategy	

of the customer and extends its area of responsibility beyond development activities to operations and maintenance. Standardized applications are provided with low customer-specific integration or installation work (Luoma & Rönkkö, 2012; Mäkilä et al., 2010). The pricing model is based on a continuous service relationship between the customer and the software vendor. Deviating from the traditional model of licenses, the Software-as-a-Service pricing schemes are based on time or usage dependent billing units (Choudhary, 2007b; Mäkilä et al., 2010; Saaksjarvi et al., 2005). The previously charged continuous maintenance and support service fees are in general embedded in the subscription fee (Cusumano, 2008). The duty of payment persists as long as a company is subscribed to the service. Subscription contracts mostly do not involve a long term commitment (Luoma & Rönkkö, 2012).

The Software-as-a-Service concept can be separated into the two building blocks: software and service. Both provide a unique perspective on the concept and emphasize on different characteristics. For this reason, the subsequent sections will discuss the characteristics of service and product separately, starting with the service characteristics as these constitute a major differentiator of the concept.

2.2.1. Software Service Characteristics

The actual service of Software-as-a-Service vendors is the direct provision of software capabilities to the end-user. This is combined with the promise to continuously enhance and extend the functionality, as well as the take-over of activities previously required to generate such software capabilities in-house by the customer or via alternative service models out of the formerly provided program-code. The value proposition of Software-as-a-Service suggests the final offering to be a service with software as a pre-product within the service process. The software component is, therefore, an enabler of the service that supports the provision of the proposed application functionalities in the moment of service consumption.

With regard to the service characteristics, the previous introduction of services in section 2.1.1 has already introduced common constitutive criteria like intangibility, the inseparability of production and consumption (simultaneity) or the existence of an external factor in the fulfillment phase. These typical service characteristics and corresponding problems can also be found in the Software-as-a-Service context. Heterogeneity, for instance, is reflected in the variance in the customers' solution scope and usage intensity. Different customers subscribe to different software modules and use them at different times with differing intensities. This leads to a variance in demand and thus in required processing capabilities of the service infrastructure. Simultaneity or inseparability of production and consumption is reflected by the requisite of a Software-as-a-Service vendor to produce the required software capabilities using the software artifact and the server infrastructure in the moment the service is consumed by the customer. As a result, the software vendor is responsible for the development and operation of the infrastructure underlying the service and the required pre-products, such as the software artifact (Saak-

Table 2.4.: Selected definitions of Software-as-a-Service in the literature

Source	Definition
Saaksjarvi et al. (2005)	*"Software as a Service is time and location independent online access to a remotely managed server application, that permits concurrent utilization of the same application installation by a large number of independent users (customers), offers attractive payment logic compared to the customer value received, and makes a continuous flow of new and innovative software possible."*
Choudhary (2007a)	*"SaaS is different from traditional software licensing, which involves the buyer's purchasing a perpetual use license from the software publisher and then making additional investments for hardware, installation, and maintenance. In contrast, in the SaaS model, users buy a subscription to the software and the software publisher (seller) runs and maintains the software on his own hardware. Users with current subscriptions can obtain access to the software using the Internet."*
Ma (2007)	*"Under the SaaS, the software system and users' data are stored off-site in a central location run by the vendor. The vendor delivers the bundle of IT infrastructure, software applications, and services to users through a network. Users pay a fee per transaction."*
Sun et al. (2007)	*"Software as a Service is a software delivery model, which provides customers access to business functionality remotely (usually over the internet) as a service. The customer does not specially purchase a software license. The cost of the infrastructure, the right to use the software, and all hosting, maintenance and support services are all bundled into a single monthly or per-use charging."*
Xin & Levina (2008)	*"A standard piece of software is owned and managed remotely by the vendor and delivered as a service over the Internet. The application is based on a single set of common code and data definitions and distributed in a one-to-many manner to all clients."*
Heart et al. (2010)	*"SaaS is a software application delivery model where a software vendor develops a web-native software application and hosts and operates (either independently or through a third party) the application for use by its customers over the Internet. Customers pay not for owning the software itself but for using it."*

sjarvi et al., 2005; Stuckenberg & Heinzl, 2010). The external factor also takes a special role in the fulfillment of a Software-as-a-Service vendor's value proposition. First of all, not only has the customer to be able to understand the features to generate value out of them, also the vendor needs to be aware of the customers' specific requirements in the moment of consumption of the solution in order to assist them in achieving the purpose associated with using the solution.

Software-as-a-Service fulfills the typical characteristics of services. An evaluation of the concept's potential impact on software vendors should therefore also include a service perspective. Instead of referring specifically to service characteristics, the Software-as-a-Service literature rather describes aspects and forms of the provided service as characteristics of the Software-as-a-Service concept. Software-as-a-Service provider, for instance, take over the responsibility for the operation and maintenance of the offered solutions (Heart et al., 2010; Manford, 2008; Mäkilä et al., 2010) and promote the service with the promise to continuously enhance and extend the provided solutions (Olsen, 2006; Saaksjarvi et al., 2005; Saeed & Jaffar-Ur-Rehmann, 2005).

2.2.2. Software Product Characteristics

The software artifact takes up a central role within the Software-as-a-Service concept. As a pre-product to the service process, its design and development is part of the capacity dimension of the service and part of the required service infrastructure. Its operation is part of the service delivery to the customer. When addressing the characteristics of Software-as-a-Service, the literature lists various methods and technologies that refer to the software artifact. Software product characteristics also refer to typical software functionality that can be found in Software-as-a-Service solutions. The following section will present such software product characteristics that are frequently attributed to the Software-as-a-Service concept.

With regard to the software component, the literature mentions a few typical technologies and approaches in conjunction with the Software-as-a-Service concept. For instance, it is being used through a web browser and has a high level of standardization (Mäkilä et al., 2010; Olsen, 2006; Saeed & Jaffar-Ur-Rehmann, 2005). Special emphasis is also put on the user interfaces to allow high usability without the need for special user training (Luoma & Rönkkö, 2012). Implementations rely on multi-tenancy architectures (Aulbach et al., 2008) and may adopt service-oriented architectures (Turner et al., 2003).

The architecture of Software-as-a-Service solutions marks an important differentiator to previous concept, like application software provisioning, and represents a crucial component of a scaling business model. Carraro (2006) presents an architecture maturity model that illustrates the development stages of the Software-as-a-Service architecture (Figure 2.4). In the first level, named "Ad-hoc" or "Custom" by Carraro, every customer is using a dedicated instance and server infrastructure. These instances may be adjusted and customized to the specific requirements of the respective customer. The second, "configurable" level, standardizes the used instance. Although every customer is still using dedicated hardware, the software instances are identical copies and customization is limited to predefined configuration possibilities. The third and fourth levels represent multi-tenancy architectures. The fourth level is further enhanced by a load balancer to provide better scalability. On these levels, every customer uses the same instance on the same hardware. In case of the highest maturity level, the hardware may be virtualized to allow further scalability (Carraro, 2006).

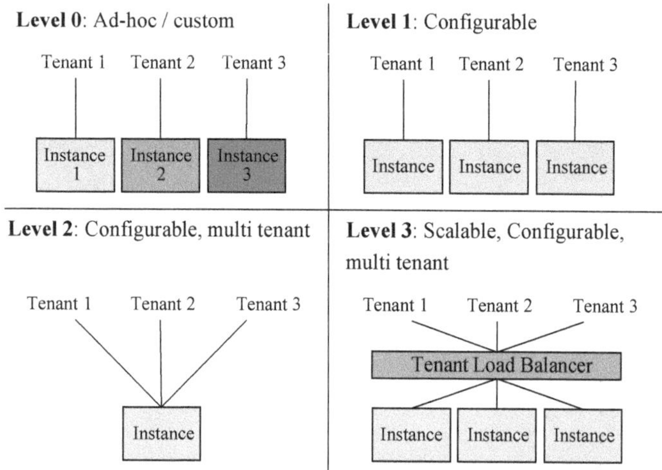

Figure 2.4.: Software-as-a-Service architecture maturity model by Carraro (2006)

Software-as-a-Service vendors rely on multi-tenancy architectures to increase resource utilization and keep operation costs low. Multiple customers are using the same instance of an application on the same infrastructure, allowing the operating cost to be spread among all customers (Aulbach et al. 2008). The costs are kept low, as no customer specific modifications to the source code are allowed that may run into update conflicts and increase the maintenance costs of the Software-as-a-Service vendor (Brehm et al., 2001; Grohmann, 2009). The use of a multi-tenancy architecture does not represent a necessity in implementing the Software-as-a-Service concept, but it is supporting vendors and, therefore, is regarded as supportive characteristics of Software-as-a-Service (Stuckenberg & Beiermeister, 2012).

Further characteristics that are commonly discussed in conjunction with the Software-as-a-Service concept can be derived from the literature (Stuckenberg & Beiermeister, 2012). Standardization, for instance, is mentioned by different authors (Mäkilä et al., 2010; Olsen, 2006; Saaksjarvi et al., 2005; Saeed & Jaffar-Ur-Rehmann, 2005, e.g.). According to these authors, Software-as-a-Service solutions should not only balance the requirements of a broad customer base by providing a core of shared features, but also need to address the specific demands of organizations to adapt the system to their own business processes. Classified as standard application software (Buxmann et al., 2008), solutions still need to provide sufficient levels of tailoring possibilities, like configuration or workflow programming that do not change any source code (Brehm et al., 2001) and, thus, do not conflict with a potential multi-tenancy approach. Solutions may rely on fine granular modules and components, as decomposing the application into smaller components increases the flexibility to adapt to changes or to specific customer requirements (Saeed & Jaffar-Ur-Rehmann, 2005). Lastly, the use of web technologies is linked to Software-as-a-Service solutions being accessible from anywhere without any extensive installation on client-side (Heart et al., 2010; Manford, 2008; Mäkilä et al., 2010; Stuckenberg & Heinzl, 2010). Therefore, the user interface of Software-as-a-Service solutions is commonly based on open web standards, providing users with the ability to access the application with a standard web browser.

2.2.3. Related Concepts

Software-as-a-Service is part of the encompassing Cloud Computing concept (Weinhardt et al., 2009). It represents the software layer in the Cloud Computing stack model (Figure 2.5). Cloud Computing is defined as *"a model for enabling convenient, on-demand network access to a shared pool of configurable computing resources (e.g. network, servers, storage, applications, services) that can be rapidly provisioned and released with minimal management effort or service provider interaction."* (National Institute of Standards a. Technology, 2011). The provided Software-as-a-Service definition is in line with this more general definition and Software-as-a-Service is considered a subcategory of Cloud Computing including solutions that focus on the computing resource *software*.

The two other concepts depicted in Figure 2.5 address lower levels of the architectural stack. Platform-as-a-Service solutions are focused on providing a middleware for developers to develop and operate software. Developers do not have to deal with issues like scalability as the platform takes care of these aspects (Weinhardt et al., 2009). The platform provides standardized application programming interfaces (API) and standard development kits (SDK) to ease development of applications that integrate into other solutions (Espadas et al., 2008). Software-as-a-Service providers use Platform-as-a-Service to provide the end-user organization and the partner network with a possibility to extend their existing Software-as-a-Service solutions. Infrastructure-as-a-Service is located at the lowest level of the Cloud Computing stack. Computing resources that are offered on this level are mainly storage and processing power (Weinhardt et al., 2009).

Due to their shared characteristics, the three concepts in practice often rely on each other. For instance, Software-as-a-Service and Platform-as-a-Service solutions may facilitate the resources provided by Infrastructure-as-a-Service to gain scalability. Even if the infrastructure is provided internally, similar technologies and approaches are used, but deployed in a private mode and not marketed to external parties (Yang & Tate, 2012). Therefore, an analysis of the implications of the Software-as-a-Service concept on software vendors cannot neglect the lower architectural Cloud Computing concepts.

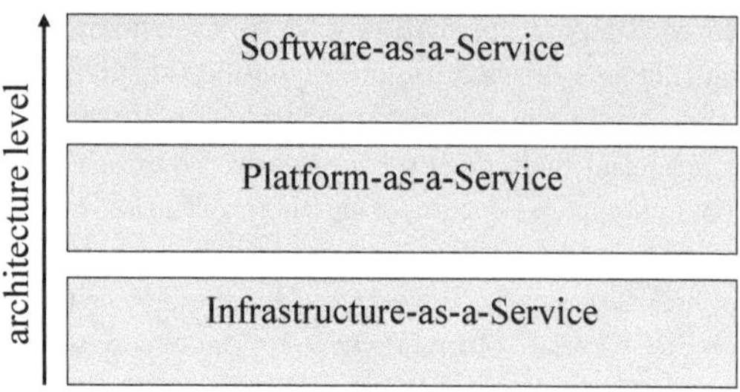

Figure 2.5.: Cloud Computing stack model

While the previously described concepts differ in the computing resource, related concepts also exist on the same architectural level. Application Software Provisioning, as discussed earlier, can be seen as a similar delivery model to Software-as-a-Service (Dimitrakos et al., 2003). Carraro (2006) argues that Application Software Provisioning represents a predecessor of the Software-as-a-Service concept of lower maturity, for instance in terms of the applied software architecture.

Luoma & Rönkkö (2012) differentiate Software-as-a-Service and ASP on a continuum between scalable and customer-specific approaches. They base their work on a cluster analysis of the Finnish software market and 172 firms. Next to the pure-play Software-as-a-Service business model, they introduce an Enterprise Software-as-a-Service model, which describes firms that address enterprise customers with complex software and complement this with integration and training services. The pure-play Software-as-a-Service model is characterized by the software being used through a web browser, a high level of standardization, a pricing model based on actual usage, low customer-specific integration or installation work, low customer-specific user training requirements, automated online purchasability and subscription contracts without long term commitment (Luoma & Rönkkö, 2012).

2.3. Previous Work on Implications of Software-as-a-Service

Although there is a considerable amount of extant literature on Software-as-a-Service and Cloud Computing, only a small number of contributions have addressed the implications of Software-as-a-Service on the software industry and software vendors in particular. Research is focused on defining the concept itself, discussing its applicability in terms of advantages and disadvantages for different stakeholders, and analyzing the adoption of the concept by customers (Juell-Skielse & Enquist, 2012; Stuckenberg et al., 2011). The implications for software vendors are broadly neglected. Existing research that takes a vendor perspective is often taking a technical perspective and is discussing specific technologies and tools.

The following section presents extant work on implications of Software-as-a-Service within the Information Systems literature that takes an industry or vendor perspective. Literature that addresses specific aspects of a vendor's business model like the implications for software pricing or development processes is discussed in combination with the findings of the exploratory field study in Chapter 4. This approach was chosen to allow a better comparison of the empirical observations with focused parts of the literature. The review of relevant literature was approached following the hermeneutic circle (Boell & Cecez-Kecmanovic, 2010). This approach was considered to be appropriate to study a relatively new phenomenon like Software-as-a-Service and also to safeguard the continuous inclusion of relevant emerging publications. A structured approach as suggested by Webster & Watson (2002) or Kitchenham (2004) was deemed not suitable due to the novelty of the study's context and the pace of new contributions emerging. For the same reason a limitation of the search to specific outlets and search terms was considered to provide too many constraints for the exploratory character of this study (Boell & Cecez-Kecmanovic, 2011).

2.3.1. The Industry Perspective

Recent additions to the Software-as-a-Service literature have studied the implications of the Software-as-a-Service delivery and pricing concept on practices and stakeholders of the software industry.

Cusumano (2008) transfers the trend to move towards service revenues in other industries to the software industry. Based on a database of 500 software companies with an average of 10 years of data for every firm, Cusumano analyzes trends and issues of the software industry. Three challenges are identified by Cusumano (2008): Finding the right mix between product and service revenues, finding new services that complement existing products, and finding more efficient ways to deliver services. The latter two challenges are termed "servitizing products" and "productizing services". The first highlighting the growing importance of services and their interplay with products. The latter is referring to the profitability problem of services, and standardization and automation are considered solution approaches (Cusumano, 2008). Software-as-a-Service is not the focus of the study and it was not explicitly considered in the data collection process, but it is seen as a part of the trend towards services. The challenges may therefore remain valid for the Software-as-a-Service context as vendors with existing on-premises software offerings need to find appropriate ways to introduce new service-based offerings, while these offerings are also needed to be delivered in an efficient way. In addition to the core service, supporting services gain importance as an accelerator for the transition towards the service model (Mohammed et al., 2010).

Contributing to the first and second challenges of Cusumano (2008)'s study, Luoma & Rönkkö (2012) analyze the Software-as-a-Service model based on a cluster analysis of the Finnish software industry. They apply the business model ontology of Osterwalder (2004) to structure their research. Though their literature review is rather limited, their data set allowed them to cluster different business models of the software industry on a continuum between scalability and customer-specificity. The results show the emergence of different variations of Software-as-a-Service business models and are considered to assist vendors in gaining a better understanding of the variations and their consequences.

On an industry level, Hilkert et al. (2010) study the implications of the "as-a-Service"-paradigm and compare two software ecosystems with CRM offerings. They assume that the paradigm shift will result in changes for all involved market players. They expect an intensified competition, with customers of Software-as-a-Service offerings being able to choose from a wider variety of software at lower prices. Due to a declining role of integrators, costs for integration and configuration will decrease. Their results are based on two case studies with expert interviews conducted with two vendors of CRM solution applying the Software-as-a-Service model. Next to interviews with managers of the software vendors, leading employees of partnering independent software vendors and system integrators are included in their data.

From an even broader perspective, Leimeister et al. (2010) analyze the Cloud Computing value network and identify different stakeholders of the industry and their changing role. They identify different new roles that emerge due to the increased service orientation of the software industry. New opportunities arise from Cloud Computing platforms that allow to offer new services and the growing integration requirements for such services (Leimeister et al., 2010). They call for more research on the client and provider perspective as Cloud Computing leads to challenges on an operational, as well as strategic business level that are yet to be investigated.

2.3.2. The Software Vendor Perspective

As this study aims on investigating the implications of Software-as-a-Service, particularly on software vendors, the extant literature applying a vendor perspective is of special interest. Existing work can be divided into those that focus on the business model of software vendors and those that analyze internal capabilities. Studies with a narrower focus, for instance those that discuss single processes or technologies of software vendors, will be presented in Chapter 4.

The potential scale of implications of the Software-as-a-Service concept on software vendors has been shown by Joha & Janssen (2012), Juell-Skielse & Enquist (2012), and Stuckenberg & Heinzl (2010). Joha & Janssen (2012) argue that there is a lack of Software-as-a-Service business model studies. They build on preliminary results of this study, published in Stuckenberg et al. (2011), and suggest eight design choices (Table 2.5) that are important in designing Software-as-a-Service business models, considered from a user perspective. These are based on an evaluation of two Software-as-a-Service customer organizations and derived from their case data by using the unified business model framework of Al-Debei & Avison (2010). Their results provide a starting point for the evaluation of implications of the Software-as-as-Service concept, but the authors agree that further research is needed (Joha & Janssen, 2012). The request for more research with regard to the Software-as-a-Service business model is also supported by Weinhardt et al. (2009). They offer a classification of different business models at different architectural layers and conclude that new business models and related research are required.

Juell-Skielse & Enquist (2012) collect a list of opportunities and challenges of the Software-as-a-Service concept for users and providers, which is based on the existing literature and a conducted field study. The focus is set on ERP solutions that are offered as Software-as-a-Service. The results are based on a field study with eight pairs of users and providers, together with an additional provider without matching user perspective. Identified implications are the opportunities to address new markets and more predictable revenue flows at a potentially greater profit. Service development is challenged by changing contractual agreements and the complexity of development of multi-tenant effective applications (Juell-Skielse & Enquist, 2012). The authors provide a broad list of potential opportunities and challenges, but do not give out further details to most of the identified implications. The list may increase the vendors' awareness of specific problems, but it is not prioritized and does provide only limited indications in preparing vendors to overcome the outlined challenges.

Table 2.5.: Design choices for Software-as-a-Service business models by Joha & Janssen (2012)

Design Choice	Description
SaaS service characteristics	Characteristics in terms of the complexity and required security, influencing whether a SaaS solution is suitable and how it needs to be designed and managed.
SaaS value source	Value in terms of the benefits that are anticipated, influencing the way the SaaS services need to be implemented and monitored.
SaaS user target group	The target group is influencing to what degree the services can be standardized and how much customization is required.
Data architecture configuration and tenancy model	The architecture is influencing the required level of security and robustness of the SaaS solution and which standards can be used.
SaaS governance and demand/supply management core competencies	These competencies are influencing the way the SaaS delivery model is designed and managed.
Cloud deployment model	The model is influencing the extent the clouds underlying the SaaS services can be outsourced and shared with other organizations.
SaaS integration and provider strategy	Strategies are influencing the way the SaaS provider(s) and application portfolio have to be managed with regard to the SaaS policy,technology, standards, tools and governance.
SaaS pricing structure	Pricing is influencing the power balance with the SaaS service provider(s) and how the costs are charged and managed internally.

Focusing on software vendors' capabilities, Heart et al. (2010) study the vendors' readiness to deliver Software-as-a-Service. Qualitative and quantitative research methods were used and a total of five interviews and 37 responses to a questionnaire were included in the data set. The data was analyzed by using an innovation classification and the Seven Fundamental Organizational Capabilities Model. The questioned companies perceive Software-as-a-Service as evolutionary innovation, rather than a revolutionary one, and, therefore, do not employ radically new business processes. The analyzed data however indicate a mismatch between perceived and indirectly measured capabilities; such mismatch therefore questions this classification. This is further supported by the SAP employees Bandulet et al. (2010), who regard Software-as-a-Service as a disruptive innovation in the enterprise application market based on the argument that the concept fulfills the characteristics of disruptive innovations defined by Christensen (1997). In the case Software-as-a-Service is regarded as a disruptive or revolutionary innovation, changes not only to limited aspects of a business model, like a new pricing model, but also to the business models as a whole can be expected. Disruptive innovations challenge existing models and processes and ask for existing knowledge to be re-evaluated and adapted to the new setting (Christensen, 1997). The studies by Heart et al. (2010) and Bandulet et al. (2010) provide strong indications for the Software-as-a-Service concept to have profound implication for software vendors' business models and applied practices. At the same time, a mismatch between the perception of software vendors and the literature on the disruptive character of Software-as-a-Service can be observed. Therefore, the studies emphasize the call for further research in this context.

After evaluating different opinions and discussing the pros and cons of the Software-as-a-Service concept, Manford (2008) is also convinced that the concept offers a valid value proposition, which is fundamentally different to anything that proceeded it and as a consequence seen to require different skills and knowledge at software vendors. Especially the shifting responsibility for the software operation, together with the increased complexity of multi-tenant applications, is seen as the drive for change (Manford, 2008).

Fan et al. (2009) and Choudhary (2007a,b) argue from the pricing model perspective and model competition between Software-as-a-Service and on-premises vendors using analytical mathematical models. Vendors are challenged by an additional success dimension. The quality dimension of Software-as-a-Service vendors includes not only functional quality, but also operational quality. Thus, Software-as-a-Service vendors are exposed to a competition with traditional software vendors on the software quality of their solutions that safeguard against any software defects and malfunction. But Software-as-a-Service vendors likewise need to fulfill the quality requirements set in the smooth operation of the solution (Fan et al., 2009). Choudhary (2007a,b) argues for the Software-as-a-Service vendors being required to continuously convince the customer of continuing the subscription of the solution. As a result, higher investments in software development are expected, which ultimately will increase the quality of Software-as-a-Service solutions. Both studies highlight the increased pressure Software-as-a-Service vendors are faced with, especially with regard to creating the internal capabilities to deliver Software-as-a-Service solutions in high quality.

The review of the extant literature provides strong indications for multiple implications of the Software-as-a-Service concept on the software industry, and software vendors in particular, that highlight the potentially disruptive character of the concept (e.g. Bandulet et al., 2010; Joha & Janssen, 2012; Juell-Skielse & Enquist, 2012; Stuckenberg & Heinzl, 2010). At the same time, existing studies indicate a misconception of software vendors with regard to the level of change required to provide Software-as-a-Service (e.g. Heart et al., 2010). Other studies emphasize the growing importance of quality in the Software-as-a-Service context (e.g. Choudhary, 2007b; Fan et al., 2009). As quality is the outcome of an appropriately designed business model and internal capabilities, the potential misconception, combined with uncertainty about the full implications of Software-as-a-Service on software vendors, point at a precarious context for vendors to be in. This situation and the numerous calls for further research (e.g. Joha & Janssen, 2012; Leimeister et al., 2010) support the objective of this study to investigate implications of Software-as-a-Service in more detail.

2.4. Summary

This chapter has presented the foundations of this study, in order to develop a shared understanding for discussing the research design and the findings from the empirical phases. Software and services have been defined and their key characteristics have been outlined. The introduction has shown the fragmentation by the architectural stack model to present a common structure within the industry. Software has been described as of immaterial nature and without being subject to any form of abrasion. As a consequence, software vendors can take advantage of low reproduction costs and the absence of reproduction limitations in terms of quality or quantity. However, large costs can occur for the initial development. The section has distinguished standard and individual software and has defined Software-as-a-Service as standard application software, which is developed to satisfy a broad set of different requirements from a large customer segment. The chapter has defined business application software as standard application software, that allows integrating transaction-oriented data and business processes throughout an organization. ERP, CRM, SCM, or BI solutions have been named as examples of this subcategory of software.

The chapter has also introduced various approaches to define services. The approach by using constitutive criteria has been argued to be compatible with the different literature streams. The constitutive criteria of intangibility, simultaneity, perishability, and heterogeneity, as well as the importance of an external factor within the service fulfillment phase, have been described and discussed. During the subsequent study, the criteria will be considered with regard to their specific influence on the organizational impact of Software-as-a-Service on software vendors.

After a basic understanding of two of the main offerings of the software industry – software and services – has been presented, the chapter has introduced different stakeholders and economic principles of the software industry. The focus has been set on software vendors that in a narrower sense are organizations that develop software. Different delivery and payment models of software vendors have been introduced. The presentation has highlighted the different possibilities of an internal and external distribution, as well as internal and external delivery and operation of software. Multiple parameters to price software, for instance, those based on the chosen delivery model have been introduced. The billing unit can for instance be based on usage-based units, like the number of transactions or used storage, or based on usage-independent billing units, like the number of CPUs or the number of concurrent users. With the help of the discussion of the different variations of delivery and pricing models, the necessary background knowledge has been presented to differentiate Software-as-a-Service from related models.

Key characteristics of the Software-as-a-Service concept have been outlined. The concept has been characterized by the software vendor being responsible for the operation and maintenance of the solutions. The customer accessing the solution with a web-browser over the internet is charged based on usage-dependent subscription fees. The concept and its characteristics have been further refined by applying a service and a product perspective separately. While the service perspective has connected the concept with the previous discussion about constitutive criteria, the product perspective has introduced key technologies, like the multi-tenancy architecture, that have frequently been associated with the Software-as-a-Service concept. After the discussion of these two perspectives, the concept has been compared with related delivery and payment concepts, as well as similar previous concept discussed in the literature. The discussion of the key characteristics of Software-as-a-Service will enable a thorough analysis of the concept's organizational impact on software vendors in the subsequent chapters.

The chapter has also provided a presentation of previous work on the implications of the Software-as-a-Service concept on software vendors. The review of the extant literature has shown that the emergence of the Software-as-a-Service concept as a delivery and pricing model for software has led to a possibly risky situation for software vendors. The review has presented initial studies that indicate implications and the potentially disruptive character of the concept. The review has at the same time provided indications for a significant amount of uncertainty among vendors and researchers about the potential implications of the concept. These indications in summary have been considered to support the objective of this study to provide further insights about the Software-as-a-Service concept.

3. Research Design

The goal of this study is the exploration of the various implications of Software-as-a-Service on software vendors, as well as the development of an in-depth understanding of the organizational impact of Software-as-a-Service on vendors offering Software-as-a-Service solutions. In order to reach this goal, the selection of an appropriate research approach is an important step. This chapter will present details with regard to the selection and application of the research strategy of this study. The research process as well as the data collection and analysis procedure will be introduced and discussed. The chapter will elaborate on the details of the applied two phase research approach that comprises out of an initial exploratory field study, followed by a second multiple-case study substantiating and deepening the initial observations.

3.1. Selection of Research Strategy

The discussion of the extant literature in the previous chapter has shown high uncertainty and a lag of research with regard to the implications of the Software-as-a-Service concept on software vendors. The goal of this study is to fill this gap and explore the organizational implications for software vendors in detail to assist vendors in providing Software-as-a-Service solutions. To approach this goal, case study research (Benbasat et al., 1987; Lee, 1989; Yin, 2009) was deemed as an appropriate research method.

Case studies as research method are commonly used within the social science to study social and cultural phenomena (Myers, 2009). It has been widely applied within the Information Systems domain (Chen & Hirschheim, 2004; Dubé & Paré, 2003; Orlikowski & Baroudi, 1991; Sarker et al., 2012b) and has led to rich contributions (e.g. Dibbern et al., 2008; Kude et al., 2012; Lazic, 2011). Case study research represents one of multiple qualitative research methods. Other research methods include experiments, surveys, or simulations (Stone, 1978). Every research endeavor asks for the selection of a research strategy that fits to the specific research setting, even though every setting may not be limited to only one method (Scandura & Williams, 2000). Extant literature proposes different taxonomies to assist with the selection process (Stone, 1978; Yin, 2009).

Yin (2009) proposes three dimensions that may support the selection process of a research strategy, as shown in Table 3.1. The raised research question and the studied context decide on the proposed research strategy. The aim of this study is to investigate *how* the Software-as-a-Service concept influences software vendors. Due to the novelty of the Software-as-a-Service concept itself, the research question is raised in a contemporary context with only little existing knowledge. The context itself cannot be controlled, as neither the specifics of the Software-as-a-Service concept, nor the behavior of software vendors, can be altered by the researcher. Based on this research setting, the taxonomy of Yin (2009) suggests case study research as suitable research strategy.

Table 3.1.: Dimensions to select a suitable research strategy by Yin (2009)

Strategy	**Form of research question**	**Requires control of behavioral events**	**Focuses on contemporary events**
Experiment	how, why?	yes	yes
Survey	who, what, where, how many, how much?	no	yes
Archival analysis	who, what, where, how many, how much?	no	yes / no
History	how, why?	no	no
Case study	how, why?	no	yes

Like Yin (2009), Stone (1978) provides additional or similar dimensions to decide on an appropriate research strategy. The control of an investigator over participants is also considered by Stone (1978) to decide on the research method. In addition, Stone (1978) argues the realism or naturalness of a research setting to be a determinant. This dimension is considering the degree of a specific research situation to be perceived as real by its participants. Replicating the context of a software vendor in an unnatural setting within this study, like an experiment, is deemed challenging. For example, simulating the proposed continuous evolution of a Software-as-a-Service solution requires an existing solution with an existing customer base, a criterion that likely exceed the scope of an experiment and the feasibility within this study. Based on this assessment, both the approaches by Yin (2009) and Stone (1978) suggest case study research as the appropriate research strategy for settings resembling those of this study. Thus, case study research is chosen as an appropriate research method for this study.

This form of selection approach is, however, not free of problems, as a research question may be formulated in different ways. The research question of this study may, for example, also be phrased as: *what are the implications of Software-as-a-Service for software vendors?* Rather suggesting the discovery of a list of implications, this variation does not cover the essence of the study's objectives, which go beyond a simple collection and aim at understanding the consequences for software vendors. The research method of surveys may not be able to lead to the required in-depth understanding, especially with only limited existing knowledge available to be built on. Qualitative case study research, on the other hand, has proven its suitability in such a setting (Yin, 2009).

3.2. Specification of the Case Study Research Strategy

After having selected the case study research strategy as suitable research approach to answer the posed research question, the following section will provide further information with regard to case study research and different design decisions made for the initial empirical phase of this study. Among these design decisions are the specification of the epistemological position of the research, the unit of analysis, the decision between single and multiple cases, and the general nature of the research in terms of an underlying explorative or confirmative character (Myers, 2009; Yin, 2009).

3.2.1. Epistemological Position

Case study research can be based on different philosophical perspectives. Various perspectives are discussed and underlying the literature. Examples are constructivism, interpretivism, positivism, or postmodernism (Chalmers, 1999). The underlying research epistemologies most often chosen by researches are a positivist or an interpretive perspective (Myers, 1997; Orlikowski & Baroudi, 1991). Epistemology refers to the nature of knowledge and how it is acquired (Hirschheim, 1992). It is important to specify a researcher's position, as it influences the interpretation of the research's findings (Brown & Dowling, 1998).

A positivistic stance assumes that reality is objectively given and it exists independently of an observer (Orlikowski & Baroudi, 1991). New knowledge is acquired through observations of the world (Chalmers, 1999). Predictive relationships between phenomena are formed and tested to increase the understanding of the raised research question (Chalmers, 1999; Hacking, 1996). Positivists assume that reality can be described by measurable properties that are not subject to any influence by the observer (Myers, 1997; Straub et al., 2004). The ability to verify or falsify formulated predictive relationships is a prerequisite of positivistic research (Chalmers, 1999; Hacking, 1996). Thus, Orlikowski & Baroudi (1991) consider research as applying a positivist perspective, as long as the research includes formal propositions, quantifiable measures of variables, or hypothesis testing and the drawing of inferences about the studied aspects from a sample.

In contrast, interpretative researchers assume that reality and the observer cannot be clearly separated. Knowledge is obtained through social interactions and is dependent on experiences, cultural background, or history of the people involved (Lee, 1991; Walsham, 1995; Weber, 2003). A phenomenon is attempted to be understood by the meanings that people assign to them (Myers, 2009). Within the Information Systems literature, interpretive research is "aimed at producing an understanding of the context of the information system, and the process whereby the information system influences and is influenced by the context" (Walsham, 1993, p. 4-5). Instead of forming and testing causal relationships between constructs, interpretive researchers aim at creating an in-depth understanding of a phenomenon (Orlikowski & Baroudi, 1991).

Even though the two described perspective have been treated as rather distinct in the past, a recent discussion challenges the clear separation of the perspectives (Dobson et al., 2007; Mingers, 2004; Smith, 2006). Mixed approaches have emerged among them, for example, soft positivism, scientific realism, or critical realism.

Critical realism acknowledges the role of subjective knowledge of social actors in a given situation but also assumes the existence of independent structures that determine a given output. Its application enables to gain detailed causal explanations of a given phenomenon respecting, both, the interviewee's interpretation as well as the underlying structures and mechanisms (Wynn & Williams, 2012). Reality is described based on the experiences observed and interpreted by the interviewees and the knowledge claims, thus, focused on those aspects of reality which must exist in order for the given observations to have occurred. The focus of critical realism is set on explaining a given phenomenon than on predicting the future (Wynn & Williams, 2012).

Critical realism matches with the assumptions of this study and is, therefore, the underlying position of this study. Primary source of information of this study are knowledgeable individuals. Thus, their statements always reflect the person's past experience with Software-as-a-Service and her implementation of problems and opportunities. Expert statements are interpreted to gain an understanding of the implications, and in the later phases to build an in-depth understanding of the phenomena and its interrelations with organizational structures of software vendors. The approach is first guided by frameworks and later by extant theory, but is still open to include unexpected findings that may emerge from the data. The mixed method approach allows conducting data analysis based on prior theory without neglecting valuable and unexpected findings emerging from the data (Ravishankar et al., 2011). This approach allows going beyond selected observations and interpretations and forming an understanding of the reasons and relations behind those (Mingers et al., 2011).

3.2.2. Case Study Design

With regard to the case study design, Yin (2009) differentiates four designs based on the two dimensions: single-case vs. multiple-case and holistic vs. embedded. The first dimension determines whether the question is studied in one or multiple contexts. The second differentiates between studies that only address a single unit of analysis and those that discuss multiple units of analysis (Yin, 2009). According to Yin (2009), a single case study design may be chosen when the selected case represents a *critical case* in testing a well-formulated theory with clearly defined propositions, an *extreme or unique case* whose rare occurrence justifies for limitations in generalizability, a *representative or typical case*, or a *revelatory case* that was previously inaccessible for investigations. Furthermore, Yin (2009) mentions a longitudinal case, which is studied at two or more different points in time. A multiple-case approach, on the other hand, can lead to more variations in the observations and are thus often regarded as more compelling and robust (Herriott & Firestone, 1983; Yin, 2009). Within the second dimension, holistic approaches focus on a single and clearly defined unit of analysis, while embedded approaches study multiple units of analysis. These units are typically embedded in a hierarchy (Yin, 2009). For example, an embedded design may study a case of an organization and different subunits of this organization.

To answer the posed research question, a single-case approach may provide valuable results. However, the case selection is challenging, as a typical case is hard to identify due to the variations of applied business models of software vendors. Examining the Software-as-a-Service consequences for a vendor that only applies the service concept may yield different results than a vendor that is active in both settings and offering on-premises as well as Software-as-a-Service solutions. Similarly, a vendor that initiates business operation with a pure Software-as-a-Service approach may have different challenges than a vendor that is transitioning from one model to the other. Extreme cases may be represented by a successful or an unsuccessful vendor. Both, however, may only provide a limited view on the full scope of implications of the Software-as-a-Service concept. In order to cover multiple perspectives on the implications of the Software-as-a-Service concept, this study takes a multiple-case approach. The selection of cases within a multiple-case study approach may be based on a literal or theoretical replication logic (Yin, 2009). A literal replication aims at confirming results based on a similar context of a second case. A theoretical replication, on the other hand, aims at observing contradicting results based on controlled variations within the context of the case (Yin, 2009). The combination of both techniques leads to the development of a better understanding of the studied unit of analysis.

The unit of analysis of this study is at the level of organizations. More specifically, the research question aims on exploring the organizational influence of Software-as-a-Service on software vendors. Thus, software vendors are in the focus of the study and a holistic approach is followed, studying every software vendor in its surrounding context. However, it has to be acknowledged that software vendors may represent large multinational organizations that offer different products and services. In these organizations, the Software-as-a-Service concept may have different implications for different organizational subunits and subunits may represent a dedicated case. Also the implications of the Software-as-a-Service concept may be influenced by aspects beyond an organizational level, for example by the software ecosystem the vendor is embedded in and the personal skills and profiles of employees. Therefore, this study focuses on an organizational level but remains open for other observations.

The nature of a case study can be descriptive, explorative or confirmative / explanative (Dubé & Paré, 2003; Yin, 2009). Descriptive case studies do not attempt to interpret a studied phenomenon with a theoretical lens, instead they rather aim at objectively presenting a phenomena and illustrate some issues of interests (Dubé & Paré, 2003). According to Kerlinger & Lee (2000), exploratory case studies may generally follow three different purposes: the discovery of significant variables, the discovery of relationships between these variables, and formation of groundwork for more systematic and rigorous future research. The purpose of confirmative case studies is testing theories that have been deduced from extant literature or emerged from exploratory empirical research (Dubé & Paré, 2003).

Case study research typically follows an iterative process within the analysis phase that may also revert to adjustments within the case design (Eisenhardt, 1989; Miles & Hubermann, 1994; Yin, 2009). A redesign may, for example, involve a change within the sampling strategy or a focus on an emerging embedded unit of analysis (Yin, 2009). Accordingly, this study anticipates potential redesign needs due to initial observations by following a two-staged approach. The approach is depicted in Figure 1.1 of Chapter 1 and outlined below.

The first phase is aiming at exploring the organizational implications of the Software-as-a-Service concept on software vendors on a rather general level. An explorative multiple-case study is conducted to gain an understanding of the Software-as-a-Service concept and its implications. It contains a descriptive character by presenting current practices of Software-as-a-Service vendors and their issues. Following the suggestion of Eisenhardt (1989), the research is initiated with no theory under consideration and a clean theoretical slate. Preconceptions about potential relationships are minimal to allow the formation of a broad picture.

Two established frameworks are used to guide and structure the exploratory research. First, a business model framework is used to understand the details of the Software-as-a-Service delivery and pricing model. A general business model framework is chosen to not only explore the concept itself, but also the context and business environment around it. An analysis from a business model perspective is expected to yield information about the situation software vendor organizations are exposed to and thus allows to systematize the analysis of the key aspects of the Software-as-a-Service concept that mark the source for organizational implications. The second research framework is expected to provide indication of implications with regard to the value creation of software vendors. Value chain frameworks not only allow to unfold the details of the prevailing division of work and orchestration of value creating activities throughout the software industry, but also within software vendor organizations. Since these two aspects represent two central aspects of organization (Kieser, 2006), their analysis within the Software-as-a-Service context is expected to yield valuable results about organizational implications of the concept. Observed findings are expected to lead to crucial implications worthy a further exploration in a subsequent phase. During the initial research phase, observations are corroborated by related literature. Like a funnel, the approach is expected to explore the impact and identify crucial implications for further analysis.

The second phase's objective is to substantiate the knowledge with regard to the identified subset of implications. A second multiple-case study is conducted. Even though the prevalent character is still of explorative character, clearer preconceptions are formed and utilized to guide and structure the exploration. Drawing on relevant extant theory, the phase aims on developing an in-depth understanding that ultimately is reflected in an initial modeling attempt of the observed constructs and relationships. While the first phase of empirical research is undertaken to lay the groundwork for more systematic and rigorous research, the second phase is conducted with the goal of theory building.

3.2.3. Data Collection and Analysis Procedure

After the previous section introduced the studies epistemological position and specified the case study design, the following section will shed some light on the details of the data collection and analysis procedure of the study. The introduction will concentrate on the general approach applied. Details with regard to the specifics of the procedure and variations applied in the two phases of the research will be provided in Chapter 4 and Chapter 5 respectively.

As outlined before, the goal of the first empirical phase is the exploration of the Software-as-a-Service concept and its organizational implications for software vendors. During this exploratory phase, a broad diversity of vendors among the studied cases is expected to ensure a variety of different observations. The introduction of the software industry in Chapter 2 has shown the multitude of different business models of software vendors and other companies in the industry. Also, it has informed about the different definitions of software vendor within the literature. The implications of the Software-as-a-Service concept may vary significantly between these organizations. Thus, a focus on a subgroup of these different players in the industry is inevitable. Software vendors that develop the core software artifacts of an offered software solutions can be considered as key value contributor. Thus, the data collection is concentrated on software vendors in the narrower sense. The foundation chapter, however, also directed the attention at the structure and underlying network effects of the software industry that lead to software solutions being composed out of multiple value activities of different stakeholders. For this reason, the first phase's sample is enhanced by partner organizations of larger software vendors. This nevertheless shall not refract the view from a focus on implications for software vendors but enhancing the scope of perspectives on the matter. To make sure the respective interviewees have collected authentic experience with the concept, only organizations that are involved with at least one Software-as-a-Service solution are included in the case sample. As implication may differ between vendors that only offer Software-as-a-Service and those that offer traditional on-premises software together with Software-as-a-Service solutions, representatives of both groups are included in the sample. The cases will be introduced in more detail in Section 4.2 and Section 5.2.

Primary source of data within both phases of research are interviews with knowledgeable persons of the case organization, as well as documents provided or received from the companies' websites. The interviews follow a semi-structured approach. Semi-structured interviews are based on a predetermined set of questions that guide the interview sessions. However, interviews remain flexible to address and adjust questions to detail interesting aspects emerging during the interview (Atteslander & Cromm, 2008; Stone, 1978; Yin, 2009). This approach is especially suitable in exploratory research settings, as it allows the questioned expert to talk freely (Stone, 1978). Furthermore, it increases the chance of discovering previously unconsidered aspects. The structure offered by the set of predefined questions safeguards for relevant aspects to be addressed during the interviews (Yin, 2009). Interviews are recorded and transcribed for later analysis.

The interview guidelines for both empirical phases of this study are included in Appendix A. Since the first phase of research aims at discovering a broad set of implications of the Software-as-a-Service concept, the guiding set of questions are equally open and touch a variety of aspects. They are following the structure provided by the used framework of business models and value chains. Within the second phase, questions become more focused and structured, reflecting the increased understanding of the context as a result of the initial phase. Nevertheless, the interview guideline remains semi-structured and open for additional observations. Structure is gained from considering relevant theories providing a frame for the collection of relevant aspects.

Next to the interview data, publicly available documents and in particular the case organizations websites are screened. This triangulation leads to an increase of the internal validity of the study (Yin, 2009). The organizations' websites provided valuable insights about the offered solution and its complexity. The websites, for example, provided information with regard to the details of the applied delivery and pricing model, possibilities of trial periods, as well as indications about the self-service functions of the solutions. This information assisted in gaining a better understanding of the scope and maturity of the offered Software-as-a-Service solution.

The transcripts of the recorded interviews are analyzed in-depth through coding relevant text passages and emerging patterns within the data (Miles & Hubermann, 1994). The software tool NVIVO 9 is used to assist this process. Codes are labels or tags that are assigned to text sections of transcribed interviews or other forms of information. These codes are used to organize chunks of text and allow later retrieval in an aggregated form (Miles & Hubermann, 1994). The collection of these codes forms the coding scheme. It has to be noted that these codes, as well as the coding scheme, is not static and will evolve and change during the analysis process. Changes may involve the relabeling of text passages or the neglect, aggregation, renaming, or extension of codes used (Miles & Hubermann, 1994).

The initial coding scheme of the first empirical phase contained the elements of the used frameworks, specifically the building blocks of the business model and the phases of the value chain. Following an iterative process, as suggested by Miles & Hubermann (1994) or Stone (1978), the interview transcripts were analyzed and text passages assigned to matching notes. The coding scheme was enhanced by emerging implications or altered by dropping or consolidating existing coding notes. This process was repeated until all interviews were coded and dominant set of implications emerged. A similar process was also followed within the second empirical phase, but instead focused on the framework deduced from the literature and extant theory. Section 4.2 and Section 5.2 will elaborate on details of the applied analysis procedure within the respective two phases.

3.3. Summary

This chapter has introduced the research design of the study. The selection of the chosen research strategy to answer the raised research question has been discussed and justified. A case study research approach has been chosen. Furthermore, the chapter has specified the research design along different design decisions. A two-staged research approach has been introduced, which consists out of two exploratory multiple-case studies. The first phase aiming at exploring the implications of Software-as-a-Service on software vendors, while the latter at substantiating the findings and focusing on emerging subtopics. Lastly, the chapter has provided details about the general data collection and analysis procedures.

The following two chapters will present the findings from the two conducted multiple-case studies. Both chapters will start with the presentation of the applied research framework and additional information with regard to the data selection and analysis procedure. These sections are followed by the presentation of the findings of the first empirical phase in Chapter 4 and second phase in Chapter 5.

4. Exploring the Organizational Impact of Software-as-a-Service

The following chapter will introduce the first phase of empirical research addressing the impact of Software-as-a-Service on software vendors. The chapter is building on the work of Stuckenberg et al. (2011) and Stuckenberg & Heinzl (2010). After an introduction to the research framework that guided the analysis, the specific sampling strategy for the first case study will be introduced. This will be followed by a detailed presentation of the case data and the matching literature.

4.1. Research Framework

To understand the potential organizational impact of the Software-as-a-Service concept on software vendors, a structured analysis approach is required. On the one hand, it is not only necessary to gain a solid understanding of the key aspects of the Software-as-a-Service concept itself, but also about the context software vendors that adopt the concept as a software delivery and pricing model are exposed to. On the other hand, knowledge about the central value creating activities of the context is needed. The research framework that guides the first phase of exploratory research should therefore incorporate these two perspectives.

With regard to the Software-as-a-Service concept, the definition of Software-as-a-Service in Section 2.2 describes various characteristics that are commonly linked to the concept. When defining Software-as-a-Service as a software delivery model that provides users with up-to-date software via the Internet on a pay-by-usage basis, the value to the customer is emphasized. In order to be able to understand the full consequences of the Software-as-a-Service concept for software vendors, it is, however, not sufficient to limit the view on the value proposition to the customer. Instead, the analysis has to take up a broader perspective and cover the value proposition, as well as the parts of an organization that lead to the capabilities to deliver this value proposition. Therefore, the analysis needs to evaluate the implications of the Software-as-a-Service concept on the way software vendors create, deliver and capture value. These aspects are commonly described by business models (Osterwalder & Pigneur, 2010). Business models help to clearly determine which value of a product or service is created and delivered by an organization (Fielt, 2011). Furthermore, they provide indications on the key activities of the value creation and the corresponding key stakeholders (Osterwalder & Pigneur, 2010). A framework that adopts a business model perspective may therefore provide valuable indications about the Software-as-a-Service concept and also about key value activities. Due to the common inclusion of a customer, competitor and partner perspective, business models in addition provide initial insights about the overall context and environment surrounding an organization. Thus, it appears promising to start the analysis of the implications of the Software-as-a-Service concept on software vendors from a business model perspective.

The requirement for a broader perspective is also supported by Cavalcante et al. (2011). They point out that it is crucial to understand the specifics of a business model and the potential change to previous similar models, as a business model revision implies that existing working practices are subject to change. Linked to changing processes, new challenges may, for instance, arise in the form of organizational inertia, resistance, uncertainty and ambiguity, or the lack of required knowledge and skills (Cavalcante et al., 2011). These aspects are likely to be neglected when focusing on a pure value proposition perspective. The business model concept instead allows to understand and analyze different business models as a whole (Osterwalder et al., 2005), and is thus considered an appropriate research framework for the initial empirical stage of this research. Section 4.1.1 will introduce the business model concept and its surrounding literature in more detail.

Even tough business model frameworks may already provide indications about the value creation; these aspects only represent one of multiple dimensions within a business model. For a more detailed evaluation it, therefore, appears promising to include the perspective of a research framework that sets the focus on the value creation. The value chain perspective is not focused on the business model of one organization, but instead takes a broader view and includes all participants of the software industry required to develop the value delivered to the customer. The introduction of the software industry in Chapter 2 has shown the existence of interdependence between different organizations offering software solutions and complementing services to the customer. The broader view of the value chain perspective compared to the business model view is considered more promising to identify potential changes due to the Software-as-a-Service concept between different organizations. A value chain perspective is expected to not only provide valuable insights on the division of work within the software industry as a whole, but also for the value activities within a software vendor organization. With various models addressing the core value activities of software creation applying a process view (e.g. life-cycle models and development methodologies), the value chain perspective, which also emphasizes a process view, may yield additional observations that are potentially neglected by a business model view. The value chain perspective is therefore considered a promising complementing perspective to a business model view. Section 4.1.2 will provide an introduction to the value chain concept.

4.1.1. Business Models

Every company has a business model, whether that model is explicitly articulated or not (Chesbrough, 2006; Teece, 2010). Business models matter; the same idea or technology taken to market through two different business models will yield two different economic outcomes (Chesbrough, 2010). Business models are required because of the features of market economies, where there is consumer choice, transaction costs, heterogeneity amongst consumers and producers, and competition (Teece, 2010). While the use of the business model concept is often fuzzy and vague, and lacks consensus on its definition and compositional elements (Al-Debei & Avison, 2010; Morris et al., 2005; Shafer et al., 2005), Ghaziani & Ventresca (2005) conclude that the business model discourse is mostly framed around value creation. Business models describe *"the rationale of how an organization creates, delivers and captures value"* (Osterwalder & Pigneur, 2010).

Next to a discussion of a proper definition, research on the business model concept is focused on business model archetypes, and business model frameworks and elements (Hedman & Kalling, 2003). Business model archetypes represent generic business models and patterns that not only may describe the entire business model, but can also be focused on specific part of it. The presentation of archetypes in the literature is often linked to the discussion of business model frameworks, as they are provided as examples of different patterns of business models illustrated with the help of frameworks (Hedman & Kalling, 2003; Osterwalder et al., 2005; Pateli & Giaglis, 2004).

Business model frameworks describe what compositional elements a business model is made of. The elements are for example also referred to as components (e.g. Pateli & Giaglis, 2004), (key) questions (e.g. Morris et al., 2005), or functions (e.g. Chesbrough & Rosenbloom, 2002). Business model frameworks and ontologies do not only define the elements, they also define the relationships between the elements (e.g. Gordijn et al., 2005). Due to their support in describing a business model, business model frameworks can also be used to compare different business models or identify differences between two business models (Osterwalder, 2004). Therefore, business model frameworks are very suitable to structure the analysis of the Software-as-a-Service concept.

Various business model frameworks are proposed within the literature (e.g. Bouwman et al., 2008; Chesbrough & Rosenbloom, 2002; Gordijn, 2002; Johnson, 2010; Morris et al., 2005; Osterwalder & Pigneur, 2010; Weill & Vitale, 2001). A discussion of these frameworks can be found in Fielt (2011). Among the more prominent and recent frameworks are The Four-Box Business Model from Johnson (2010) and the Business Model Canvas from Osterwalder & Pigneur (2010).

The Four-Box business model from Johnson (2010) is based on an earlier version by Johnson et al. (2008). It aims on providing assistance in revealing and structuring issues that are linked to a business model innovation to a previously unaddressed market an organization has limited existing knowledge about (Fielt, 2011). The model is divided into the four components: Customer value proposition, key resources, key processes, and profit formula (Johnson, 2010). Within the profit formula component, Johnson (2010), for example, asks for an analysis of the revenue model and cost structure of a business model. This analysis may be on the level of detail of target unit margins and the resource velocity. Though the model may also be applicable on a higher level, it appears more appropriate for the analysis of a concrete business opportunity, rather than the analysis of a more general innovation evoked by a new software delivery and payment model.

Table 4.1.: The business model building blocks of Osterwalder & Pigneur (2010)

Building Block	**Description**
Customer Segments	The *Customer Segments* building block defines the different groups of people or organizations that an enterprise aims to reach and serve. In order to better satisfy customers, a company may group them into distinct segments with common needs, common behaviors, or other attributes. An organization must make a conscious decision about which segments to serve and which segments to ignore.
Value Proposition	The *Value Proposition* building block describes the bundle of products and services that create value for a specific *Customer Segment.* It solves a customer problem or satisfies a customer need.
Channels	The *Channels* building block describes how a company communicates with and reaches its *Customer Segments* to deliver a *Value Proposition. Channels* comprise the customer interface with touch points that play an important role in the customer experience.
Customer Relationship	The *Customer Relationships* building block describes the types of relationships a company establishes with specific *Customer Segments.* A company should clarify the type of relationship it wants to establish with each *Customer Segment.*
Revenue Streams	The *Revenue Streams* building block represents the cash a company generates from each *Customer Segment.* A company must ask itself, for what value is each *Customer Segment* truly willing to pay?
Key Resources	The *Key Resources* building block describes the most important assets required to make a business model work. These assets allow an enterprise to create and offer a *Value Proposition*, reach markets, maintain relationships with *Customer Segments*, and earn revenues.
Key Activities	The *Key Activities* building block describes the most important things a company must do to make its business model work. Like *Key Resources*, they are required to create and offer a *Value Proposition*, reach markets, maintain *Customer Relationships*, and earn revenues.
Key Partnerships	The *Key Partnerships* building block describes the network of suppliers and partners that make the business model work. Companies create alliances to optimize their business models, reduce risks, or acquire resources.
Cost Structure	The *Cost Structure* describes all costs incurred to operate a business model. Creating and delivering value, maintaining *Customer Relationships*, and generating revenue all incur costs. Such costs can be calculated relatively easily after defining *Key Resources*, *Key Activities*, and *Key Partnerships.*

Osterwalder & Pigneur (2010) divide their model into nine building blocks that are summarized in Table 4.1. Their framework is widely applied and supported (for example, it was co-developed with 470 practitioners) and it is based on the already well-founded ontology of Osterwalder (2004). It is generic enough to reflect the Software-as-a-Service as well as the traditional on-premises business models. The Business Model Canvas presents a shared language for describing, visualizing, assessing and changing business models (Fielt, 2011; Osterwalder & Pigneur, 2010). The ontology offers a clear structure and allows studying business models at different levels of detail. It therefore promises to be a valid means for structuring the exploratory case study on the influence of Software-as-a-Service on software vendors.

4.1.2. Value Chains

The concept of disaggregating the creation of a product, which brings value to a customer, into a chain of various activities that generate this value, was initially introduced by Porter (1985). The value chain concept was developed as a tool for firms to analyze and sustain their competitive advantage. With value chain analysis, the value creation process of a firm is disaggregated into discrete activities that contribute to the firm's competitive advantage (Stabell & Fjeldstad, 1998). The underlying assumption of looking at different activities is that they are assumed to be the building blocks that create the value for the customer. Different activities may have different underlying constraints and provide different contributions to the characteristics of the firm's output, perceived as valuable by the customer (Stabell & Fjeldstad, 1998).

Porter (1985) proposes to disaggregate the value chain into activities that have different economics, have a high potential for differentiation, or represent a main cost component (Porter, 1985; Stabell & Fjeldstad, 1998). Based on these criteria, Porter (1985) suggests five generic primary activity categories of the value chain. *Inbound logistics* cover activities dealing with handling the inputs to a product. *Operations* include all activities dealing with the transformation of inputs into the final product. Outbound logistics comprise all activities undertaking the delivery of the product to the customer. *Marketing and sales* covers activities that inform the customer about the product and convince the customer to purchase it. The last category is termed *service* and includes activities that provide services to enhance or maintain the value of the product (Porter, 1985).

Although the value chain concept was developed to describe the value generation within one firm, it can also be applied to more holistic level on entire industries or supply chains (Barnes, 2002; Li & Whalley, 2002). The production of a single product often relies on a network of companies working together to create the end-product, with every participant of the supply chain adding value to the final product. Similarly, a software product relies on a network of software vendors, integrators, or consultancies to deliver its value to the customer (Messerschmitt & Szyperski, 2003). The value chain concept can be used to get a simple and high level view on a firm or industry with a simple model of the activities performed to generate value (Pussep et al., 2011). For a software vendor, a big portion of the value is created within the software development process, for instance, as defined by Sommerville (2011). However, the value chain perspective includes additional activities that are required to not only develop a software artifact, but also to put it into operation in order to create the customer value. For the software industry, Pussep et al. (2012, 2011) offer a list of generic activities that form the software value chain. The authors derive these activities from a literature review, a pre-test, and a subsequent Delphi study. Table 4.2 provides an overview of the activities they have identified including a short description.

Table 4.2.: Activities of the software value chain based on Pussep et al. (2012, 2011)

Activity	Description
Research	This activity covers the development of a product vision, decisions about the major technologies and components, as well as a general proof of concept.
Development	This activity covers the actual software development process, including requirements engineering, software analysis and design, software coding and the subsequent tests.
Production	This activity deals with the printing and packaging of the documentation and software on the distribution media.
Marketing	Marketing and sales of the solution and the increase of the awareness of potential customers of the solution.
Implementation	This activity covers the installation, configuration and adaptation of the software to the customers' business processes and needs.
Education	This activity involves the training of users and other stakeholders, like partners.
Operations	This activity covers the hosting of the software to ensure the end-user can use it and upgrading of the software to new releases during the lifecycle.
Maintenance	This activity is covering similar aspects as development, just that it does not address new features, but bug fixing and enhancements to existing software without disruptive changes.
Support	This activity covers the support of the end-user and the technical support for the stakeholders operating the software.
Replacement	This activity covers the decision to replace a potentially outdated software and the activities to backup and migrate data to a potential new software.

The activities of a value chain are following a sequential order (Stabell & Fjeldstad, 1998). The generic activities of a value chain are, however, not the same as organizational functions. Activities may span several organizational functions (Stabell & Fjeldstad, 1998). Activities may also be executed by different organizations. Nevertheless, a value chain analysis can provide valuable information with regard to the organizational structures and processes of a firm. In the software industry, a software solution may be developed by a software vendor, who relies on his network of partners to sell and implement the solution at the side of the customer. Other partners may then address the user training needs of the customer (Buxmann et al., 2013). A value chain analysis can provide indications for the added value of an organization to a product or service and that of other involved parties.

Similarly to the business model framework by Osterwalder & Pigneur (2010), the value chain activities can be used to structure different observations. The different activities suggested by Pussep et al. (2012, 2011) are thus taken as a research framework for the analysis of the case study.

4.2. Data Selection and Analysis

As outlined in Chapter 3, this study aims on investigating the implications of the Software-as-a-Service concept on software vendors by conducting multiple case studies. The following section will introduce the details of the case sites and data collection, as well as analysis procedure.

Table 4.3.: Case study sample

Case	Business model	Company size	Description	Number of interviews
Case A	pure	large	Leading software vendor of complex business application software	2
Case B	hybrid	large	Leading software vendor of complex business application software	3
Case C	hybrid	large	Leading software vendor of complex business application software	2
Case D	partner	medium	Sales and implementation partner of leading Software-as-a-Service vendor	1
Case E	partner	small	Sales and implementation partner of leading hybrid software vendor	1
Case F	pure	small	Business application for financial processes	1
Case G	pure	small	Business application for invoice processing	1
Case H	pure	small	Solution provider for collaboration services	1
Case I	pure	small	Solution provider for e-commerce	1
Case J	pure	small	Solution provider for collaboration services	1
Case K	hybrid	small	Business application for logistics and warehouse processes	1

Based on the outlined research strategy of Section 3.1, selected organizations were identified to provide empirical insights for the first phase of the study. To collect valid insights on the implications of the Software-as-a-Service concept, the focus was set on companies with experience in such field. A company was seen as experienced, when it had at least one Software-as-a-Service solution available for subscription by potential customers in the market. The type of solutions was limited to enterprise solutions, excluding solutions that target a private end-customer. Solutions targeting private end-consumers were considered to differ in complexity, security requirements, or pricing model, and were therefore excluded to reduce the diversity and increase the comparability of applied business models. A list of potential organizations was created by aggregating entries from a published Software-as-a-Service solution catalog for the German market (see Grohmann, 2011).

In an initial set, leading software vendors were identified to form the basis of the sample. These vendors offer complex business applications as a Software-as-a-Service solution and can be considered as market leaders, either with their Software-as-a-Service or product offering which they now complement by a Software-as-a-Service variation. Complex business applications in this context refer to software like customer relationship management systems or enterprise resource planning systems. The three initially identified vendors (Case A, Case B, and Case C) are of large size with more than 7500 employees. As illustrated in Table 4.3, company A applies a pure Software-as-a-Service business model, while the other leading vendors (B and C) also sell software in the traditional approach (on-premises) and have its origin in this area. Company A already extended its Software-as-a-Service solution with a platform offering, allowing third-parties to enhance the solutions by complementary applications. This can be regarded as an indication for a matured state of Software-as-a-Service concept implementation.

In order to gain a better feeling for the position in the market and the relationships to other organizations, two partner companies of leading software vendors were included in the sample. While D represents a sales and implementation partner of A, Case E is working together with Case C. Both are classified as "partner" in Table 4.3.

With the organizations A - E, the case sample included a set of leading software vendors and their partners, both for a pure Software-as-a-Service, as well as for a hybrid approach of software delivery. In a second step, the sample was extended to also include smaller organizations with experience in the development and operations of Software-as-a-Service solutions. With a focus on complex business application software, the Software-as-a-Service solution catalog was queried to provide a list of smaller Software-as-a-Service vendors to complement the findings of the large software vendors. The number of employees was taken as a measure for the size of the case organization. Table 4.3 classifies the size as "large", "medium", or "small" based on whether the organization has more than 7500 employees, between 7500 and 20 employees or less than 20 employees.

The identified organizations were approached by email with a letter describing the purpose and objective of the study and a copy of the simplified interview guidelines. Those organizations, which did not react to the first written inquiry, were re-approached via telephone. One organization was approached on a trade fair. Table 4.3 provides an overview of the final case sample of the first empirical phase of this study.

The job positions varied from senior sales consultants to technology and process experts. In case C, the interview partners belonged to departments dealing with lower layers of the architectural stack model. This was expected to allow further insights into operations and infrastructure related implications, in addition to contrast Software-as-a-Service and Infrastructure-as-a-Service business models. For the smaller software vendors, the interview was conducted with the director of the company. Table 4.4 provides an overview of the interview partners.

Table 4.4.: Interview partners in the case study

Case	Interview partner(s)
Case A	Senior Director Alliances (A-1) Director Marketing (A-2)
Case B	Director Business Development (B-1) Manager Service Business Development (B-2) Director Platform Solutions (B-3)
Case C	Solution Architect (C-1) Director Network Solutions (C-2)
Case D	Chief Technology Officer (Founder) (D-1)
Case E	Director Consulting Services (E-1)
Case F	Director Research Development (F-1)
Case G	Managing Director (Founder) (G-1)
Case H	Director Operations (Founder) (H-1)
Case I	Director Research and Development (Founder) (I-1)
Case J	Marketing and Sales Consultant (J-1)
Case K	Managing Director (Founder) (K-1)

The interviews were partly conducted in person and on-site, and partly by telephone. The conversations were held in German and had an average duration of around 75 minutes. All interviews were tape recorded and fully transcripted to allow a better analysis. In addition, notes were taken during the interviews. The conducted interviews resulted in more than 75.000 words of qualitative data. For triangulation purposes, the expert interviews were complemented by publicly available documents, especially the companies' Internet pages (Yin, 2009). These were especially useful in providing an understanding of the scope and complexity of the offered solutions. The information on the companies' website was also beneficial in assessing the companies' understanding and level of implementation of the Software-as-a-Service concept. Typical aspects, like the possibility to subscribe to trial-versions, provided an indication for the adoption of a one-to-many delivery approach. This was considered as a possible hint on a multi-tenancy architecture. On the other hand, the lag of such possibility or its compensation by offering test systems with test data that were shared by all prospective customers, pointed at a less sophisticated implementation of Software-as-a-Service. The websites also provided hints on whether Software-as-a-Service is rather used as a marketing term.

The analysis of the data was conducted in an iterative manner: by using the two research frameworks of a business model and the value chain. For both frameworks, chunks of text were coded to notes summarizing and aggregating similar aspects. New codes were introduced for emerging concepts, while others were redefined or dropped in the process of sense-making.

For the business model framework, the analysis was done using descriptive codes, structured according to the nine elements of the business model ontology proposed by Osterwalder & Pigneur (2010). Codes were created for aspects describing a change within the business model or implications for software vendors or other stakeholders. Relevant text was firstly assigned to one of the nine business model blocks. In a second step, the codes for every building block were sorted and coded according to similar aspects. New codes were added to the coding scheme as new aspects or implications emerged during the analysis (Miles & Hubermann, 1994). In case implications matched more than one building block, the relevant text was linked to all relevant building blocks. During the aggregation process, implications were assigned to the building block providing the biggest fit to the described changes. The same process was also done for the second framework. Instead of the business model building blocks, the text passages were assigned to the different phases of the value chain. Figure 4.5 shows the initial coding scheme for both research frameworks.

Table 4.5.: Initial coding scheme of first empirical phase

Framework	Nodes	
Business Model	Cost Structure	(BM-CS)
	Customer Relationship	(BM-CR)
	Customer Segments	(BM-CS)
	Channels	(BM-C)
	Key Activities	(BM-KA)
	Key Partnerships	(BM-KP)
	Key Resources	(BM-KR)
	Revenue Stream	(BM-RM)
	Value Proposition	(BM-VP)
Value Chain	Development	(VC-D)
	Education	(VC-E)
	Implementation	(VC-I)
	Maintenance	(VC-M)
	Marketing Sales	(VC-MS)
	Operation	(VC-O)
	Production	(VC-P)
	Replacement	(VC-R)
	Research	(VC-RE)
	Support	(VC-S)

4.3. Results and Observations

The following sections will provide the results and observations from the first empirical phase of the study. Aspects that emerged during the analysis of the case study will be presented and underpinned with selected quotes from the interview partners. With the help of the label at the end of the quote, the respective expert and corresponding organization can be identified using Table 4.4 and Table 4.3. Following the two perspectives of the research framework, the presentation of the findings will first concentrate on the business model perspective in Section 4.3.1, and then address the value chain perspective in Section 4.3.2. The results are discussed for every perspective individually as well as in a combined form.

4.3.1. The Business Model of Software-as-a-Service

To evaluate the Software-as-a-Service concept and its implications for software vendors with the help of a business model perspective, an appropriate starting point appears to be the discussion of the customer-facing buildings blocks of a business model, especially the *Value Proposition*, as well as the targeted *Customer Segments* and the respective *Revenue Stream*. These define the customers, who are addressed with the offering, as well as the value that is promised to these customers. Their general boundaries are defined by the market and the general understanding of the Software-as-a-Service concept, though there may be limitations to the full potential of variations within these building blocks, due to missing internal capabilities that do not allow a specific value proposition at this stage. Afterwards, the relationship building blocks are addressed. The *Channels*, *Customer Relationship*, as well as *Key Partnership* building blocks, deal with links between the software vendor and external entities, e.g. the customers and potential partners. Finally, the vendor internal building blocks *Key Activities* and *Key Resources* are outlined before the bottom line *Cost Structure* is discussed.

Value Proposition

In general, the value proposition describes the bundle of products and services that create value for a specific customer group in terms of that it solves a customer problem or satisfies a customer need (Osterwalder & Pigneur, 2010).

Case study observations: The value proposition of Software-as-a-Service to the customer covers the core elements of the concepts defining characteristics. A remotely operated software solution is provided to the customer and priced by applying usage-based pricing models. Software-as-a-Service offers the customer a changed delivery and pricing model of software.

With regard to the pricing model, it can be observed that the Software-as-a-Service concept markets transparent pricing models that are geared to customers.

> *"The value proposition creates a setting that allows the customer to not care about maintenance and updates anymore and that has a quite transparent pricing structure that is really geared towards the user."* (B-2)

Related to the usage based-pricing is the provided flexibility with regard to the usage-intensity and scope of the solution. Elastic capacity is one of the selling points of Software-as-a-Service. It allows the dynamic assignment of resources like computing power or data storage.

> *"In a nutshell, the flexible provision of IT resources is an advantage compared to traditional operations, where building up IT resources is a time-consuming activity. Hardware has to be organized, has to be configured, and has to be administrated. That often overruns its time."* (C-1)

With this flexibility advantage, the customer can generate real-time BI reports or master seasonal demand peaks, without the need to reserve dedicated resources or run batch processes in periods of low system usage e.g. during the night. This flexibility is core to the value proposition of Software-as-a-Service.

> *"In the discussion with a director of a medium sized company, enabling a view on the customer's business and this in real-time, is actually the main sales pitch."* (B-1)

The second aspect with regard to flexibility is the adjustable implementation scope of Software-as-a-Service solutions. It is a major differentiator and change to traditional approaches, that vendors allow flexibility in the scope of the implementation of a customer. Customers may start with a small set of features and extend the adopted solutions scope over time as needed.

> *"The whole implementation approach does not target on a Big Bang, instead [a customer] can start with small functionality, and thanks to the scalability of the software regarding users, but also regarding the flexible unlocking of additional functions, [a vendor] can sell the software gradually."* (B-3)

These flexibility gains are not only beneficial to the customer, but also have implications for software vendors. Implementation projects are getting smaller and initial projects, particularly, may be realized within shorter time frames. For the vendor, this change has the advantage of sales activities not binding as much long-term resources as in traditional approaches, in which projects can easily take several months. Therefore, the customer can expect less implementation costs. Solutions in addition are marketed to require less user training, as vendors put a lot of effort into archiving a high usability of their solutions.

> *"The whole thing is paired with a very strong focus on usability, user-friendliness of the solution."* (A-2)

With regard to the changes to the delivery model, customers are attracted by the promise that they do not need to take care of the operation and maintenance of software solutions anymore. The complete architectural stack of software is taken care of by the vendor. This reduces the complexity from the customer's point of view.

> *"For the customer, the difference is a complexity reduction. The customer simply has a lot less to take care of compared to on-premises software."* (B-1)

Problems that may occur because of the software underlying architectural layers, like the middleware or hardware, are not affecting the customer anymore. At the same time, the customer is provided with the latest state of development and the software solution is continuously kept up-to-date by the vendor. The customer can take advantage of the newest extensions and improvements without the need to invest in resources.

Table 4.6.: Key observations within *Value Proposition*

Key observations	**Description**
Flexibility	Solutions provide customers with flexibility in terms of elastic resources, solution scope, and implementation time.
Complexity reduction	Complexity is moved to the vendor.
Smaller implementation projects	Implementation at the customer takes less time and binds fewer resources.

Literature discussion: Aspects concerning the value proposition are well discussed within the Software-as-a-Service literature, due to the overlap and similarity of these aspects with common Software-as-a-Service definitions. Aside of the contributions presented in Section 2.3 that addressed implications of the Software-as-a-Service concept on a general level, a limited number of researchers discussing implications, with a focus on the value proposition, can be found in the literature.

Joha & Janssen (2012) found that small providers, who are new in the market and do not yet have signed a representable customer base, may be perceived as less mature players in the market by a potential customer during a potential provider selection process. Therefore, these providers may need to provide detailed contingency plans as part of their value proposition that address and account for change in control and potential provider failure (Joha & Janssen, 2012).

Enquist & Juell-Skielse (2010) studied Software-as-a-Service vendors and found two taxonomy types of value propositions within their sample of vendors. They differentiate between the holistic approach and the niche approach. The first is used by vendors to address customers who want a comprehensive solution, including full support for ERP. Small and medium sized enterprises are the target customers of this type. The niche approach is directed to large customer organizations and offers a limited number of specific functions of ERP. The customer remains responsible for integrating the functions into its operations and IT architecture (Enquist & Juell-Skielse, 2010).

Compared to the typical on-premises model, the observed and outlined value proposition of Software-as-a-Service includes various changes that are reflected in modifications of the delivery and pricing model. The different aspects imply multiple implications for the other building blocks of a software vendor's business model. Some aspects may even change the structure of the entire software industry. The value proposition is more complete in satisfying the customer's wish for software to provide functionality to support his business, rather than undesirably increasing complexity by software handling related issues. The general value proposition of software, that a customer can implement a business process with it, can be achieved more efficiently with a service model, as knowledge and experiences of required but no direct value creating activities of operating the software can be left to the vendor. The implications of the outlined value proposition for the entire business model are discussed in the following sections.

Customer Segments

Customer segments specify the different groups of people or organizations that an enterprise aims to reach and serve with its offerings (Osterwalder & Pigneur, 2010). A company may group customers into distinct segments with common needs, common behaviors, or other attributes in order to better response to differences among potential customers.

Case study observations: The case study data indicates that Software-as-a-Service may not be limited to a specific customer segment. The lower required up-front investments allow to target new customer groups, which previously could not afford the offered solutions because they were too expensive or too complex to deploy. Target customers are the functional departments, but with involvement of the IT departments. As defining and implementing an aligned strategy concerning Cloud Computing related concepts and technologies is promoted by companies' IT divisions, those days, when the IT department was bypassed, are said to be over. Apart from the mentioned extension of possibly targeted customers, companies of all sizes and domains are addressed by Software-as-a-Service vendors. There is no clear focus on a specific customer segment. On the other hand, quite the opposite can be observed as the market is increasingly global. The global reach is enabled for instance by platforms and integrated marketplaces.

> *"Due to the underlying technology, we do not have size limitations to specific customer segments. We also don't have a certain industry focus."* (A-1)

The limitations with regard to the customizability of Software-as-a-Service solutions also confine the customer segments. Vendors cannot satisfy all customer requirements without creating customer-specific workarounds that may influence the vendor's efficiency and profitability.

> *"And there it's easy to let go customers. In the past, it happened a few times that we had to let go big customers because their requirements required us to do too big of trade-offs."* (K-1)

Other observed limitations are based on the objectives to protect existing products and their accompanying service revenues from being cannibalized by the new offering.

Table 4.7.: Key observations within *Customer Segments*

Key observations	**Description**
No focus on specific segments	Software-as-a-Service can be used by companies of all sizes and all industry.
Additional customer groups	The pricing model reduces the investment barrier and companies with less resources can be targeted.
Limited fulfillment of customization requests	Customers with too many customization requirements cannot be addressed.

Literature discussion: The literature also does not reveal any clear indications for a specific customer segment. Characteristics of Software-as-a-Service adopting organizations have been studied, including companies of all sizes. There seems to be a trend that Software-as-a-Service is especially suitable for small and mid-sized companies. However, small corporations are also among the adopters (Benlian & Hess, 2009, 2010). Tyrväinen & Selin (2011) discovered a link between the customer and the provider size, with small providers targeting also smaller customer organizations, and large providers addressing larger customer organizations or the entire range of small to large organizations. The market is further widened by the emergence of Software-as-a-Service platform accompanying extension marketplaces, which allow vendors an easier access to a global market (Hilkert et al. 2010). Additional revenues may also be generated from customer segments, those of which were previously not able to afford complex solutions (Anding, 2010).

Looking inside the client's organization, a vendor may even want to distinguish the actual users of the system of one customer. As a client's solution may be accessed by internal and external users of that specific client, the requirements with regard to customization and security may vary considerably (Joha & Janssen, 2012). According to Luoma & Rönkkö (2012), simple and non-customized software of pure-play Software-as-a-Service leads to lower fees that appeal to the customer segment of small and medium sized enterprises. The actual persons buying a Software-as-a-Service solution are business managers or the top management (Tyrväinen & Selin, 2011). This is also supported by the cases of Enquist & Juell-Skielse (2010), where CEOs and CIOs initiated the consumption decision of solutions.

The case study findings, as summarized in Table 4.7, are in line with the discussion in the literature (Table 4.8). While Software-as-a-Service adoption factors are heavily discussed within the literature, it appears that there are hardly any customers that can be excluded from the target group of Software-as-a-Service solutions. Limiting factors of an adoption of Software-as-a-Service solutions are specific requirements of customers, which may not be fulfilled by current Software-as-a-Service solutions. While some aspects that hinder the adoption of Software-as-a-Service solutions by customers may be ascribable to customer reluctance, others may rather be the consequence of current technical limitations. Limited customizability can be seen as an example for the latter. Software vendors

Table 4.8.: Literature topics with regard to *Customer Segments*

Key topics	Description	Selected sources
Software-as-a-Service adoption factors	Studies discussing the adoption of Software-as-a-Service by organizations of different sizes	Benlian & Hess (2009, 2010); Luoma & Rönkkö (2012); Tyrväinen & Selin (2011); Wu et al. (2011); Xin & Levina (2008)
New customer segments	Studies discussing new markets and customer segments	Anding (2010)
International markets and platform	Studies discussing the international availability or possibilities of platforms	Hilkert et al. (2010)

may take advantage of reaching new customer segments and increasing the potential customer base but may also face increasing competition from competitors previously active in unconnected markets and countries.

Revenue Streams

Since the value proposition of Software-as-a-Service promotes a change in the pricing model as a central element, the *Revenue Stream* building block of the Software-as-a-Service business model is closely linked to the value proposition. The *Revenue Streams* building block specifies the prices charged for the value proposition offered by a company (Osterwalder & Pigneur, 2010). The prices may be different for each *Customer Segment*, as customers may have a different willingness to pay.

Case study observations: The interview partners mentioned the typical advantages for customers. The move towards variable instead of fix costs, as a result of the usage or time based subscription fees. In addition, vendors can charge for the additional activities that were previously done by the customers themselves. But customers are not charged for updates, which are already included in the subscription fee. Similarly, a basic support is in general included.

> *"There is a standard support that is already covered with the subscription fee. This means that the customer can raise questions that will be answered within a specified time. If the customer wants a quicker response time or a dedicated support contact, the customer has to pay a premium"* (A-1)

Enhancements to the software solution in form of new modules and entirely new features, on the other hand, may lead to additional fees. Because of the continuous evolvement of the solutions, a simple and consistent pricing model becomes harder to maintain.

> *"When I look at our price list, it becomes obvious that we have way too much modules that partly have a bad description, are partly obsolete, partly have been*

> *bundled with other modules to form reasonable packages. We have quite some difficulties with this because on the one hand, the customer is demanding new features, but on the other hand we do not want to overstrain the general user with this mass of possibilities."* (K-1)

Vendors need to identify the appropriate measure to link the usage-based pricing model to, and that are dependent on the benefits the customer may achieve from using the solution.

> *"The challenge is to evaluate which pricing model to choose. Which pricing model makes sense? What is the value driver for the customer? In our case, the value driver is not the number of users using the solution. This may be the case in CRM solutions. In our case, this doesn't make sense because the usage frequency between users varies significantly. Some users may access the solution daily, some may only log-in once a year. The value driver is the linchpin of the pricing model. And in our case it is not the number of users but the number of reference entities created in the solution. The more of these the user can manage with the solution, the bigger the value he gains from the usage of our solution."* (F-1)

Next to the changes to the pricing model, in terms of a move from fixed to variable pricing, the case data was focused on the complexity that the design of consistent pricing schemes may imply.

Table 4.9.: Key observations within *Revenue Streams*

Key observations	**Description**
Continuous revenue streams	Move towards a variable cost offering with subscription fees, which include the operations and maintenance of the solution, with potential updates and a basic support included.
Revenue model complexity	Pricing models are influenced by the evolutionary character of Software-as-a-Service solutions. Consistent and easy to understand pricing models are more complex to maintain.
Importance of value driver	The usage-based pricing model needs to be linked to the appropriate measures, which depend on the delivered value to the customer.

Literature discussion: The literature, which discusses aspects associated to the *Revenue Stream* building block, focuses on general implications of changing the pricing model of software. Cusumano (2008) expects service based revenues to substitute product revenues, while the price for standardized products is estimated to drop dramatically. His data reveals product revenues to account for only 50% of software companies' revenues in 2003. The profitability of software vendors seems to be positively influenced, if service revenue takes up below 20% or more than 60% of the total revenues. The potential new customer segment that is opened up by the reduced complexity and smaller up-front investment requirements may generate further revenues. However, these extra revenues are not expected to offset missing license revenues (Anding, 2010).

Apart from the pure subscription fees, costs or charges for existing contracts may play an important role, as they create not only a log-in effect, but at the same time adoption barriers (Ma, 2007). In addition, supporting services are supposed to account for a major share of profits and costs (Mohammed et al., 2010).

With a mature pricing model that evaluates fine grained software usage, the transaction volume and volatility of customers is influencing the competiveness of Software-as-a-Service to traditional solutions. In such a context, decreasing software quality is asked to be counter measured with increased prices (Ma & Seidmann, 2008). However, a recent study has revealed that currently vendors do not apply actual utility pricing schemes and mainly charge user-based, per-month subscription fees instead. Pricing therefore is still very similar to traditional license models (Gartner, 2009). These findings are supported by Enquist & Juell-Skielse (2010), who observed a dominance of monthly fees that varied according to the content used, per user, per month and combinations of these in their case studies. As Eurich et al. (2011) point out with a focus on Platform-as-a-Service solutions, current revenue models neglect various revenue possibilities by focusing on subscription models. Vendors may also take advantage of revenue streams from service consumers and other service providers that are, for instance, based on transactions, forms of revenue sharing, or advertisements (Eurich et al., 2011).

From a user perspective, Joha & Janssen (2012) argue that a transparent pricing model is important to set the right incentives for the customer. This may include a distinction between one-time implementation costs, expected recurring costs, potential additional costs for additional services or changes in volume, and the termination fees (Joha & Janssen, 2012).

For the vendor perspective, Bauer (2012) shares the experience, that the new pricing models and their resulting large number of smaller payments require significant adjustments to vendor's processes and methods. However, he does not provide any indications for a proper implementation. Instead, a rather large part of the literature, which addresses aspects from a vendor perspective, takes a rather technical focus and discusses dynamic pricing models for Cloud Computing in general without differentiating into Software-as-a-Service and other architectural layers. These contributions are concerned with the problem of optimal resource utilization under uncertain customer demand and provide mathematical optimization models and algorithms (e.g. Anandasivam & Premm, 2009; Mazzucco & Dumas, 2011; Pueschel et al., 2012; Sewook, 2011).

Compared to the findings from the case study (Table 4.9), the literature (Table 4.10) is focused on the general implications of a change in the pricing model of software, and does not directly address the raised question of growing complexity in communicating the pricing model that was dominant within the cases. Though complexity is seen as the reason for a lag of pay-per-use pricing models (Ojala & Tyrväinen, 2012), the literature

Table 4.10.: Literature topics with regard to *Revenue Streams*

Key topics	Description	Selected sources
General implications of new pricing model	Literature discussing the implications of the changing pricing model of software for the software industry	Anding (2010); Choudhary (2007b); Cusumano (2008); Ma (2007); Mohammed et al. (2010)
Trends and dominant pricing models	Literature discussing different pricing models and discussing prevalent patterns	Enquist & Juell-Skielse (2010); Eurich et al. (2011); Gartner (2009); Ojala & Tyrväinen (2012)
Administrative complexity of pricing model	Literature discussing the complexity to implement variable pricing models	Bauer (2012)
Dynamic pricing models	Literature discussing dynamic pricing models for Cloud Computing	Anandasivam & Premm (2009); Mazzucco & Dumas (2011); Mazzucco et al. (2010); Pueschel et al. (2012); Sewook (2011)

does not discuss the organizational requirements to facilitate pricing models that result in continuous small payments from a large number of customers. Such aspects are touched within rather practice oriented articles (e.g. Bauer, 2012), but not further discussed or analyzed. In summary, the findings form the case study and the literature indicate a complexity increase of the design and management of revenue streams.

Channels

The following sections will move on to the relationship centric building blocks that focus on the links between the software vendor and external entities. The *Channels* building block describes how a company communicates with and reaches its *Customer Segments* to deliver a value proposition (Osterwalder & Pigneur, 2010). *Channels* comprise the customer interface with touch points that play an important role in the customer experience.

Case study observations: The main channel a Software-as-a-Service vendor facilitates to interact with customers is the Internet. Solutions are delivered over the Internet and customers access them by using standard web-browsers.

Aside of the main delivery of solutions, the Internet is also heavily used as a channel to interact with customers. Software-as-a-Service vendors intensively use direct sales channels, like their websites, to attract new customers and initiate a sales process. Often additional documents and reports, that require the customer to provide contact information prior to access or download, are offered and the collected data utilized to start further sales activities.

> *"A high percentage of our leads originate from our homepage."* (A-1)

This is further supported by the popular possibility to offer trial periods to potential customers, which allow the latter to extensively test the software with its full functionality without any further obligation or setup requirements. Trial periods typically range from 7 to 30 days.

> *"For the software vendor, the flexible deployment of resources enables the possibility to, for example, offer test installations to its customers. A customer that is interested in the software can very easily try a test installation for a few weeks with just a click of a button. If the customer likes it, the test installation can easily be altered into a productive version. In case the customer doesn't like it, the test installation can easily been dismounted."* (C-1)

The test systems are established without much effort from the software vendor and provide a very simple way to inform the customer about the functions and features of the system and allow the customer to precisely evaluate the capabilities of the software solution against the set business requirements. Once the customer is convinced of the solution, transparent self-service sales processes can be initiated.

> *"Right from the demo system, the customer can open an order form. The customer just has to enter the number of users required and a calculation of the expected subscription fee is provided. The customer may add additional modules and at the end of this process the costs of the system are shown including a decomposition of the different cost components. It is very transparent and the customer in that moment knows exactly what do expect."* (J-1)

In development, product ideas are provided by the customer base or partners using idea platforms and are used to enhance the offering. Seamlessly integrated solutions are also used to provide help or to train the users. These functions go beyond static pages and include forums, videos and interactive tutorials.

> *"I don't need to open a separate channel. In on-premises software, there is a media transfer. In on-demand it is much easier to offer help over the internet and to provide the customer with a much better overall experience."* (B-3)

For the distribution and sales of the Software-as-a-Service solution, vendors can take advantage of marketplaces with standardized subscription processes. These marketplaces are offered by the larger Software-as-a-Service providers that have extended their solutions with platform offerings. On the platforms, smaller vendors can deploy their solutions and provide complementing functionality to the core Software-as-a-Service provider of the platform.

> *"Electronic marketplaces are especially attractive, as they allow an easy and straightforward possibility to make a Software-as-a-Service solution available and visible to customers. For the customer the acquisition of software is significantly eased by this."* (C-1)

"Marketplaces have a lot of potential. They are pretty much sales-promoting methods. When a vendor currently sells software for small- and medium-sized enterprises, such platforms suddenly offer the possibility to address foreign market and a fast and easy way. Vendors can perform a relatively easy market-entry." (C-2)

Table 4.11.: Key observations within *Channels*

Key observations	**Description**
Internet as delivery channel	The Software-as-a-Service solutions are delivered via the Internet and the customer accesses the solution using a web-browser.
Website as sales channel	A major share of sales are initiated by the customer on the software vendors website
Trial periods and demo systems	The customer can test drive Software-as-a-Service solutions for a period of time without any costs involved. Demo systems can easily be converted to paid systems.
Self-service functions	The customer can manage the solutions using self-service tools.
Feedback channels	Solutions have integrated feedback channels that allow customers to request and retrieve help with regard to functions or provide feedback.
Marketplaces as sales channels	Marketplaces provide sales channels especially for smaller Software-as-a-Service vendors.

Literature discussion: Within the literature, the prevalent consequence with respect to *Channels* is the use of the Internet and related technologies as the primary delivery channel (Saaksjarvi et al., 2005). Apart from the core service delivery, the Internet is also considered to act as major communication channel with regard to information provisioning, training or support activities, facilitating web collaboration platforms like webcast or forums (Stuckenberg & Heinzl, 2010).

Initial studies analyzing the role of the Internet as a sales channel in the Software-as-a-Service context can be found in the literature. Luoma & Rönkkö (2012) associate online channels for marketing, sales and delivery with the Software-as-a-Service concept and see a high level of automation within these activities as a consequence of the concept. Customer relationships may be established either through push-oriented high-pressure sales or as pull-oriented self-service. Tyrväinen & Selin (2011) also expected the Internet to be the main sales channel for Software-as-a-Service providers, but they found contradicting results within their conducted multi-case study, claiming that personal sales is the dominant channel to address new customers. Within their study, only one out of six providers used the Internet as channel for new customer acquisition. Thus, the costs to sign new customers are seen as important key performance indicator for Software-as-a-Service vendors. The market is claimed to be not mature enough for self-service to be an effective, rational and scalable alternative (Tyrväinen & Selin, 2011).

Table 4.12.: Literature topics with regard to *Channels*

Key topics	Description	Selected sources
Internet sales channels	Literature discussing the role of the internet as sales channel for Software-as-a-Service	Luoma & Rönkkö (2012); Tyrväinen & Selin (2011)

Table 4.11 and Table 4.12 provide a summary of the main findings from the case study and the identified literature respectively. The literature is limited to suggesting new or enhanced channels in the Software-as-a-Service context, but researchers do not analyze the implications in detail. The Internet is defined as main sales and delivery channel for Software-as-a-Service by articles defining the concept (e.g. Ma, 2007; Mäkilä et al., 2010; Saaksjarvi et al., 2005), the implications, for instance, in terms of the role of self-service systems in interacting with the customer are, however, rarely touched. This is especially important, as there appears to be a mismatch between the observations that self-service tools are heavily used and the literature suggesting that the market is not mature enough for such tools.

Customer Relationship

The *Customer Relationships* building block describes the types of relationships a company establishes with specific *Customer Segments* (Osterwalder & Pigneur, 2010). The type of relationship may, for example, vary for different customer segments or based on the applied pricing model.

Case study observations: The partly new or intensified communication channels already indicate a changed customer relationship, which is also signaled by a few other interesting facets that emerged during the interviews. As already indicated by the direct sales channels, further aspect suggesting a closer and more continuous relationship between the vendor and the customer can be observed.

> *"In fact, you are much closer to the customer and much closer to the customers' problems, when you operate [the software] yourself."* (B-1)

In the support departments, questions regarding installation specifications are obsolete. In fact, the support staff can directly look into the Meta information of an incident, and is then aware of the latest interactions with the system and can provide a quick solution. In the on-premises world, this was limited by the high number of possible variations of configurations.

The usage/user related information can be further utilized to prioritize development activities, putting more resources on aspects that are used heavily. At the same time, usage information may identify problems the users have when using the software.

> *"That means, I have the chance to develop the perfect application. This chance did not exist before, because I had to spend a lot of money to gather this data using traditional market research techniques."* (B-1)

On a more general level, the information gains can be facilitated to increase customer satisfaction.

> *"Because with the system operation, we have a good insight into how much a customer works with the system. We can't see what he does, but we can see if he uses it. And an indicator for an unsatisfied customer is one, who doesn't use the system that frequently."* (A-1)

A closer customer relationship is further expressed by the requirement to have an increase awareness of customers' processes and problems.

> *"It is called impact management. It already exists in the hosting area, you for example know when your customer runs critical processes, like the end-of-quarter closing, and take special care of the customer during these times."* (B-3)

Overall, the relationship between the customer and the software vendor is more continuous than before.

> *"With Software-as-a-Service, you sell a service. With on-premises, you first of all sell a license, with a transfer of rights from the vendor to the customer. There is of course a service afterwards, the maintenance contract. But with Software-as-a-Service the whole offering is a service and that is why the customer relationship is much more continuous."* (B-3)

Table 4.13.: Key observations within *Customer Relationship*

Key observations	Description
Continuous customer relationship	Software customer and software vendor are in a continuous relationship.
More customer insights	Software vendors have more knowledge about their customers and their usage of software due to the operation of the solution.

Literature discussion: Within the literature, the continuous relationship with the customer is only partly picked up. The accumulated responsibility of the complete architecture stack in the role of the Software-as-a-Service vendors is said to strengthen its position in the industry. The customer channel is owned by the vendor and providers of lower architectural layers are not required to maintain a communication channel with the customer anymore (Anding, 2010). Then again, lower switching costs are considered to weaken the relationship and as a result to cater for an increased investments in customer loyalty to compensate the effect (Hilkert et al., 2010). Examples are higher investments into software development with the result of an increased software quality that continuously convinces the customer to remain with the vendor (Choudhary, 2007b).

A closer customer relationship in phases like requirements engineering is expected as a consequence of the hybrid software and service character (Berkovich et al., 2010). Analogously does the direct customer relationship make additional user and interaction related information available that can be facilitated to increase the customer's satisfaction or further intensify the communication (Saeed & Jaffar-Ur-Rehmann, 2005). This is also supported by Luoma & Rönkkö (2012), who regard an increased focus on customer acquisition and retention to be a consequence of Software-as-a-Service.

Table 4.14.: Literature topics with regard to *Customer Relationship*

Key topics	Description	Selected sources
Changing customer relationship	Literature discussing changes in the customer relationship	Anding (2010); Hilkert et al. (2010); Luoma & Rönkkö (2012)
Facilitating customer relationship	Literature discussing the benefits of a changed customer relationship in the Software-as-a-Service context.	Berkovich et al. (2010); Saeed & Jaffar-Ur-Rehmann (2005)

Table 4.13 and Table 4.14 provide a summary of the main findings from the case study and the identified literature respectively. The case study findings indicate a closer relationship between the Software-as-a-Service provider and the customer. The continuity of the relationship is emphasized and the findings suggest that the provider may obtain a much more detailed knowledge about its customers. Within the literature, a changing customer relationship is identified and initial scenarios, like requirements engineering activities, are discussed that may benefit from the new form of relationship.

Key Partnerships

The value proposition of an organization typically relies on components or services of other companies. Within the partnership component of a business model, the relationships to other organizations are described (Osterwalder & Pigneur, 2010). From an organizational perspective, this component provides indications of the added value from external organizations to the value proposition.

Case study observations: The observations concerning partnerships can be distinguished between implications for the Software-as-a-Service vendor and those that affect the business model of the partners. For example, partner organizations that offer complementary products and service to the software vendors customer base. Even though partners were not in the focus of this study, some findings are worth mentioning since they have an indirect influence on the vendors' business model.

For the Software-as-a-Service vendor, the partner relationships are getting closer. Depending on the service of the partner, the two provided services are closer integrated.

> *"Processes need to be closely aligned and integrated because you deliver a joined service. In the end the customer gets a solution that is as consistent as possible."* (B-3)

This implies that similar to the vendor, the customer relationships of partners are also aiming on long-term relations.

The Software-as-a-Service concept makes certain business models of partners redundant or let the vendor enter into a direct competition with value propositions of partners. One example is integration activities, which can be offered very easily by the vendor. Due to the central infrastructure approach, the vendor can integrate its solution with other applications once and that integration is afterwards available to all its customers. The previously local integration in every customer's system is not required anymore. Integrators specialized in these activities are left with small scale application integrations that are not accomplished by the vendors yet. Similarly, partners that offer integration services for lower architectural layers lose business. Software-as-a-Service vendors not only offer a software solution to the customer, but also take care of the underlying infrastructure. The customer receives the entire architectural stack of a software solution from one vendor and does not need to deal with integration activities on lower levels anymore. The integration between a database system, middleware and business application software, for instance, is all dealt with by the vendor and not of concern for the customer.

> *"The partners, whose business models target on making money from configuration or the infrastructure, won't exist anymore in the future."* (A-1)

On the other hand, the concept also offers new revenue possibilities to partners. The changes require the partner to standardize and scale their services. The specific services need to be productized and offered to the global customer base of the Software-as-a-Service vendor.

> *"Partners need to use their specific added value know-how to form new own products that they offer on marketplaces and that are operated on platform solutions."* (B-1)

One example in this context could be integration functions, which are offered to the customer as a service and link two Software-as-a-Service solutions together. The implementation can, due to the standardization and accompanied acceleration of the process, be regarded as a productized, classic IT-service. It is charged as a fixed price and requires the partners to generate more volume by more implementation projects.

Literature discussion: The identified articles addressing the partnership component of a Software-as-a-Service business model are often discussing an industry perspective. Due to the increasing number of partners that are not necessarily bound by contracts to the provider and instead more market-organized, Hilkert et al. (2010) expect a growing requirement of developing new skills in the management and orchestration of partner

Table 4.15.: Key observations within *Key Partnerships*

Key observations	**Description**
Closer relationship	As partners and vendors provide joint services, the relationship between the two becomes closer and also more continuous.
Obsolete business models	The responsibility shifts of Software-as-a-Service enable software vendors to take over activities that were previously left to partners.
New business opportunities	New business opportunities emerge or gain significance with the Software-as-a-Service concept.

relationships. They argue with a higher degree of market coordination in "as-a-Service" ecosystems, since a coordination implementing a market would result in comparably lower absolute transaction costs in the relationship between provider and partners. Cusumano (2008) predicts an increased direct competition of partners and vendors regarding activities that previously were not addressed by vendors.

The business model of partners may differ from models of traditional software vendor partners. The role of the conventional integrator, responsible for composing and configuring software solutions or providing the market with information, will decrease because major parts of these activities are taken over by the Software-as-a-Service vendors themselves. On the other side, trust building activities, legal counseling or risk consulting services may create new business opportunities (Hilkert et al., 2010). Lassila (2006) analyzed the role of system integrators and outline how they may take advantage of the Software-as-a-Service business model and transform their business models into more service oriented ones without ignoring associated risks.

Leimeister et al. (2010) and Ojala & Tyrväinen (2011) outline suggestions for the design of the value network of Cloud Computing. For instance, Leimeister et al. (2010) describe the new role of customers, service providers, infrastructure providers, aggregate services providers, platform provider, and consultants. They demand more research on the partner networks as roles are changing and Cloud Computing is often considered as disruptive innovation. Service value networks may require different approaches to manage and maintain the partner network. Conte et al. (2010), for instance, suggest that revenues may be shared among partners, even if they did not actively participate in a transaction. Revenues may be shared among service providers that actually contribute to a complex service offering, but also with those partners who are on standby and, for instance, contribute to the network's variety and stability.

The existing literature agrees that further research in Software-as-a-Service eco-systems and the implications of Software-as-a-Service for the software market is required (Lassila, 2006; Leimeister et al., 2010).

The main findings with regard to Software-as-a-Service partner networks from the case study and the identified literature are shown in Table 4.15 and Table 4.16.

Table 4.16.: Literature topics with regard to *Key Partnerships*

Key topics	Description	Selected sources
Software ecosystems	Literature discussing implications and changes to existing partner networks and potential forms of a Software-as-a-Service ecosystem	Conte et al. (2010); Cusumano (2008); Hilkert et al. (2010); Ojala & Tyrväinen (2011)
Roles of different partners	Literature discussing the role of different partners in a Software-as-a-Service provider's network / platform	Hilkert et al. (2010); Lassila (2006); Leimeister et al. (2010)
Partner platforms	Literature discussing the role of platforms and marketplaces	Conte et al. (2010)

Key Resources

After the discussion of business model building blocks that focus on relationship aspects, the next sections address rather vendor internal aspects instead. The business model building blocks *key resources*, *key activities*, and *cost structure* focus on internal capabilities and describe how the promised value proposition is created. The key resources describe the most important assets required to make the business model work, while key activities focus on the activities and processes involved.

Case study observations: Building up competence regarding infrastructure and operation activities is considered as an important implication of the Software-as-a-Service concept. These are required to drive innovation and assure an efficient service delivery at manageable costs.

> *"A big investment is the investment in building up know-how. Training people to understand the technologies and be able to work with these."* (C-2)

Being responsible for the operation of the service also affects the core competencies of the vendors, as security aspects are now perceived as key capabilities.

> *"We are a company that considers IT security as its core competence. We think of IT operations as our core competence."* (A-2)

But also competence regarding technologies and methods that allow to efficiently scale is highly demanded. Software-as-a-Service providers need to be able to flexibly react to changes in demand. For that, not only the right people and skills are required, but also the organizational requirements are needed to assign resources dynamically.

> *"It may well happen that due to a successful marketing campaign, the customer base is increased by a factor of 2 or even 10. When you in this situation don't have enough support staff to answer telephone calls, then it can happen that the customers are gone again quicker than you can count. That means that*

you have to be aware of the employees and organizational structures you need as a provider to satisfy customers and to tie them to your solution." (G-1)

Software-as-a-Service requires vendors to build up additional resources that are linked to new responsibility of operating the software solutions. This includes infrastructure related aspects like the scalability of the entire solution and the required physical hardware, but also the skills and knowledge of involved people dealing with the new aspects.

Table 4.17.: Key observations within *Key Resources*

Key observations	Description
Additional physical assets	Due to the additional responsibilities of software vendors new assets (e.g. server infrastructure) are required.
Additional know-how and skills	The new responsibilities require additional skills and know-how.

Literature discussion: The literature suggests that the control of the complete architecture stack requires building up capabilities on all layers. For current application software companies, especially infrastructure or ecosystem management related capabilities may not have been in the focus before (Anding, 2010). The service availability and elasticity aspects both drive complexity of service provisioning and call for altered mind-sets in development of the software and operation of the service (Benefield, 2009). New skill profiles and jobs may emerge (Manford, 2008). The capabilities to deliver Software-as-a-Service and especially those that are not directly adoption related are not addressed appropriately. Vendors currently seem to overestimate their capabilities and do not expect Software-as-a-Service to challenge existing practices (Heart et al., 2010).

Delivering Software-as-a-Service helps to protect the intellectual property of vendors and reduce the chance of competitors to reproduce resources. For example, software piracy is avoided as source code is not leaving the control of the vendor anymore (Saeed & Jaffar-Ur-Rehmann, 2005).

The literature offers various contributions in form of methods and tools to optimize the provisioning process of Cloud Computing resources (e.g. Chaisiri et al., 2012; Chard & Bubendorfer, 2013; Khazaei et al., 2012) or assuring its reliability (e.g. Zheng et al., 2012). Especially, research concerned with architectural problems, like multi-tenancy architectures, can be frequently found in the literature (e.g. Aulbach et al., 2008; Bobrowski, 2011; Fehling et al., 2010; Liang-Jie & Jia, 2009.

Table 4.17 and Table 4.18 summarized the key findings from the case study and the literature. While the findings point at the requirement to build up additional resources and knowledge, the literature lacks providing assistance with integrating those resources into the organization, and with disseminating the required knowledge within the organization.

Table 4.18.: Literature topics with regard to *Key Resources*

Key topics	**Description**	**Selected sources**
Changed resources and skills	Literature discussing changes to required resources and skills	Anding (2010); Benefield (2009); Heart et al. (2010)
Technologies and methods	Literature discussing specific technologies or methods that assist in developing and delivering Software-as-a-Service	Aulbach et al. (2008); Bobrowski (2011); Chaisiri et al. (2012); Chard & Bubendorfer (2013); Fehling et al. (2010); Khazaei et al. (2012); Liang-Jie & Jia (2009); Zheng et al. (2012)

Instead, the discussion is often focused on technical aspects assuring balanced resource utilization.

Key Activities

Key activities describe the activities and processes required to deliver the value proposition, reach markets, and maintain customer relationships (Osterwalder & Pigneur, 2010).

Case study observations: With regard to activities and processes, the most obvious implication is of course the extension of the process of value creation with operation related activities.

Parts of these latter steps, especially the process to get a customer using the system, are highly standardized and tool-supported.

> *"All providers make a living automating as much as possible. That means, every support call, every individual move for a specific customer costs money and should be avoided."* (C-1)

Perceived complexity increases exist with regard to update cycles, as updates or enhancements affect the whole customer base at once, due to the central multi-tenancy architectures. A disruption of customers' processes, however, has to be avoided.

> *"I can't just add new functions and the user does not recognize his work environment on the next day anymore. Enhancements have to work in a complete different way."* (B-3)

Compatible and continuous development is required and is challenging existing release-based development cycles. This is especially important, since the customer does not have the possibility to choose if he wants an update. The advantage for the vendor, however, is that it can focus all its resources on one release, without being required to reserve developers for the support of older versions. This is perceived to accelerate the development and innovation process. Innovation priorities move from functions to performance and cost efficiency.

Table 4.19.: Key observations within *Key Activities*

Key observations	**Description**
Process extension	The software development process does not end with the finalization of a new release, as the software vendor in the Software-as-a-Service concept also takes care of the operation and maintenance of the solution.
Automation of processes	To be scalable and profitable, vendors need to automate processes and avoid customer individual work.

Literature discussion: Within the literature, the discussion of the implications of the Software-as-a-Service concept on the key activities is divided into mainly two streams. The first focusing on the analysis of implications on a process or organizational level, the latter proposing development processes that fit to the Software-as-a-Service concept or specific characteristics of the concept.

Key activities of Software-as-a-Service vendors are the software development, deployment and operations processes, since these are essential for the value creation of the company. In the service context, the value creation is archived to a considerable degree in the later of these activities (Ramaswamy, 1994). Significant changes to the processes are expected (Espadas et al., 2008; Saeed & Jaffar-Ur-Rehmann, 2005; Stuckenberg & Heinzl, 2010).

Among the envisioned implications are continuous, integrated processes of development and operations, a changed quality understanding, or information quality improvements, gained from the direct end-user relationship (Stuckenberg & Heinzl, 2010). Existing development methodologies that aim on supporting and organizing development activities are expected to not fit to the new Software-as-a-Service context (Stuckenberg & Heinzl, 2010). An evaluation of existing software development methodologies and a review of the literature are provided by Stuckenberg & Heinzl (2010) and Stuckenberg & Beiermeister (2012).

The emergence of Software-as-a-Service accompanying platform offerings may, for example, predefine architectural or technological aspects and affect related evaluation and design activities (Espadas et al., 2008). Espadas et al. (2008) develop a software development method focusing on Software-as-a-Service platforms by comparing the software life cycle of traditional and service-based software. Following a sequential waterfall-model, they analyze the different phases of software development and suggest, for instance, that requirements engineering has to be extended by scalability and vendor platform specific requirements and analysis.

Saeed & Jaffar-Ur-Rehmann (2005) analyze, from a rather technical perspective, the requirements which are related to a paradigm shift from a product-based model to Software-as-a-Service. The authors consider ultra-late binding of services as the key point of service-based software engineering, highlighting the fine-granularity of solutions. Other impacted aspects are the maintenance of software, service configuration, and how customers are involved in software development and evolution. Building on these results, Olsen (2006) discusses the software engineering practices comparing three aspects (planning, versioning, and maintenance) of product and service-based offerings applying also a management perspective. He concludes that practices need to be adjusted to the new context to compete in the marketplace and to allocate resources appropriately, for instance by shifting the focus from new customers to maintaining long-term stable relationships with the existing customer base.

Haines (2007) analyzes the impact again from a more technical perspective and places a special focus on the common Software-as-a-Service enabling technology: web services. The author declares five influences on methodology choice: environment, technology, organization, individual and task. The analysis and conducted case study indicate required changes in development skills, roles, process and organizational culture, all pushed by the use of web technologies (Haines, 2007).

Singh (2008) discusses the limitations of traditional SCRUM in the context of Software-as-a-Service, as the end-user interaction with the application and the frequent product releases challenge the development processes. Benefield (2009) analyzes lean practices of the manufacturing industry and how they can be applied on software, in order to help the software industry to cope with the arising challenges connected to Software-as-a-Service. Guo & Wang (2009) define incident management models for Software-as-a-Service grounded on ITIL, which include the customers with their users and the Software-as-a-Service providers with integrators and independent software vendors. Berkovich et al. (2010) take a focused approach on the requirements engineering phase of the software development process and argue similarly with the emergence of a second stakeholder, the service provider that requests operations related requirements. The requirements engineering methods, therefore, need to incorporate software and service aspects and domain knowledge, continuous processes with tight customer integration and be capable of multiple requirement sources and stakeholders. Further software development processes specifically designed for Software-as-a-Service are suggested by Agarwal (2011) or La & Kim (2009). Stuckenberg & Beiermeister (2012) point out that most of the existing research suggesting development processes for Software-as-a-Service only address a subset of characteristics of the concept. Studies tend to take a technical perspective and focus on characteristics like standardization, web-technologies, multi-tenancy or the fine granularity of functions (Stuckenberg & Beiermeister, 2012).

Next to the processes, the Software-as-a-Service concept also moves the development focus towards criteria like reusability, scalability, and availability (La & Kim, 2009). Commonly used technologies, like multi-tenancy, further support this change. The development prioritization switches from feature enhancement to operational cost decreasing functionality (Aulbach et al., 2008).

The potential and benefit of appropriate internal processes and structures for vendors are indicated by Luoma & Rönkkö (2012), as they explicitly define Software-as-a-Service as a business model to organize software development, deployment and operation in an efficient manner.

Table 4.20.: Literature topics with regard to *Key Activities*

Key topics	Description	Selected sources
Changing processes	Literature discussing requirements to change processes to fit to the Software-as-a-Service context	Benefield (2009); Haines (2007); Olsen (2006); Saeed & Jaffar-Ur-Rehmann (2005); Stuckenberg & Beiermeister (2012); Stuckenberg & Heinzl (2010)
Focus of development	Literature discussing a changing focus of development activities	Aulbach et al. (2008); La & Kim (2009)
Development methodologies	Literature suggesting Software-as-a-Service development methodologies or tools	Agarwal (2011); Berkovich et al. (2010); Espadas et al. (2008); Guo & Wang (2009); Kapuruge et al. (2011); La & Kim (2009); Singh (2008)

Key activities are subject to multiple implications of the Software-as-a-Service concept. The identified aspects of the case study are shown in Table 4.19. Table 4.20 includes those topics discussed within the literature.

Cost Structure

The *Cost Structure* building block describes all costs incurred to operate a business model. The costs depend on the specifications of every component of a business model and, for instance, include the costs to create and deliver value, or maintain customer relationships.

Case study observations: Implications regarding the cost structure of Soft-ware-as-a-Service vendors are a consequence of the previously described changes. The focus on direct and shorter sales cycles, for example, leads to reduced costs for customers and vendors.

> *"In the end, the cost savings of the shortened sales cycle are beneficial for the customer but also for the provider"* (B-3)

However, the Software-as-a-Service concept and related technologies require a certain scale to be able to be operated at manageable costs and to take full advantage of its potentials.

> *"With Software-as-a-Service, we made the experience that the costs do not scale proportionally. You only have to add a new server every thousand customer or so and if you are doing good with FAQs and the like then you may save on the number of required support employees. Costs do not necessarily scale proportional with the number of customers or the revenue as you have possibilities to work very cost efficient, especially when you are aware of the main cost drivers."* (G-1)

The investment risk for vendors is higher than before, because vendors have to make the specific investments and are exposed to a hold-up risk. The major implications of the Software-as-a-Service concept, however, are anticipated efficiency gains throughout the whole value chain.

> *"The bottom line is that Software-as-a-Service as a deployment and operation mode is much more efficient than traditional on premise software, furthermore it allows to develop better software. For this reason, in the long run it has to be more profitable."* (B-3)

Table 4.21.: Key observations within *Cost Structure*

Key observations	**Description**
Changed cost structure	Due to the new responsibilities and added activities, additional cost components arise on the vendor side.
Importance to scale	Scaling the service and offering solutions to a large number of customers with efficient resource usage becomes crucial.

Literature discussion: The literature also provides contributions with regard to the cost structure of Software-as-a-Service. Fan et al. (2009) observed Software-as-a-Service vendors to experience an increased cost pressure, as they have to compete with traditional vendors and invest in software quality to be competitive, while at the same time handle operational costs. To achieve a sufficient perceived quality by the customer, high quality features and functions as well as efficient service operations, and therefore a competition on two fronts, is required. Both are significant cost drivers (Fan et al., 2009). Operational expenses replace capital expenses in the improvement priority list (Aulbach et al., 2008). The 'productization' of services, in the sense of standardizing services for a more efficient delivery, is of equal importance as the 'servitization' of products (Cusumano, 2008).

Focused on productivity, Huang & Wang (2009) and Ge & Huang (2011a,b) postulate that Software-as-a-Service vendors will benefit from greater productivity increases due to maturing technologies and R&D investments.

Table 4.21 and Table 4.22 summarize the key findings from the case study and the key topics discussed in the relevant literature. Both streams provide support for an increased cost pressure for software vendors. The changed pricing model and the importance to

Table 4.22.: Literature topics with regard to *Cost Structure*

Key topics	Description	Selected sources
Total cost of ownership	Literature discussing the cost structure and total costs of ownership of Software-as-a-Service vendors	Aulbach et al. (2008); Choudhary (2007b); Fan et al. (2009); Susarla et al. (2009)
Productivity analysis	Studies discussing the productivity of Software-as-a-Service for vendors	Ge & Huang (2011a,b); Huang & Wang (2009)

reach economies of scale are discussed as key drivers of this situation. However, vendors in the long-term may profit from productivity gains as a consequence of the increased control over large parts of the value chain.

Discussion and Summary

The observations from the case study as well as the review of the literature within the last section have revealed different implications of the Software-as-a-Service concept for the business models and practices of software vendors. They raise new challenges for software vendors offering Software-as-a-Service. Table 4.23 summarizes the findings and discussion on a business model element level. It shows that the Software-as-a-Service concept affects every building block and, thereby, confirms its disruptive character. It underlines the need to assess the impact of Software-as-a-Service in an integrated, holistic manner, for instance by means of the business model concept, and to move beyond a focus on isolated aspects such as adoption factors or risks. A subset of the presented findings, which has been published in Stuckenberg et al. (2011), is confirmed by a later study of Joha & Janssen (2012).

From a cross-element perspective, the impact is driven by the customer-facing elements: it centers on the *Value Proposition* (the service concept) and it originates in particular from the *Channels* (delivery model) and *Revenue Streams* (pricing model) components. As the majority of the Software-as-a-Service concept definitions comprise the delivery and pricing model as key differentiating factors to the on-premises business, this is hardly surprising. More interesting, though, are the implications of the residual, vendor-internal elements, as some of the identified consequences fundamentally challenge existing practices of software vendors. Based on the previously discussed findings, the *Key Activities*, *Customer Relationship* and *Key Partnership* aspects are particularly challenged. Key activities, as the value generation is not limited to software development anymore but also originated from an efficient service delivery involving all architectural layers. Existing development methodologies may not address the delivery aspects appropriately and cumber a tight integration of development and operations. The customer role is further strengthened, as the vendor establishes a long-term direct relationship when delivering Software-as-a-Service. It is required to respond to customer wishes as vendors continuously need to convince the customer to stay with the service. On the supply side, the Software-as-a-Service concept challenges parts of the existing structures of the partner ecosystem.

It can be observed that the customer/demand oriented elements (*Value Proposition*, *Channels*, *Revenue Streams* and *Customer Segments*), in particular, indicate similarities regarding the applied business model, e.g. with regard to the pricing scheme. The vendor/supply oriented elements vary more significantly. This is further supported by a focus of the Software-as-a-Service related discussion in the literature and in practice on how to foster customer adoption and solve related problems. Most attention is, therefore, attracted by the customer oriented components. It can however be speculated, that the main changes and challenges for software vendors concern supply oriented components like *Key Activities* and *Key Resources*. Supporting arguments for this hypothesis can, for example, be found in current price models, as most of these are not yet applying real usage-based pricing schemes and are mainly based on fixed time periods like monthly payments. A usage-based pricing model, that for example charges the number of times when a certain function is used, may require changes to underlying internal processes or resources. To be measurable, this may, for example, require appropriate software architecture. But also from an administrative perspective, practical contributions within the literature indicate that the format of payments, as small and frequent amounts, challenge internal processes and require building up the necessary handling capabilities. A second innovation wave of customer/demand oriented components with new forms of *Value Propositions*, *Revenue Streams* or *Customer Segments* may be expected once the supply-related issues have been resolved. For example, introducing innovative functionality, extending customization options and new, needs-based customer segmentation.

Concerning the evaluation of the impact of Software-as-a-Service, the previous discussion makes clear that the concept strongly influences business models of Software-as-a-Service vendors. However, the impact can differ, in particular for the vendor/supply oriented business model elements. The evaluation revealed a preliminary list of implications. Some of these have already been addressed by the vendors; others are yet to be resolved.

To a certain extent, the co-existence of either both delivery models or the focus on a pure Software-as-a-Service model seem to have an impact, in particular on the *Customer Segments* and the *Key Partnerships*. Vendors with two business models may create sufficient differentiation factors to avoid conflicts with existing product revenues. Similarly, the partner ecosystem inherits possible disputes, as partners of the on-premises business may be in a situation of direct competition in the service model. However, offering software in a product, as well as service mode, may also create synergies with regard to resources or the cost structure, as the increased Software-as-a-Service related investment risks may be balanced with established revenue streams of the product business.

In summary, the analysis of the Software-as-a-Service concept from a business model perspective has revealed different implications. The Software-as-a-Service concept is expected to have major implications on the business logic of a software vendor in terms of

Table 4.23.: Summary of implications on different business model components

Building Block	Implications
Customer Segments	Customer segments are manifold and an increasingly global market is addressed by vendors. Various adoption barriers and risks have been identified in the literature and it seems as if vendors themselves further support and propagate limitations because of their desire to protect existing product revenues.
Value Proposition	The value proposition promises flexibility and carefree service delivery with regard to resources, updates and enhancements, and even implementation scope. The literature and the cases, however, indicate that this requires fundamental changes to processes and mindsets, e.g. version-free software, to be realized.
Channels	Communication, distribution and sales channels are making extensive use of the Internet and vendors are utilizing subsequent opportunities, e.g. forums, idea platforms, or video streams to automate processes and to increase efficiency.
Customer Relationship	The customer relationship is expected to be closer, more direct and with a more continuous orientation. As a consequence of the direct feedback channel, the information base regarding customer requirements is strengthened.
Revenue Streams	Revenue streams of Software-as-a-Service vendors are dependent on the variable pricing model of subscription fees and challenge existing practices of consulting or implementation services.
Key Resources	Infrastructure and operation related capabilities gain importance and extend the key resources of a software vendor.
Key Activities	The processes to develop, deploy and operate the service require integrating development and operations activities and seting a focus on efficiency in the whole end-to-end process. Existing release-based development cycles are challenged.
Key Partnerships	The competition between the vendors' and partners' business models, as part of the existing value propositions of partners are absorbed by the vendors. The cases not only reveal concrete examples of conflicts, but also point at opportunities for partners to engage in new fields. However the service delivery increasingly requires a joint and consistent integration of vendor and partner processes.
Cost Structure	The cost structure is pressurized by the additional operations related activities and obligation to investment in software as well as service quality. The regarded organizations, however, are convinced that the possible – maybe yet to address – efficiency gains will result in a profitable business model in the long-term.

how it creates, delivers and captures value when implementing the concept. While most attention is focused on the impact on the value proposition, channels and revenue model, as they form the more visible part of the Software-as-a-Service concept, the impact on key activities, customer relationship and key partnerships of software vendors should not be underestimated. Some of the specific issues for software vendors related to these building blocks are the integration of development and operations activities, a focus on efficiency in the whole end-to-end process, closer and more direct relations with customers with a more continuous orientation, and a more balanced perspective of partners. They are not only the possible threats of redundancies, but they also create the need for closer collaboration and, thus, new revenue opportunities have to be considered. The evaluation from a business model perspective has shown that more research, especially with regard to the internal capabilities and processes, is required.

4.3.2. The Software-as-a-Service Value Chain

The second perspective to evaluate the implications of the Software-as-a-Service concept on software vendors is the value chain perspective. As outlined in section 4.1.2, value chains contain activity categories that disaggregate the value creation into rather distinct subgroups. The following section will present the observations from the case study with regard to the different value activities of a software vendor in the Software-as-a-Service context. In comparison to the analysis from a business model perspective, the observations of the value chain perspective are more focused on the value creation during the process of developing and providing a Software-as-a-Service solution. Thus, the focus is set on the activities that develop the capabilities to deliver the promised value proposition. Since the value chain of the software industry, as developed by Pussep et al. (2012), is used for the analysis, the scope is not necessarily limited to one organization. Instead, the perspective includes indications about the orchestration of responsibilities among all participants involved in the delivery of the value proposition to the customer. As a consequence of this focus, an overlap with previously presented observations within the *Key Partnership* and *Key Activity* building blocks may occur. In this case, the focus of the subsequent section is set on a process view, emphasizing the sequence and connections between different activities of the value chain. As outlined within Section 4.1.2, the activities of a value chain follow a sequential order, thus the presentation of observations within the different activities in the subsequent section will comply with this general assumption.

Research

The research activity covers the development of a product vision and decisions about major technologies (Pussep et al., 2012). Among them is the decision to use a multi-tenancy architecture. Like in other developments, architectural decisions are difficult to change in later stages of development.

Dependent on the scope of the research phase, the advertised continuous evolution of Software-as-a-Service solutions leads to changes. With regard to the research phase providing the initial idea and prototyping of a new product, the continuous evolution leads to a longer life-cycle of solutions. Creating initial ideas remains the starting point of the Software-as-a-Service value chain, however, incremental innovation gains importance. A continuous research phase that provides development with new solution enhancement and improvement ideas appears more appropriate in the Software-as-a-Service context than a onetime initial activity.

> *"OnDemand tries to get rid of release cycles and tries to develop compatible enhancements. This is a fundamental difference to OnPremises."* (B-3)

Innovations need to be incremental rather than disruptive. The characteristics of Software-as-a-Service may allow increasing the information quality innovations and incremental improvements to solutions are based on, as vendors with their direct customer relationship can take advantage of observing and learning from their customers.

> *"You have access [to your customer base], instead of having to conduct and extensively analyze a classic market research study with a random sample, you have basically access to you entire customer base. You can work with the complete data set. That means you can develop a significant competitive advantage by knowing more about your customer than any competitor."* (B-1)

Based on this observation, it can be expected that research activities, not only move closer to development, but also operations activities.

Development

The previous discussion within the business model building block of *Key Activities* has already revealed various implications of the Software-as-a-Service concept on the development phase and its processes (see Section 4.3.1). From a value chain perspective, one of the most obvious changes is the amalgamation of the phase with other phases of the value chain. Due to the continuous evolution and the decreasing role of releases, the development phase is, for instance, mixed with the maintenance phase. The frequency of delivering new updates is undermining the former separation between core development and maintenance.

Furthermore, the gained responsibility for operation activities leads to the opera-tion-related software features to gain importance. Development and operations may work closer together to provide Software-as-a-Service solutions.

> *"You cannot say you develop software and later you think about its implementation and operation, instead you actually right from the beginning think of the ideal way to implement the software at the customer and how it is operated and how it is consumed."* (B-3)

Production

The production phase is concerned with preparing the delivery of software. Software-as-a-Service solutions are not packaged on a physical media and sent to the customer anymore. Instead the solutions are delivered to the customer via the Internet. As a consequence, the traditional value chain activities of *production* are no longer required. Documentation is embedded in the solution, making shipment to customers not necessary.

However, the production activities that aim on preparing the solution for delivery to the customer, for instance by creating physical distribution media, can still be found in the Software-as-a-Service context. Even though in this context, they take quite a different form. Instead of creating physical distribution media and accompanying documentation, production is concerned with the establishment of the basic service capacity. This includes all aspects of preparing the necessary capabilities to provide and deliver the offered service with exception of the software artifact itself.

Though there is no need to create a (physical) distribution media for every customer, the activities of production phase may need to safeguard the scaling of the solution for additional customers. Similar to development activities being closely linked to maintenance activities, the production activities are interlinked with aspects that concern the operation of the solution.

Marketing

The marketing phase is concerned with activities that increase the awareness of the solution for customers in order to sell it (Pussep et al., 2012). As discussed within the building block of *Channels*, Software-as-a-Service providers tend to use the Internet within this phase. From a value chain perspective, a link between activities of marketing and implementation activities can be observed. Initial projects are used to convince the customer and to generate further projects with additional revenues.

> *"Our aim is to get the customer productive as quick as possible and by proving our capabilities, be able to collect further requirements to be implemented subsequently."* (A-2)

The flexible scope of Software-as-a-Service solutions is used to exploit first implementation projects at the customer as marketing tool for further sales activities. The characteristics of the solutions allow gradually selling the solutions.

> *"The whole implementation approach does not target on a Big Bang, instead [a customer] can start with small functionality and thanks to the scalability of the software, regarding users, but also regarding the flexible unlocking of additional functions, [a vendor] can sell the software gradually."* (B-3)

In addition, the sales processes are standardized and automated. Potential customers can use self-service systems to sign-up for trial periods or directly subscribe to the solution.

Implementation

As outlined within the *Value Proposition* building block, implementation projects become smaller and are completed within a shorter time frame.

The standardization of the solutions and the multi-tenancy architecture result in a basic system to be ready for the customer within automated steps. Implementation is, therefore, not concerned with the underlying infrastructure anymore and concentrated on the fine-tuning of the solution to the needs of the customer.

> *"The software is simply activated, it doesn't need to be installed any more, it is just activated and users are created and log-in information is sent to the customer."* (A-1)

As typical for standardized solutions, customers can make various configurations using self-service functions of the solutions.

> *"Using business-related questionnaires within the system, the system is scoped to the specific requirements automatically based on the customer's answers. That is a revolutionary step forward."* (B-2)

Education

The education phase is concerned with user training. Within the Software-as-a-Service context, the cases indicate a strong emphasis on usability. Vendors try to reduce the training requirements of its users to a minimum.

> *"Then there is the necessity of trainings so that the users know how to use the system appropriately. But the need for training is actually extremely small. Everything has a very intuitive user interface."* (A-1)

Remaining training requirements are often tool supported and directly embedded in the solutions.

> *"Either the software is simple enough that you don't need training or you use other training methods. For instance, by providing continuous assistance with the help of e-learning tools. With on-demand software, the possibilities to integrate web 2.0 concepts are much bigger. That you don't just offer a static help page but instead include forums and videos. These can be uploaded continuously. Something like demo videos or tutorials. I don't need to open a separate channel. In on-premises software, there is a media transfer. In on-demand it is much easier to offer help over the internet and to provide the customer with a much better overall experience"* (B-3)

Operations

A major change within the software value chain is the shifting responsibility of operations activities from the customer to the software vendor. As described in the concept's core idea, the vendor is now responsible for the development and the operation of the Software-as-a-Service solutions.

> *"And that, I think, makes the change, how the value chain is altered. By adding an additional element, software developers are now also software operators."* (C-2)

Linked to the responsibility for the operation of solutions are various other aspects that like indicated in the *Key Resources* building block become core competencies of software vendors.

> *"On the one hand, certain tasks do not take place at the customer or end-customer anymore and instead are executed by the provider. That includes the operation but that also includes risk management and emergency management of data and backups. There are a lot of services that need to be executed by the provider itself that previously lay within the responsibility of the customer."* (B-3)

Maintenance

The distinction of the maintenance phase within the value chain of Pussep et al. (2012) is based on the characteristics of the software component developed. Maintenance focuses on bug-fixing and disruptive free enhancements. Within the Software-as-a-Service context, however, enhancements may always not disrupt the customer. As the operation and maintenance of the solutions is done by the Software-as-a-Service vendor, updates and their timing are based on the decision of the vendor. The customer's control of the process is minimal.

> *"In the OnDemand context, the customer cannot choose whether he wants or doesn't want a new release, instead he is automatically and continuously kept on the latest state of the software. That is also why I need to avoid that something changes in a way that the customer has to adjust or requires new training."* (B-3)

It is the responsibility of the software vendor to assure that customers can proceed in their daily business activities with the software solution. The continuous evolution of Software-as-a-Service solutions, in addition, leads to updates, including enhancements and bug-fixing, being made available on a continuous basis. The maintenance activities as a consequence move closer to the general development activities and both groups of activities are less resoluble.

Support

The support activities cover the end-users and the stakeholders operating the software. The latter are now an internal unit of the organization, the related support is thus likely to be very close to the operations units. At the same time, operation-related questions and issues do not reach the vendor from the customer anymore.

> *"I can image, that things like maintenance and problems that are based on different software releases or because some system administrator made a bad installation that leads to reliability issues, that these things don't come up anymore"* (B-2)

Keeping the entire customer base on one software release, in addition, enables the support to increase its efficiency.

> *"Since you pretty much have all your customers on one state of development, a lot of support requests get simpler, as you do not have to ask the customer on which database the system is running, of which release the system is. If you find an error, you can pro-actively fix it before other support requests come in."* (B-2)

Aggregating the responsibility for operations, development, and support within one organization may in addition to the potential efficiency gains, also benefit the customer, as vendors get a better understanding of customer problems.

> *"Certainly, the one-stop approach for operations, development and support has the priceless advantage that if something happens, you can immediately look into the customer's system. That means you have the Meta information of an incident and may be able to fix it with an unbeatable resolution time. I can forward the incident to development. You are actually much closer to the customer, much closer to the customer's problems when you operate the solutions yourself."* (B-1)

But the Software-as-a-Service model also requires vendors to standardize the support as much as possible and embrace additional channels that allow providing customer support in a one-to-many instead of a one-to-one approach.

> *"In the Software-as-a-Service mass market, we cannot deal with this on a personal level, instead we need to facilitate other possibilities. Communities, Twitter, Facebook and the like. Social networks will gain significance that is for sure. That also affects the contact to the customer. Personal contact becomes less frequent and is replaced by other channels."* (B-2)

In summary, support activities may become more efficient by closer ties between development, operation, and support stakeholders, as well as being standardized with the help of additional channels and more efficient communication.

Replacement

The replacement phase includes activities covering the decision to replace an existing solution with a new one and the activities to backup and migrate the data. Within the Software-as-a-Service context, all activities remain the responsibility of the customer.

The cases do not provide any details with regard to the replacement phase but highlight the importance of the existence of features to extract data from the solutions. As the solutions are hosted on the servers of the Software-as-a-Service vendor, customers deciding on a Software-as-a-Service solution are afraid that data may get lost, may be assessed by unauthorized parties or cannot be received from the systems. To compensate for this adoption barrier, vendors offer tools that assure a safe and reliable extraction and backup of data.

> *"When the customer doesn't want a software anymore, we as a Software-as-a-Service provider are responsible that the customer is able to obey to all legal obligations. That means we can't just flip the switch and the system is off, instead we have to assure that the customer's auditors are happy for the next ten years."* (B-2)

Discussion and Summary

Looking at the implications of the Software-as-a-Service concept on software vendors from a value chain perspective points at mainly two aspects. First, the responsibility for activities within the value chain is changing, and second, different activities appear to move closer together. The most obvious example for the first change is the shifting responsibility of operations activities from the customer to the software vendor. This can be considered as a form of vertical integration of value chain activities by Software-as-a-Service vendors. To a certain point it enables the second major observation that different activities of the value chain move closer together. Having development and operations of software in one hand appears to enable a more efficient and quicker response to problems within the software. As such, the maintenance departments can deliver bug-fixes with the support of the operations department without the customer being involved or required to react and install something. Also, support activities may take advantage of information accessible through the in-house operation and provide more efficient and reliable assistance to problems. Activities of creating some sort of distribution media for software become obsolete and instead production activities are closely linked to operation activities.

A third aspect that appears to play an important role within the Software-as-a-Service context is the promoted continuous evolution of the solutions and the goal to reduce the number of simultaneously existing software release at the customers. The first leads to the necessity of an increased innovation speed. Continuous innovation is required, bringing activities of research and those of development closer together. The latter, aims on reducing the variety of different system states that such increased innovation otherwise would generate, but also enables all customers to take advantage of the latest state of development at the same time. As a consequence, for example, support activities are eased as the software environment of all customers are standardized.

The clear distinction between development and maintenance activities, as defined within the value chain of Pussep et al. (2012), is vanished, as the increased innovation speed and the release-less state of the solutions make it unnecessary to distinguish between the two. All customers are on the same state-of-development making maintenance activities of old releases obsolete, as they do not exist anymore once the vendor has updated its systems. Software bugs are dealt with within the continuous development activities of the software vendor. Thus, maintenance becomes a part of development.

The observation of different activities of the value chain to vanish or somehow interact differently with other activities is very interesting and points at a major organizational implication of Software-as-a-Service on software vendors. Though, the activities of the value chain do not necessarily represent departments within an organization (Stabell & Fjeldstad, 1998), an aggregation of similar activities within organizational units is not uncommon in the software industry. For example, the involvement of developers in marketing and Sales activities is rather small. Thus it appears promising to investigate the implications of Software-as-a-Service on the interdependency and link between different organizational units. For instance, how are operation and development activities integrated within one organization? The case study findings indicate that the activities move closer together, partly because of the shared responsibility for both activities within one organization, but also because the context and the surrounding market require this move.

4.3.3. Discussion

The presented two perspectives on the implications of the Software-as-a-Service concept on software vendors have revealed multiple aspects. The Software-as-a-Service delivery and pricing model has an impact on the entire business model of software vendors. Organizations adapting the Software-as-a-Service as a delivery and pricing model for their software are exposed to a new context which is different in a variety of organization internal and external factors. The business model analysis has, for instance, indicated the emergence of new technologies that lead to internal changes. Furthermore, Software-as-a-Service customer structures or segments are different altering external context factor.

The objectives of the first empirical phase were to explore the implications of the Software-as-a-Service concept and to identify aspects that require further investigation. Within the Software-as-a-Service business model analysis, two aspects in particular appear to be in need for a closer examination: The internal capabilities required for the value creation, as well as the changed relationship to the customer. As outlined within the discussion on the *Key Activities*, the value generation is not limited to software development anymore. Instead, it is made up of a combination of continuous development and efficient service delivery. Existing approaches and processes require a re-evaluation as initial studies expect a misfit with the new context. Especially the interplay between development and operation is considered to be not appropriately covered in existing practices.

The changed customer relationship, as the second identified aspect, is based on Software-as-a-Service vendors, as solution operators, having a direct relationship with their customers. This relationship follows a long-term perspective with the objective to establish a lasting relationship between the vendor and its customers. Software-as-a-Service vendors are required to continuously convince customers of the benefits of their solutions and are, thus, in need to continuously enhance solutions and keep the quality on a high level. Quality in this context may refer to the software quality, but also includes operation quality and, thus, includes an additional dimension which had not been in the focus of software vendors previously. The direct character of the relationship enables vendors to observe their customers while interacting with the solution on its infrastructure. If approached appropriately, Software-as-a-Service vendors may gain a much better understanding of their customer base and their needs. However, suggestions on how to take advantage of the direct relationship are rarely found and potential problems related to it are not further discussed.

The value chain analysis has pointed at changing responsibilities for specific activities of the value chain, but more surprisingly also at different activities of the value chain to move closer together and to be subject to new forms and levels of interaction. Due to the vertical integration of software vendors, not only the execution of the majority of activities lies within the responsibility of the vendor, but also the design and management of interactions between these activities. The observations of increased interactions between activities like operations and development point at influences of Software-as-a-Service on the organization of related departments and thus on the organizational structure of software vendors.

Together, the two selected research frameworks have helped to highlight two aspects in particular. The frameworks have supported the identification of changes to the context software vendors that adopt Software-as-a-Service are a part of. Furthermore, they have pointed at changes to the structure of value creation within this context. The analysis has disclosed various phenomena that indicate changes to the division of work between organizations of the software industry but also within software vendor organizations. Selected value chain activities, like software operation, are executed by different stakeholders indicating changes to the orchestration of the value creation in the software industry but also within software vendor organizations. With the division of work and the value creation the changes address two central aspects of organization. Thus, the findings provide initial indications about organizational implications of Software-as-a-Service. However, the frameworks are not sufficient to provide enough details to evaluate the entire organizational implications and require a more detailed assessment of the observed phenomena with a more focused perspective.

4.4. Re-evaluation from a Coordination Perspective

As the previous discussion of the findings from the business model and value chain perspective has shown, the Software-as-a-Service concept may result in multiple organizational implications for software vendors. It changes the business environment of software vendors. The concept is likely to influence the division of labor and the value creation of organizations that adapt the concept as a software delivery model. The previously used frameworks have helped to structure the initial analysis, however, they are not sufficient for a detailed analysis of the observed organizational implications. The following section will, thus, provide an introduction to different theoretical perspectives on organizations that may yield more detailed insights into the observed phenomena. The different perspectives are discussed before an appropriate perspective is selected to re-evaluate the observations from the multiple case study.

4.4.1. Theoretical Perspectives on Organization

The organization literature discusses a list of different theoretical lenses to analyze organizations (Kieser, 2006; Kieser & Walgenbach, 2003; Picot et al., 2002). Organizations may for example be studied using a human relations perspective, a bureaucracy perspective, a behavioral perspective, a contingency perspective, or a transaction cost perspective (Kieser, 2006). Despite their partly contradicting underlying assumptions, all perspectives have their right to exist. Shared by all perspective is the objective to help understanding the purpose, the development, the existence, the change and the function of organizations (Kieser & Walgenbach, 2003). Each perspective sets a different focus on selected aspects of organizations and can assist in providing new insights (Kieser & Walgenbach, 2003). This study aims to address the research question of how Software-as-a-Service influences organizational structures and processes of software vendors (compare Section 1.2). For this reason, a perspective that puts a special emphasis on organizational structures is deemed most suitable for the analysis.

The behavioral perspective, for instance, studies decision processes within organizations and views these processes not as specified decision logic but as decision behavior that can be observed and studied with empirical methods. The main interest of this theoretical perspective is the question, how organizations secure their existence in an uncertain and changing environment (Kieser & Walgenbach, 2003). A central assumption is the concept of bounded rationality that stops decision makers from making rational decisions due to incomplete knowledge about decision outcomes and alternatives (Kieser & Walgenbach, 2003; Simon, 1945). Organizational structures are viewed as instrument to reduce complexity and uncertainty. They simplify the decision environment of members of the organization and support them in making more rational decisions (Kieser & Walgenbach, 2003, p. 40–43). The behavioral perspective appears promising to study how organizational structure may reduce uncertainty of the new Software-as-a-Service context and ease decisions within the organization but it may not necessarily be the optimal perspective to study how Software-as-a-Service influences organizational structure or which structures fit to the Software-as-a-Service context.

Compared to decision processes, the contingency approach puts organizational structures into the focus of the analysis. According to the contingency approach, organizational structures influence an organization's efficiency. As such, organizations need to adjust their structure to adapt to different situations. Organizational theories may suggest organizational structures that fit to selected contingency variables and may also predict needed adjustment requirements induced by a changing environment (Kieser, 2006, p. 169). Compared to other approaches, the contingency approach considers the characteristics of organizational structures to be flexible rather than static. Furthermore, it neglects the assumption that there is a universal structure that is efficient in every situation (Kieser & Walgenbach, 2003, p. 43). A central interest of the contingency approach are the questions of the influences of situation-specific influencing factors on organizational structures and ultimately on organizational efficiency (Kieser, 2006, p. 171).

The contingency perspective on organizations matches the objectives of this study. Software-as-a-Service is considered to change the environment of an organization and a central objective of this study is to investigate the influence of this change of situation on organizational structures. A situation is defined to include internal dimensions, like production techniques and technologies but also external dimensions, like customer and competitor structures (Kieser & Walgenbach, 2003, p. 44). Section 4.3.1 and Section 4.3.2 have provided various indications that the Software-as-a-Service concept is influencing such dimensions, thus Software-as-a-Service likely poses a change of situation to organizations. The contingency perspective is in line with this study's objective, as it studies the influence of factors of the environment on organizational structures. Furthermore, the approach is considered suitable, as the underlying reasoning for organizational structures appears feasible and matches those of practitioners (Kieser & Walgenbach, 2003, p. 45). As this study relies on information and experiences from practitioners this may be of advantage. In addition, Kieser & Walgenbach mention that the perspective is especially suitable to establish an understanding of organizational structures and that it is very flexible and allows to incorporate additional contextual factors previously not studied. As such, it allows to study a newly emerging context like the one created by Software-as-a-Service.

To study the influence of Software-as-a-Service on organizational structures it is, furthermore, necessary to establish a common understanding of potential ways to describe organizational structures. The literature suggests five dimensions that assist in understanding important aspects of organizational structures (Kieser & Walgenbach, 2003; Lawrence & Lorsch, 1969). The subsequent sections will provide a brief introduction of these different dimensions (specialization, coordination, configuration, delegation, formalization).

Specialization

Specialization is also called division of work and is based on the problem that goals of organizations are too complex to be handled by a single person. Tasks have to be split up and be executed by different members of the organization (Kieser & Walgenbach, 2003, p. 77). Organizations subdivide tasks that are required to accomplish the organization's goals and allocate them to different members of the organization. Specialization stands for a form of division of labor that leads to sub-tasks of different kinds. It can be distinguished between the kind or extend of specialization. The specialization can be based on the specifics of a task but also on the object a task is performed on. For example, a member of an organization that produces furniture may be allocated to execute the task of painting the furniture or the task to build a specific type of furniture like chairs. As the rules of specialization provide a long-term assignment of tasks to positions of the organizations, they are considered to be part of the formal organizational structure. These assignments are furthermore independent of the actual person taking up the position in the organizational structure. In larger organizations specialization is not limited to single positions but may also aggregate to specialized organizational units. Similar to single work profiles these unit may, for instance, be differentiated by the function they fulfill within the organization or the product or market they address. Important criteria for the establishment of divisions is that the unit can reach a maximum level of autonomy and is as independent as possible from other units in its task execution (Kieser & Walgenbach, 2003, p. 78–100).

Coordination

A second dimension of organizational structures that is directly linked to specialization is coordination. The division of work leads to the need of coordination to align the specialized stakeholders on the goals of the whole organization. With specialization, one member of the organization may not be capable of overseeing all activities executed by every other specialized unit. However, the members own work can only contribute to the organization's goal if it is executed in alignment with the activities of other members (Kieser & Walgenbach, 2003, p. 100-101). Specialized sub-units of an organization may depend on the outcome of other units or provide the input to other units of the organization. These interdependencies need to be managed and to be aligned on the organization's goals by coordination.

The role of coordination within the organization literature is highlighted by authors using coordination synonymous with organization (Urwick, 1963). Table 4.24 provides a brief list of different definitions of coordination within the literature. As coordination is researched in various fields the variance within the scope and subject of the definitions can partly be traced back to different focal interests of the corresponding research. Despite the multiple definitions, Okhuysen & Bechky (2009) point out that most definitions share a common pattern. Commonalities among the definitions are the following three aspects that coordination includes: "(1) people work collectively; (2) the work is interdependent; and (3) a goal, task, or piece of work is achieved" (Okhuysen & Bechky, 2009, p. 469).

Specialization and coordination represent the two central principles and mechanism of organizational structures (Mintzberg, 1983). However, in order to paint a complete picture of organizational structures three additional dimensions are often mentioned (Kieser & Walgenbach, 2003).

Configuration

Configuration describes the shape of the role structure within an organization (Pugh et al., 1968). The configuration can be summarized by an organization chart (Kieser &

Walgenbach, 2003, p. 137). It shows how the authority to give directions is distributed within the organization. In case a member of an organization has the authority to give directions, he can order other members of the organization to execute a task. The specification of who has an authority to give directions and the sub-group of members this authority is valid for is part of the configuration dimension. This line of command creates a hierarchy between different members of the organization (Kieser & Walgenbach, 2003, p. 77). A member may, for example, supervise a specialized sub-unit and take up coordination tasks with other sub-units. In more complex configurations the authority to give direction may be differentiated by different dimensions with the result that members of the organization may receive directions from multiple supervisors. Next to a general supervisor, a member may also receive directions from a functional supervisor (Kieser & Walgenbach, 2003, p. 136–163). An accountant of a production plant may, for example, be supervised by the director of the plant but may also get directions from members of the financial department of the organization's headquarters.

Table 4.24.: Definitions of coordination in extant literature

Definition	Source
"The Adoption of all members of a group of the same decision"	Simon (1945, p. 8)
"In a situation of interdependence, concerted action comes about through coordination"	Thompson (1967, p. 55)
"The integration or linking together of different parts of an organization to accomplish a collective set of tasks"	Van de Ven et al. (1976, p. 322)
"[T]he additional information processing performed when multiple, connected actors pursue goals that a single actor pursuing the same goals would not perform."	Malone (1988, p. 5)
"The joint efforts of independent communicating actors towards mutually defined goals."	NSF-IRIS (1989)
"Activities required to maintain consistency within a work product or to manage dependencies within the workflow."	Curtis (1989)
"[T]he act of managing interdependencies between activities performed to achieve a goal"	Malone & Crowston (1990, p. 361)
"Coordination has been defined as the direction of 'individuals' efforts toward achieving common and explicitly recognized goals"	Kraut & Streeter (1995, p. 69)
"[A]t its core, coordination is about the integration of organizational work under conditions of task interdependence and uncertainty"	Faraj & Xiao (2006, p. 1156)

Delegation

Closely linked to the dimension of configuration is the dimension of delegation. Delegation addresses the decision rights of members of the organization. Members may have the right to make binding decisions for the organization. These decision can be internal, for example, the decision to use a certain technology, or external, for example, a contract to sell a product to a customer at a specified price. The right to make decisions for the organizations is closely linked to the authority to give direction but it still can be differentiated. A decision means, that a member of the organization makes a binding decision to take certain measures or work to achieve a certain goal. Following the decision directions to other members of the organization may be given. Members of an organization that have the authority to give directions, however, do not necessarily also have the right to make the decision that preceded an execution (Kieser & Walgenbach, 2003, p. 163–168).

Formalization

The last dimension describes the degree organizational rules, procedures or communication are documented in form of charts, manuals, job descriptions or other documents. (Kieser & Walgenbach, 2003, p. 169–175). Potential sub-dimension are formalizations of roles, communication or role performances. Formalizations of roles may document a role definition that prescribe a certain behavior of organizational members. Example documents may be job descriptions or manuals of procedures. Communication between different members of the organizations may also be documented, for instance, using memo forms or meeting minutes. The performance of a role may include the notification or authorization of accomplishments in written form, like records that document the proper maintenance of an equipment (Pugh et al., 1968).

Discussion

The brief introduction of the five dimensions of organizational structures (specialization, coordination, configuration, delegation, and formalization) in the previous sections shows the diversity of perspectives on organizational structures. The dimensions are rather interrelated. Specialization directly implies coordination, as members of an organization that execute specialized task still need to ensure that their actions are in line with the overall objectives of the organization. Although departments are formed with the goal of maximum autonomy and a high level of independence from other departments, coordination is still required to accomplish the organization's goals. Maximizing the autonomy and independence of departments can also be seen as minimizing the required coordination between departments. Specialization, however, always requires some level of coordination to handle remaining dependencies between units. Finding the right levels of specialization and the resulting coordination needs are therefore a question of balance. As a result, studying coordination and interdependencies within an organization may provide a good indicator for suboptimal arrangement in the specialization dimension of organizational structure.

Even though, all introduced structural dimensions may need to be considered to investigate structural implications of a changed context like Software-as-a-Service, looking at coordination is considered to be a promising starting point for an evaluation. The discussion of the findings in Section 4.3.3 has highlighted the implications to the division of work, not only within the software industry, but also within software vendors. A new task, the operation of software solutions, is added to the responsibilities of software vendors. This responsibility shift from the customer to the software vendor challenges existing organizational structures. Some vendors may already have a unit that is specialized on executing software operation task, for example, those vendors that also offer hosting services or have a large own software infrastructure to manage their own processes. Other vendors may need to build up such operation units. To be able to decide on the appropriate organizational structure, knowledge about the interdependencies and resulting coordination requirements is needed. Thus, in this exploratory study it appears promising to focus the analysis on coordination and interdependencies to prepare for a more detailed analysis.

4.4.2. Coordination & Interdependence

The previous section has already indicated the close connection between interdependencies of organizational units and coordination. Thompson (1967) suggests appropriate forms of coordination for different types of interdependencies between organizational units. Similarly, Malone & Crowston (1994) suggests coordination approaches based on the interdependence of activities or resources. This second stream of research is claiming to provide a "Coordination Theory" that offers approaches for process design that are based on the chosen coordination mechanisms to manage dependencies among tasks and resources involved in the process (Crowston, 1997). Although, the authors call it "Coordination Theory", its potential to explain relationships is questionable (Strode et al., 2012). Crowston et al. acknowledge this criticism in a review of extant literature building on their original work by describing it as a pattern model that links phenomena to known patterns (Crowston et al., 2006). Nevertheless, the typology of dependencies and coordination mechanisms that authors like Thompson (1967) or Malone & Crowston (1994) provide can assist in identifying and categorizing dependencies, as well as identifying coordination mechanisms (Strode et al., 2012). With an emphasis on software engineering, Malone & Crowston (1994) are focused on tasks and single resources rather than on an organizational level. Despite of the context fit, the taken perspective appears too focused for the objectives of this study. Instead the more general typology of Thompson (1967) is used. Thompson (1967) discusses different interdependencies between organizational units and suggests appropriate coordination mechanisms. The following section will provide a short overview.

Types of Interdependence

Thompson (1967) distinguishes between three types of interdependence: *pooled*, *sequential*, and *reciprocal*. The three types are illustrated in Figure 4.1. *Pooled interdependence* exists in a situation with two activities or organizational parts, each delivering their own discrete contribution to the whole, while at the same time being supported by the whole. Thompson's example is a setting with different branches of the same chain. Each branch is independent and delivers its own value to the whole organization, but a failure of one branch may still threaten the whole organization including the other branches. A damage to the image of the organization that is caused by one branch may also impact the image of all the other branches of the organization. *Sequential interdependence* refers to a situation that has activities or organizational parts with interdependency of serial form. One activity is dependent on the output of another and cannot be executed without the preceding activity being completed. A clear order of the interdependence can be specified. *Reciprocal interdependence* exists in situations with activities or organizational parts accessing the output of each other for their own input. The output of activity A represents the input of activity B and contrariwise the output of activity B is the input of activity A. "The three types of interdependence are increasingly difficult to coordinate because they contain increasing degrees of contingency" (Thompson, 1967, p. 55). The three types of interdependence contain each other in the introduced order. As a consequence, organizations with activities with reciprocal interdependence also have pooled and sequential interdependence (Thompson, 1967).

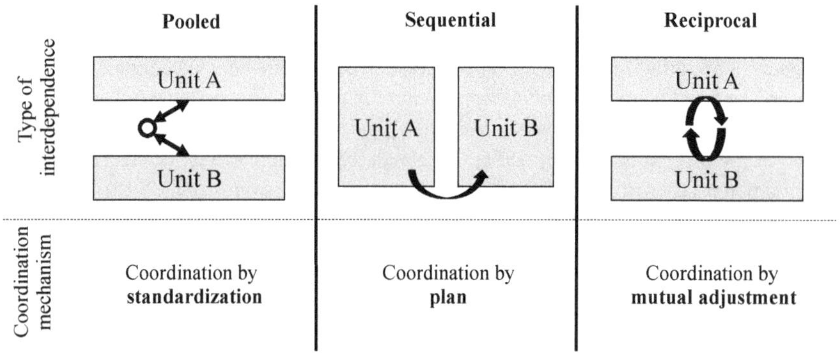

Figure 4.1.: Types of interdependence and suggested coordination mechanism

Coordination Mechanism

While the change of an activity with pooled interdependence does not affect other activities unless it is breaching the organization, changes to activities with sequential or reciprocal interdependence require to reassess and readjust other activities (Thompson, 1967).

Thompson (1967) introduced three different forms of coordination that fit to the three types of interdependence. While *standardization* is appropriate with pooled interdependence, *coordination by plan* is appropriate with sequential interdependence, and *coordination by mutual adjustment* is required in situations with reciprocal interdependence. *Coordination by standardization* involves the establishment of routines or rules. They assure that actions taken by each unit do not conflict with those of other units and are consistent. Coordination by standardization requires a relatively stable context. *Coordination by plan* relies on aligned schedules that coordinate the actions of every interdependent unit. This coordination mechanism may also deal with more dynamic situations. *Coordination by mutual adjustment*, the appropriate response to situations with reciprocal interdependence, involves the communication and sharing of information between units and activities during the execution of interrelated activities (Thompson, 1967). With the increasing degree of variance and uncertainty of a situation, coordination by mutual adjustment becomes more important (March & Simon, 1958). Communication requirements in terms of volume and frequency increase along the three types of coordination. While standardization only requires infrequent communication between units, the demand for communication rises with coordination by plan. Coordination by mutual adjustment, eventually, requires frequent communication and decision making (Thompson, 1967).

For the design of organizational structures or work systems, activities with more complex forms of interdependence, like reciprocal interdependence, should be managed within the same unit or group to reduce communication costs (Thompson, 1967). Communication within units or groups is assumed to be achieved with more ease and less involved costs than communication between units and groups. As a consequence, activities with reciprocal interdependence are better managed within one specialized unit. Sequential interdependent activities can be managed with less coordination costs, if they are grouped in the smallest possible cluster, as planning for small units can be done much easier than for large units. In case of pooled interdependence, organizations should focus on grouping units that perform similar activities. "Homogeneity facilitates coordination because one set of rules applies to all positions in the group; and when changes in rules are necessary, one set of changes applies to all." (Thompson, 1967, p. 59).

In the software industry, coordination has already been researched by various researchers, supporting the applicability of coordination research from the organization science for software vendor organizations. However, it has to be noted that the level of analysis may vary as not all research is positioned at an organizational level but also discussion coordination at a project level. In such project setting, time constraints may be of importance and may prose limitations (Barki et al., 2001). As an example for coordination research within the software industry, Staudenmayer (1997) has studied interdependence of software development activities. In distributed settings, software developers have to deal with coordinating interdependence arising from the software architecture and artifacts used by multiple developers simultaneously. Examples for the latter may be task-specific tools or software artifacts and their documentation (Staudenmayer, 1997). Kraut & Streeter (1995) provides a classification of different coordination techniques for distributed software development. They distinguish between impersonal and interpersonal, as well as formal and informal settings. For example, they suggest group meetings for interpersonal and informal settings (Kraut & Streeter, 1995). Gattiker & Goodhue (2005) investigate the influence of interdependence and differentiation between organizational units on the benefits an ERP implementation may yield for the organization. Within the study, ERP systems are considered to provide a form of standardization that requires a certain level of fit with the degree of interdependence and differentiation in an organization.

By applying a coordination perspective on the collected case study data, the previously discussed observations can be enhanced by additional explanations. A coordination perspective assists in understanding the role releases play in the observed dependencies between value chain activities. As such, the coordination perspective provides hints on an explanation as for why software vendors in the context of developing and operating Software-as-a-Service may need to rely on different coordination mechanisms. The following section will discuss this aspect in more detail.

4.4.3. The Role of Releases in Software-as-a-Service Development and Operations

Within software development, a software release typically represents an aggregation of changes or enhancements to a software (Ruhe & Saliu, 2005). The scope and size of the changes and enhancements may vary between major and minor releases. A software release is a collection of software code that is ready to be deployed and installed (Messerschmitt & Szyperski, 2003). Table 4.25 shows four generic types of software releases. Releases can be differentiated by different characteristics, like coverage, frequency, architectural change, or installation requirements (Messerschmitt & Szyperski, 2003). With regards to a release, software vendors do not just refer to the changes, but the entire source code that comprises the changes and typically represents the latest state of development. From a customer perspective, releases are identified by a version number or entirely new product name. Versions in this context are, however, not to be misunderstood as versions in the sense of the marketing tool of different packages that differ in scope and pricing. Messerschmitt & Szyperski (2003) refers to this type of release as variant release. Examples for different versions are Windows XP, Windows Vista or Windows 7 and for software variants are Windows Vista Home, Windows Vista Home Premium, and Windows Vista Professional.

The software development process is instantiated with every release. And a new release is typically traversing the different generic phases of software development, like requirements engineering, development, or testing (Sommerville, 2011). Similarly in a wider perspective, a release can also be found in the software value chain. A major release, for instance a version release, is passed through the different activities of the value chain until the cycle starts anew. A release may also initiate training of customer support personnel, preparing appropriate distribution channels, and a potential new marketing campaign (Messerschmitt & Szyperski, 2003).

Table 4.25.: Generic types of software releases (Messerschmitt & Szyperski, 2003)

Type	Description	Purpose
Patch	Replacement code that repairs a defect or shortcoming, usually in a small portion of the deployed code.	The supplier wants to correct defects that may affect the stability or security of the software as quickly as practical.
Service	A cohesive, synchronized release of a whole collection of patches, many of which were never made available separately.	The supplier not only wants to correct defects but also to ensure that all customers have deployed the same set of patches, simplifying customer service. This is also an opportunity to deploy patches that interact with one another. Often, patches require prior installation of the most recent service release.
Version	A replacement of all or most of the code embodying new features and capabilities or removing or modifying undesirable characteristics of the previous version.	The latest version release (incorporating also the most recent service release) is sold to new customers. Charging existing customers for a new version release (usually voluntarily and at a price discounted relative to new sales) as well as new sales provides a revenue stream to pay for the ongoing development cost of keeping the software competitive.
Variant	A variation on the same software differing in features or capabilities that is offered to the customer as an alternative.	Offering variant releases that differ in features or capabilities is one basis for price discrimination, allowing customers to self-select the price they are willing to pay. Thus, all variants are offered for sale at the same time.

Within the Software-as-a-Service context, the previous discussion indicates that the practice of release-based development is challenged. Most Software-as-a-Service vendors aim on a reduction of the simultaneously available software releases.

The earlier analysis also indicated that the Software-as-a-Service concept leads to a change of existing interdependence between different activities. Examples include activities of support, operations, or development. The coordination perspective can assist in finding reasons for the observation that different activities move closer together. In particular, this perspective provides explanation for the role releases play in this context. More importantly, the literature on coordination indicates that with changing interdependence, the applied coordination mechanisms are likely to require a re-evaluation. Thus, the coordination perspective indicates that an appropriate reaction of software vendors to the change is essential. The suggested coordination mechanisms can guide vendors in their decisions.

Within the collected data, changing inter-dependencies of selected activities can be observed. Most noticeable are the inter-dependencies between development and operations, and the interplay with sales and implementation. The following section discusses

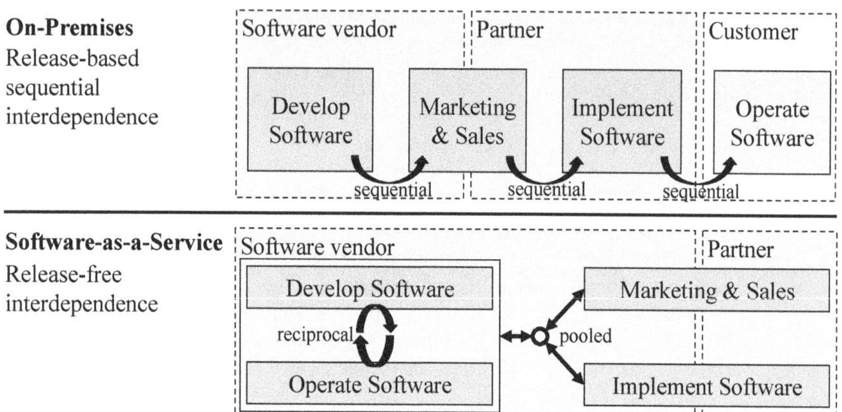

Figure 4.2.: The role of releases in Software-as-a-Service development and operations

the changing dependencies of these activities from a coordination perspective. Figure 4.2 provides a simplified overview of the changing interdependence between these selected activities.

Development – Operations

The interdependence between the activities of development and operation is changing from a sequential interdependence towards a more complex reciprocal interdependence. While in the traditional on-premises context, the existence of releases lead to a prevalent sequential order, the lag of releases in the Software-as-a-Service context is changing this situation.

An on-premises release is not ready for shipment to the customer before the development is completed and the release has been thoroughly tested. The input for operations is the output of the development activity that may however pass through intermediate activities before reaching the operations department at the customer. The operations department, however does not maintain direct dependencies to the development department. Potentially raised wished to make changes to the distributed release are not covered within the lifespan of this release, but are potentially addressed by development in a subsequent release (Messerschmitt & Szyperski, 2003). The overarching interdependence between the activities of development and operations in the on-premises context can thus be considered as of sequential type.

With Software-as-a-Service, the interdependence between development and operations is loosing its prevalent sequential character. The anticipated missing aggregation of changed features and enhancements to releases leads to a continuous output of development that is continuously deployed by operations. The missing distinction into releases brings about a dilution of development and maintenance activities.

> *"The advantage is that all developers are working on the next enhancements because all customers are always on the same release and nobody is using an older release. Thus, there is no need to do any bug-fixing of old software"* (A-1)

Development takes in maintenance activities and as a consequence is fed by operations with new tasks to perform. These are based on emerging issues and problems within the operations department. The interdependence between development and operations in the Software-as-a-Service context can be seen as more complex than in the on-premises context. On top of the existing sequential interdependence, the Software-as-a-Service context introduces additional sequential interdependence of reversed direction, forming reciprocal interdependence.

As a consequence of this changed complexity of interdependence, coordination literature suggests a required change in the appropriate coordination mechanisms to deal with the occurring interdependence. In the on-premises context and its sequential interdependence between development and operations, coordination by plans is suggested (Thompson, 1967). Releases are planned and a release date is scheduled. Operations can adjust the timing of the deployment of the release based on this time-line. The Software-as-a-Service context and its reciprocal type of interdependence requires coordination by mutual adjustment (Thompson, 1967). This coordination mechanism involves an intensified level of communication and joined decision making. This setting suggests that development and operations move much closer together than it would be necessary in an on-premises context.

In the Software-as-a-Service model, the responsibility for operations is moved from the customer to the software vendor. The Software-as-a-Service vendor is now responsible for the maintenance and operation of the solution and, as outlined earlier, has to build up the required resources to provide this service to its customers. The operations activity needs to be integrated into the organization. With reciprocal inter-dependencies in place, it can be expected that close cooperation and integration with development is required. The collected data indicates that operations departments move closer to the development departments.

> *"Simultaneous Engineering gains importance; that you do not just develop the software but simultaneously with software development, consider the operations infrastructure. [...] I can't say, I develop software now and later I think about implementation and operations aspects. Instead I have to think about these things during the development."* (B-3)

Thompson (1967) states that activities and units with reciprocal interdependence shall be grouped together to ease communication. The Software-as-a-Service context, with vendors being responsible for both developing and operating, and fading organizational boundaries between the activities and units, open up the opportunity to exploit new levels and forms of integration. However, a more detailed analysis of the communication and coordination links between development and operation is required to better understand the dependencies and requirements, and to provide more profound suggestions for appropriate integration approaches.

Marketing – Development and Operations

The interdependence between marketing the software solution and the two interrelated activities of development and operations is changing from a sequential interdependence to a less complex pooled interdependence. While the existence of releases lead to a prevalent sequential order in the on-premises context, missing releases in the Software-as-a-Service context may ease these dependencies.

The public announcement of a new release initiates a new sales cycle. At this stage, the development department has finished or is about to finish a new version of the software solution that now can be advertised and sold to customers. New marketing materials are produced including the major innovations and key features of the new release. When the development of the new release is finished and thoroughly tested, sales activities can be initiated.

With continuous enhancement without releases, the sequential order is potentially opened up. Software-as-a-Service solutions do not need to be differentiated into versions anymore (Olsen, 2006). All Software-as-a-Service vendors in the case study sample did not promote a version number or release state on their sales websites. This has different potential reasons. Due to the vendor operating and maintaining the solution, the entire customer base can be kept on one software release state. The vendor can influence the timing of the update process and as a consequence determines the time an old release state is vanished from being used by any customer.

> *"All customers are on the same release and nobody can use an old release anymore"* (A-1)

The distinctive function of software version numbers, to characterize a software solution as outdated and inform about the availability of a new release is not required anymore.

> *"There is no need to sell releases anymore. Instead, the solutions are continuously enhanced in functionality."* (B-3)

Customers subscribe to Software-as-a-Service solutions instead of buying licenses for a software version as up-front investments. They pay continuous subscription fees that generate a steady flow of revenues for software vendors. Revenues from licenses do not exist anymore in the Software-as-a-Service context. Software vendors, therefore, do not need to persuade customers to invest into a new software version any longer. Versions loose their sales-driving character. Instead, marketing promotes the Software-as-a-Service solutions as a whole. Similar to websites, like Facebook, that also do not have a version number. Marketing is focused on the value a user can gain from using the solution and not on the advantages over previous versions. Therefore, new and existing customers are addressed equally.

The interdependence of marketing with development and operations in the Software-as-a-Service context matches Thompson (1967) definition of a pooled interdependence. Both marketing as well as development and operation add a discrete contribution to the software vendor as a whole but can act rather independent from each other. Failure of one of the activities, however, will threaten the whole organization with all its parts (Thompson, 1967).

Without a release-driven sales cycle, marketing is not dependent on development to finish a release, instead it can continuously advertise the promise of an always up-to-date solution. New features that are produced by development may support the sales process, as the solution may gain competitiveness and appear more compelling to prospective customers but customers will automatically take advantage of new features once they are made available and, therefore, do not need to delay their buying decision in anticipation of a new and potentially better software version.

> *"Within the whole delivery organization, something like a release is totally vanished. There is no release to be sold anymore, instead functionality is actually enhanced continuously, in very short software release cycles, if you call it a release at all."* (B-3)

In the traditional setting, with the responsibility for operating the licensed software solutions at the customer side, the interrelations between marketing and operations are of rather sequential character. The marketing and sales process has to be completed before the customer has the license rights to install, operate and use the software solution. Due to the different organizational boundaries, additional complexity is added that is not covered in this study, as operations activities are out of the control of a software vendor. In the Software-as-a-Service context, the operations activity is internalized and the interrelations between marketing and operations becomes the internal issue of a vendor. Even though, direct interdependence between the two activities is less obvious. Instead both activities deliver an independent contribution to the software vendor's organization. Marketing and sales generate new customers and make sure existing customer stay with the software vendor. The operations department on the other hand, takes care of the smooth operations of the solutions and makes sure the solution scales with new customers.

Problems for all activities emerge, however, when one of them fails to deliver. In case marketing and sales are not able to win new customers for the Software-as-a-Service solution, software vendors may not reach the required level of profitability as the business model is relying heavily on economies of scale.

> *"I think, if you want to develop and operate a successful cloud solution, you need economies of scale. That means, if you do it, you need to do it big, because otherwise you won't be able to cover the expenses."* (C-2)

A failure within operations will result in a potential downtime of the Software-as-a-Service solution that may damage the trust of customers in the solution and the image of the vendor.

> *"If [server downtimes] occur constantly, our customers will cancel our solution rather quick, that's for sure."* (K-1)

Operations also need to create the necessary capabilities to scale the solution and enable it to manage a large number of customers. Errors of development or badly designed software functions may result in unsatisfied customers that over the long-term will replace the vendor's solution with one that promises better usability or a better fit to the customer's processes.

For pooled interdependence, Thompson (1967) argues for coordination by standardization as an appropriate communication instrument. An integration of the involved units is not necessarily required. Instead, routines and rules that govern the individual actions and their congruence with the overall organizational goal are sufficient. Coordination theory lets expect the marketing and sales activity to be relatively independent from development and operations. The case study includes different observations that support this surmise. On the one hand, cases indicate the heavy reliance on partners as a sales channel but on the other hand the case companies stated a strong use of direct website-based sales activities that are often free of personal interactions and fully automated.

> *"We have partly direct sales but after a contract has been signed, we always include a partner to accompany the delivery"* (C-2)

> *"A major percentage of our leads are coming in via our website"* (A-1)

> *"We also have a major share of the generated leads reaching us from partners."* (A-2)

Without the consolidated introduction of new features within releases and the general role of releases vanishing, it can be speculated that less specific knowledge about the output of development is needed. Marketing, therefore, does not require as much awareness of the upcoming output of development to execute its sales activities, as with a stronger emphasis of releases. The necessary knowledge can be communicated by documentations and standardized sales materials. As a consequence, the activities may also be performed by partners of the software vendors.

A second observation that indicates a coordination by standardization are the self-service capabilities of solutions. The customer can subscribe to the website via the Software-as-a-Service vendor's website without interacting with any sales personnel of the vendor.

> *"Right from the demo system, the customer can open an order form. The customer just has to enter the number of users required and a calculation of the expected subscription fee is provided. The customer may add additional modules and at the end of this process the costs of the system are shown including a decomposition of the different cost components. It is very transparent and the customer in that moment knows exactly what to expect."* (J-1)

Self-service tools are used to guide the customer in the process. As self-services require a certain degree of standardizeability, it can be assumed that the underlying process are characterized by a high level of standardization. By coordination with standards interactions can be minimized.

> *"Software-as-a-Service is something for the mass market. That means that I have less personal interactions. We are currently discussing this. You may have a technical problem and previously you had a dedicated contact person. In the on-demand mass market, a vendor cannot provide a personal contact anymore, instead the vendor needs to use other methods, like communities, Twitter, Facebook and the like. The contact to the customer will become less personal and rely more on other channels."* (B-2)

4.4.4. Discussion

The re-evaluation from a coordination perspective has provided additional explanations for the observed phenomena. The analysis from a coordination perspective points at certain interdependence between activities to lose in complexity while others become more complex. While maintenance activities are more or less absorbed by development, dependencies between marketing and development and operation appear to loosen their prevalent sequential character and, thus, also lead to a reduction of the complexity of managing the interdependence of the associated activities. The dependencies between development and operation, on the other hand, appear to gain complexity due to more intense and bidirectional communication requirements.

The analysis supports the previous finding that especially the link between development and operation is crucial for developing and delivering Software-as-a-Service solutions. The change from a sequential to a more complex reciprocal interdependence highlights the importance of vendors to reconsider the applied coordination mechanisms between the two activities. Rather than a coordination by plan, the Software-as-a-Service context may require a coordination by mutual adjustment between the activities. It can therefore be expected that the communication and coordination requirements between development and operation increase drastically.

In an organizational context, such communication and coordination links between different departments are commonly referred to as organizational integration. It is defined as the interconnectivity and coordination between different departments involved in the innovation process (Barki & Pinsonneault, 2005). A high degree of organizational integration consequently stands for a high communication and coordination intensity between departments. Intensive communication and coordination are also characteristics of coordination by mutual adjustment (Thompson, 1967). Therefore, organizational integration may be seen as an example of a coordination mechanism that is based on mutual adjustment. Based on the observations within this initial phase of research, it can be speculated that software vendors, which are offering or planning to offer software as Software-as-a-Service, may need to take special care of organizational integration aspects. However, to gain a better understanding of the specific requirements more knowledge is required.

Further observations and new insights from additional case studies that set a dedicated focus on an organizational integration perspective are necessary to substantiate the current expectations. Thus, it is deemed promising to concentrate subsequent research activities on this aspect.

It has to be noted that the analysis of the re-evaluation of the first research phase's empirical data is limited to a selective view on only a subgroup of interdependence of activities and not covering the entire relationships from all potential perspectives. For example, the relationship between marketing and operation may also be analyzed on the basis of a legal perspective. However, legal constraints are not in the scope of this study and the perspective from which the dependencies are looked at, is focused on the internal development and operation process. Therefore, the previous discussion can only be seen as an indication for important aspects rather than a universal explanation.

Even though, the interpretation of changing interdependence is based on rather high level observations and still includes a high degree of speculation, it can be taken as an indication to direct the subsequent analysis of this study. At this point, the collected data of the initial multiple-case study is, however, not sufficient to explain the entire phenomena. Nevertheless, the findings and the application of the well-established coordination perspective on the observations, provide enough support to justify a closer look on the coordination and communication links between development and operation within a second case study.

4.5. Summary

Within this chapter, the findings from the first phase of this study's two-staged research approach have been presented and discussed. The multiple case study data has been reviewed by applying three different perspectives. In an initial step, the data has been analyzed and structured by using two research frameworks taking a business model, as well as value chain perspective. The presentation of the case study data has been enriched by the introduction of relevant contributions from extant literature. Observations have been discussed, put into perspective and compared with extant knowledge of related research articles. This approach has led to obtaining a broad overview of the implications of Software-as-a-Service for software vendors and the identification of potential research gaps within extant literature.

The findings of the business model perspective have pointed at various implications for all components of a business model. The general value proposition has been considered to allow customers of Software-as-a-Service solutions to focus on their respective core competence, instead of operating software solutions. Customers can take advantage of software supported business processes without the need to build up the required knowledge and expertise to execute non-core activities, like IT operations. Software vendors may get access to new customer segments and may increase the potential customer base but may also face increasing competition from competitors, who were previously active in unconnected markets and countries. Limitations may, however, arise from the limited technical capabilities, which restrict the degree of adaptability of solutions to individual customer wishes. With regard to pricing models, the findings have indicated an increased complexity to specify the appropriate pricing model and to identify the right underlying pricing units, as well as the complexity to manage the billing processes internally. Channels to interact with the customers are based on heavy usage of the Internet and automated self-service systems. The interaction with partners becomes, on one hand, closer as a result of joined service delivery, but on the other hand also more competitive due to the overlap between the providers' and partners' business models. In addition, the case study findings have indicated a closer relationship between the Software-as-a-Service provider and its customers. This relationship is characterized by continuity and the findings suggest that the provider may obtain a much more detailed knowledge about its customers. With regard to the internal building blocks, the findings have pointed at the requirement to build up additional knowledge and resources, in particular concerning operations related activities and technologies. Furthermore, the findings have indicated multiple implications for the internal processes of software vendors. The cost structure is challenged by additional cost components and an increased cost pressure, but the findings at the same time hint at the potential to improve the efficiency over the long-term, based on the increased control over the software value chain.

The value chain perspective has pointed at three different key observations. First, responsibilities for selected activities change between vendors and customers of the software solutions. As such, the responsibility for operation activities has been identified to move to the software vendor. Second, selected activities of the value chain have appeared to move closer together. Findings have indicated that development and maintenance activities become more difficult to separate, and operation activities to have closer ties with other activities of the value chain, like development. Last, the findings have pointed at the continuous evolution of Software-as-a-Service solutions to play a key role for the observed changes.

Based on these findings, the case study data has, as a third step, been re-evaluated by using a coordination perspective. This perspective has provided further indications for changing dependencies between selected activities relevant for developing and operating Software-as-a-Service solutions. Furthermore, the perspective has assisted in selecting subsequent research activities and the focus of those activities. While the prevalent character of dependencies of marketing and sales activities with other activities of the value chain appear to become less complex, the coordination and communication requirements between development and operation gain complexity instead. Since the data from the initial multiple-case study has been considered not rich enough to provide a clear explanation for this phenomena, a second round of case studies has been initiated to explore these aspects. The second phase is expected to create an in-depth understanding of the coordination and communication requirements between the activities of developing and operating Software-as-a-Service solutions. The findings of this second research phase will be presented in the following Chapter 5.

5. The Role of Organizational Integration for Software-as-a-Service

5.1. Research Framework

The first research phase in the previous chapter has identified reasons for integration aspects to gain importance in the development and operation of Software-as-a-Service solutions. Figure 5.1 summaries the changed setting of Software-as-a-Service providers compared to traditional on-premises vendors. While in the on-premises model, software is developed and shipped to the customer to be installed, customized, operated and eventually used, the vendor takes over the operation activity in the Software-as-a-Service context and offers a ready-to-use systems (Luoma & Rönkkö, 2012). The service character of Software-as-a-Service stresses the importance of the fulfillment phase, as the value creation of services is typically concentrated in this phase (Ramaswamy, 1994).

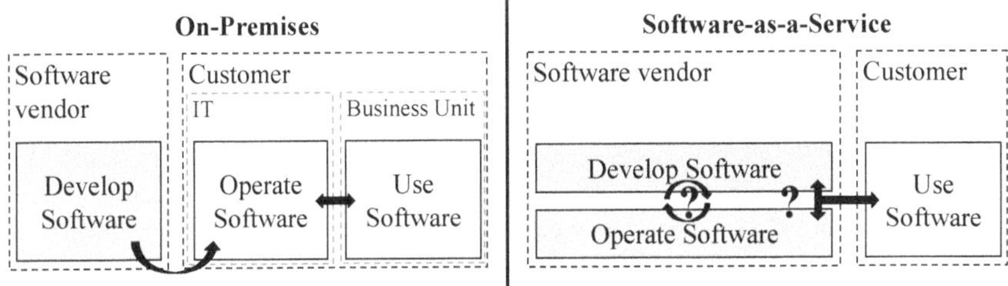

Figure 5.1.: Changing business model

Given that both the responsibility for software operations and the direct customer relation are closely linked to internal and external communication and coordination aspects, the second phase of empirical research in this chapter draws on an organizational integration perspective to further analyze the implications of the Software-as-a-Service concept for software vendors. More specifically, by drawing on the literature on organizational integration, it aims at providing a better understanding of the consequences of a software vendor's responsibility for operations, as well as its new task to directly communicate with the end-customer or end-user (see question marks in Figure 5.1). In line with the discussion in the previous chapter, the focus remains on the coordination dimension of organizational structures. The organizational integration concept is linking the dimensions coordination and specialization by looking at coordination between specialized organizational units (Barki & Pinsonneault, 2005). While the re-evaluation in Section 4.4 has suggested coordination mechanisms based on the prevalent interdependencies between organizational units, organizational integration directly looks at the coordination and communication between organizational units. Thus, analyzing organizational integration in the Software-as-a-Service context may yield valuable insights on the coordination and communication requirements and forms of coordination between organizational units. This chapter is based on Stuckenberg et al. (2014) and organized as follows: First, organizational integration is introduced and its relevance in the Software-as-a-Service context is discussed in order to deduce a consistent framework for further analysis. After an introduction to the data selection and analysis approach, the framework is filled with empirical findings on the nature of organizational integration in the context of Software-as-a-Service. The chapter concludes with a discussion of the findings.

5.1.1. Organizational Integration

Organizational integration is a central construct within different fields of research (Barki & Pinsonneault, 2005; García et al., 2008; Pinto & Pinto, 1990; Song et al., 1997, 2000). It has been defined as the interconnectivity and coordination between different departments involved in the innovation process (Barki & Pinsonneault, 2005). More specifically, organizational integration reflects the extent to which communication and coordination links between two distinct organizational subunits exist (Barki & Pinsonneault, 2005; Ettlie & Reza, 1992; Millson & Wilemon, 2002). Although organizational integration has been researched most prominently in the context of new product or service development, the research results are deemed transferable and applicable in the context of software development (Nambisan & Wilemon, 2000).

It is important to note that organizational integration is set on an organizational level, as opposed to the technical perspective on integration issues that focus on the integration of systems or standardized, IT-supported processes (Barki & Pinsonneault, 2005; Goodhue et al., 1992; Sun et al., 2007). In the latter context, information systems often play the role of a facilitator that supports integration. Given that within this study, a technology-based service solution is the output of the development and operation processes under investigation, rather than the object of integration, the focus is on an organizational perspective on integration.

Organizational integration takes a central role as a determinant of successful product and service development. The relationship between integration and success is well researched in the new product and new service development literature (Troy et al., 2008). A positive relationship of collaboration and communication between organizational units involved in the development and the performance of that product or service was found in various studies (Adler, 1995; Atuahene-Gima & Evangelista, 2000; Cordon-Pozo et al., 2006; Ettlie & Reza, 1992; Froehle et al., 2000; García et al., 2008; Gupta et al., 1986; Kahn, 1996; Millson & Wilemon, 2002; Pinto & Pinto, 1990; Song & Montoya-Weiss, 2001; Song et al., 1996, 2000). In particular, previous studies suggest a positive impact on firm success for internal integration of value creating activities, as well as for market-directed integration in form of customer orientation and integration. The positive effect of internal integration is explained by the amount and variety of information available during the process and, as a result, the team's broadened understanding of problems. Such a broadened understanding was associated with the diverse functional backgrounds of individuals within integrated teams (Froehle et al., 2000; Milliken & Martins, 1996; Schilling & Hill, 1998). The influence of external integration on success were traced back to the possibility to develop products or services that fit with customer needs and requirements or to identify new ideas and innovations (Alam, 2002; Lundkvist & Yakhlef, 2004; Magnusson, 2003).

Previous research in software development suggests a link between the integration of focused activities or functions of software development and solutions success (Botzenhardt et al., 2011; Tiwana, 2004). Evidence also exists for the positive effect of customer-orientation and customer integration, considered within this study as external organizational integration (Keil & Carmel, 1995; Kujala, 2003). However, a theory-driven understanding of the role of organizational integration in developing and providing Software-as-a-Service is still missing. In order to fill this gap, the next section ties the concept of organizational integration to the characteristics of services, resulting in a framework that allows for theory-driven empirical exploration.

5.1.2. Organizational Integration in the Software-as-a-Service Context

Based on the previous discussion on constituent characteristic of services in Chapter 2 as well as organizational integration in the previous section, a framework can be deduced that integrates the two streams in the context of Software-as-a-Service. More specifically, the integration of the two streams results in a matrix with four cells that categorizes organizational integration into inward-oriented and outward-oriented transformation challenges and evolvement opportunities. The framework is depicted in Figure 5.2 and discussed subsequently.

The distinction between an internal and external perspective is in line with the organizational integration literature (Barki & Pinsonneault, 2005). While internal organizational integration involves communication and coordination between firm-internal units, external organizational integration comprises the communication and coordination of internal units with entities outside the firm (Millson & Wilemon, 2002). Transferred to the context of Software-as-a-Service, the distinction between inward-oriented and outward-oriented perspectives on organizational integration can be linked to (1) simultaneity and (2) the existence of the external factor as two constituent characteristics of services.

First, the simultaneity characteristic of Software-as-a-Service entails the internalization of operation activities and is, therefore, deemed as a main origin of internal integration efforts and requirements. Simultaneity describes the service characteristic that the production and consumption of services happen at the same time (Zeithaml et al., 1985). Production in the Software-as-a-Service context covers all activities of the service provider required to offer the specified service. This includes the pre-production of components

	Internal / inward-oriented	**External / outward-oriented**
Transformation **challenges**	Inward-oriented transformation challenges caused by simultaneity	Outward-oriented transformation challenges caused by the existence of an external factor
Evolvement **opportunities**	Inward-oriented evolvement opportunities enabled by simultaneity	Outward-oriented evolvement opportunities enabled by the existence of an external factor
	Simultaneity	**External factor**
	Driving service characteristic	

Figure 5.2.: Dimensions of organizational integration

necessary for service delivery, in this case the software artifact. Consumption stands for the satisfaction of the value proposition of a service. From a customer perspective, the value of a Software-as-a-Service solution is thus not created when the underlying software artifact is developed, but in the moment the provided software functions are used. Hence, simultaneity leads to the requirement to execute both development and operation appropriately and to manage the activities' interrelations. In other words, in the context of Software-as-a-Service, inward-oriented integration focuses on integration aspects that relate to the links between development and operations functions that now reside within one organization (see also Figure 5.1). Thus, simultaneity can be considered the main driver of internal organizational integration in the Software-as-a-Service context.

Second, services are characterized by the existence of an external factor within the fulfillment phase and concentrate the value generation within this phase (Fitzsimmons & Fitzsimmons, 2011; Ramaswamy, 1994). In the Software-as-a-Service context, the external factor is the customer in form of the end-user consuming the solution. Next to the adoption-related aspects of solution design and feature scope definition, the customer is directly involved in the service process. Thus, the customer is more than a sales target to license software to. The end-user is directly interacting with the software provider by using the software capabilities based on the provider's infrastructure. The interaction becomes part of the value proposition of a Software-as-a-Service offering. The involvement of the external factor can therefore be considered a main driver of integration topics of the external/outward-oriented perspective in the Software-as-a-Service context, given that external integration addresses the communication channels and interfaces with an external customer consuming the Software-as-a-Service solution (see Figure 5.1).

In addition to the external and internal perspectives on organizational integration, the framework depicted in Figure 5.2 distinguishes between transformation challenges and evolvement opportunities.

Challenges refer to all aspects that are below a certain threshold of minimum accomplishment and rather immanent steps of a transition to a service model. Following existing literature on organizational integration, these challenges may result from specialization as a barrier of organizational integration (Lawrence & Lorsch, 1969). Goal and frame of reference differences among organizational units lead to greater implementation effort of organizational integration (Barki & Pinsonneault, 2005). Units tend to be oriented towards locally focused goals that reflect their corresponding core competency and expertise. At the same time, units can have different underlying structures, assumptions, knowledge, and expectation that also hinder integration (Barki & Pinsonneault, 2005). Internalization of a previously external activity implies the integration of resources in form of people, processes, and technologies that followed a potentially different goal orientation and stem from a different frame of reference. Therefore, integration challenges in connection with specialization are likely to be of importance in the Software-as-a-Service context. Taking over the responsibility for software operation may lead to dealing with a potentially different frame of reference and goal orientation.

In addition to these challenges, providing Software-as-a-Service may also imply opportunities for software vendors stemming from organizational integration. Specifically, Barki & Pinsonneault (2005) argue that external integration requires greater efforts to achieve than internal integration. This means that external development or operations partners will require a greater effort to be integrated than internal development and operation units. The internalization of previously external activities and processes inherent in the Software-as-a-Service model may thus provide opportunities for software vendors resulting from easier integration. Within the Software-as-a-Service context, vendors can benefit from internalizing the previously external activity of software operation. The entire solution can be developed, deployed and operated under one roof, aggregating activities previously undertaken by multiple stakeholders. In doing so, opportunities may emerge from characteristics of the Software-as-a-Service model that are not feasible in a traditional setting.

The previous discussion integrated the literature on service characteristics and organizational integration into the framework shown in Figure 5.2. The resulting matrix categorizes the role of organizational integration in developing and operating Software-as-a-Service into inward-oriented and outward-oriented transformation challenges and evolvement opportunities. In this second research stage, this framework is used to guide the empirical exploration. The following section presents the chosen research design in more detail.

5.2. Data Selection and Analysis

The goal of this chapter is to provide an in-depth understanding of how the adoption of Software-as-a-Service influences the organizational integration of software vendors. After having theoretically deduced a classification of the potential influences of Software-as-a-Service on software vendors, a second empirical study is conducted. This aims on obtaining an understanding of the nature of inward-oriented challenges and opportunities that result from simultaneity, as well as outward-oriented challenges and opportunities resulting from the existence of an external factor. Specifically, the second empirical study aims at unearthing and structuring different themes that populate the cells of the matrix depicted in Figure 5.2. These themes are manifestations of the implications of the characteristics of Software-as-a-Service and its service properties (simultaneity and existence of an external factor) on the challenges and opportunities that software vendors face when deploying software in the Software-as-a-Service mode. In addition to clarifying what the cells of the matrix in Figure 2 mean for Software-as-a-Service providers, the study is targeted at the discovery of contingency factors that act as enabler or inhibitors of the different emerging themes.

In order to achieve this goal, a multiple-case study design was chosen (Kerlinger & Lee, 2000; Yin, 2009). The study's aim of unearthing themes as well as enablers and inhibitors resembles Sarker and colleagues' recent study on value co-creation (Sarker et al., 2012a). Similar to the study of Sarker et al., qualitative data gathered via case study research is used to distill themes and enablers/inhibitors. In contrast to Sarker et al's research who conducted a single-case study, this study relies on multiple cases in order to account for differences across organizations. The multiple-case study consists of six organizations. In line with the level of analysis of this study, each of these organizations represented a singular case. Table 5.1 provides an overview of the analyzed cases.

In order to obtain a comprehensive picture of the influence of Software-as-a-Service on software vendors, the sample included Software-as-a-Service vendors of different size and with varying commitment to the Software-as-a-Service business model. Providers with a full commitment to the service model offer only Software-as-a-Service solutions and are referred to as pure Software-as-a-Service vendors. Providers that also have a traditional on-premises solution in their portfolio are referred to as hybrid providers. Including these hybrid vendors allowed to draw from the expertise and experiences of developing and marketing software in the traditional way, and to reflect on the changes induced by the Software-as-a-Service deployment model. Organizations of varying size were included for two reasons. First, organizational integration aspects can be assumed to vary with the size of organizations. Second, given the novelty of the business model, pure Software-as-a-Service provider are often of smaller size. Generally, hybrid organizations tend to be rather large due to the level of resources that is required to simultaneously provide software via both deployment models.

All analyzed vendors are developing complex business software applications such as ERP or CRM. This focus ensured comparability among the cases, as the complexity of knowledge-intensive goods like software solutions is reflected in the underlying processes and organizational structures (Ivari et al., 2001; Walz et al., 1993). Complex solutions were deemed particularly adequate to reveal aspects of organizational integration.

Semi-structured expert interviews with knowledgeable members of the organizations formed the major source of empirical data (Appendix A shows a high-level interview guideline). The decision to rely on semi-structured expert interviews is in line with the nature of the study that is exploratory, but structured by an a priori framework. Semi-structured interviews offer the advantage of a theory-driven data collection, but still allow open answers and the flexibility to respond to interesting aspects that emerge throughout the interviews (Stone, 1978; Yin, 2009). In total, 13 expert interviews were conducted within the six case companies. Within the two smaller companies, one knowledgeable expert was considered sufficient to obtain a comprehensive picture. In contrast, several interviews were required to conceive all facets within the larger case companies. Except for two interviews within case companies A and B, all interviews were conducted in German. All interviews were recorded and transcribed, resulting in more than 90.000 words of qualitative data.

Table 5.1.: Analyzed companies and conducted interviews

Case	Company Size	Business Model	Interview partners
A	Large	Hybrid	- Developer (A-1), - Program Director Cloud Services (A-2), - Vice President Cloud Services (A-3), - Solution Architect (A-4), - Developer (A-5)
B	Large	Hybrid	- Program Manager (B-1), - Technology Consultant (B-2)
C	Large	Hybrid	- Director Online Services (C-1), - Director Customer Service (C-2), - Quality Manager (C-3)
D	Large	Pure SaaS	- Vice President Customer Relations (D-1)
E	Small	Pure SaaS	- Director Development Operations (E-1)
F	Small	Pure SaaS	- Director Research Development (F-1)

The qualitative data was analyzed using the software tool NVivo (Miles & Hubermann, 1994). The analysis of the gathered data was structured by the theoretically deduced framework that is tied to extant literature. The underlying rationale for this approach was to structure the data analysis, but at the same time leave enough flexibility and openness to obtain an understanding of what the different cells of the framework depicted in Figure 5.2 mean in the studied context. More specifically, the qualitative data was initially coded referring to the dimensions of the framework. Hence, text fragments were coded that relate to the four cells of the matrix depicted in Figure 5.2, that is, "inward-oriented challenges resulting from simultaneity", "inward-oriented opportunities resulting from simultaneity", "outward-oriented challenges resulting from the existence of an external factor", as well as "outward-oriented opportunities resulting from the existence of an external factor". In an iterative process of sense-making, the text fragments were labeled according to different emerging patterns, similar patterns were aggregated and relabeled, and redundant labels were dropped. Eventually, five consistent themes emerged that represent manifestations of the influence of Software-as-a-Service on software vendors and relate to the a priori framework. The themes allow to gain and structure an in-depth understanding of challenges and opportunities of Software-as-a-Service vendors that result from the constituent characteristics of services. In addition, the data analysis revealed three types of enablers and inhibitors that aggravate or facilitate organizational integration in the context of the five themes. The five themes as well as the enablers and inhibitors are discussed subsequently, liberally referring to the qualitative data that instantiate these themes and the enablers and inhibitors within the case companies.

5.3. Results and Observations

5.3.1. The Role of Organizational Integration in Software-as-a-Service Development and Operations

In the following, five themes are outlined which are found to reflect the changing role of integration within the Software-as-a-Service context. Figure 5.3 provides an overview of the identified themes that relates to the theoretically deduced framework. It has to be noted that it is not claimed that these themes of organizational integration are completely independent of each other; rather they represent different perspectives on organizational integration, as well as different underlying rationales and objectives. The inward-oriented themes *awareness*, *continuity*, and *increment* are focused on the interplay between development and operations. The outward-oriented themes *timing* and *feedback* are addressing integration aspects relating to the external service consumer. While *awareness*, *continuity*, and *timing* represent transformation challenges, *increment* and *feedback* are evolvement opportunities.

Awareness

The first theme of integration addresses the communication between the software development units and the departments responsible for the operation of the software and the delivery of the service. The simultaneity characteristic of Software-as-a-Service leads to vendors being responsible for both activities. Integration aspects of this theme are centered on the knowledge and awareness both provider-internal parties have about each other and their corresponding key activities and problems.

Due to the formerly rather separated processes of developing software and operating it within the traditional on-premises business model, developers, for instance, may lack a proper understanding of the complexity and costs involved in operating software. The

	Internal / inward-oriented	Exernal / outward-oriented
Transformation **challenges**	**Awareness** Increase the operation-related knowledge of developers **Continuity** Synchronize activities and processes to reduce bottlenecks between development and operation	**Timing** Consider customers' business activities in scheduling updates
Evolvement **opportunities**	**Increment** Increase innovation capabilities and reduce cycle times of new software releases	**Feedback** Leverage usage-data to improve the solution
	Simultaneity	**External factor**
	Driving service characteristic	

Figure 5.3.: Themes of organizational integration in the Software-as-a-Service context

focus of developers in the traditional context is often set on features and the scope of the software. After development and quality checks, the software artifact is licensed and sent to customers for their IT-departments to handle installation, customization, and deployment. In contrast, operating the artifact is a prerequisite to deliver the offered service in the Software-as-a-Service context. It is the responsibility of the vendor to install, operate and maintain the software artifact and to bear the respective costs involved. Adding the additional primary activity of operations to the value chain of a software vendor implies that optimizing operation and delivery costs is brought into focus.

Company A describes the problem as follows:

> *"In the past, it always had the flavor of software being developed in the classical way and thrown over the fence to be operated. Then, it's too late of course, as you can't influence the way the software works any more. Not from an application logic, but operations perspective."* (A-2)

In the traditional model, developers did not put much priority on the cost of operations. Even though initiatives to reduce the total cost of ownership (TCO) of software solutions may also have existed in the past, the sustainability of these efforts can be questioned.

> *"There have been TCO programs in the past, but they never really interested anybody because it did not hurt the company itself. Even when the customers kept on shouting as loud as they could."* (A-2)

Also, developers may lack the understanding of operations complexity to be able to estimate the implications of programming a software artifact in a certain way.

> *"The typical games happened: 'you're too stupid to operate [our solution], you just make it expensive.' It was a very long process to convince [the other side] that it is just not possible to do it cheaper."* (A-2)

The Software-as-a-Service context reinforces the need to keep operations costs low.

> *"We have a fixed price for the customer, that's why we, of course, want to significantly reduce the fixed cost on our side in terms of systems operations costs."* (A-3)

An increased awareness of operations is required because of the implications of Software-as-a-Service on the revenue as well as on the cost basis of software vendors. Operating and maintaining the software solutions lies within the responsibility of the software vendors and thus the costs of operating need to be covered by the incoming revenue streams. However, compared to the on-premises model, these revenue streams are much smaller and distributed over the entire usage period instead of the upfront investment of traditional software solutions.

> *'It was a rude awakening how expensive the operation of our systems can be. This was previously unnoticed by the company as the customer took care of it. Now, with a Software-as-a-Service offering the company suddenly bears the costs."* (A-2)

To be able to effectively reduce costs, a developer is required to build up additional knowledge about operations to understand the key cost drivers and challenges of this domain.

> *"That the software provider itself bears the cost of operation, leads to completely new discussions with the developer that they did not know before. It is definitely fruitful and often an eye-opener."* (A-2)

> *"Developers are just not used to deal with Euros. It is a complete new experience for them to get to know the financial impact of their code."* (A-2)

> *"Developers have to know more operations-related aspects than with on-premises software. They have to understand software operations."* (F-1)

Close cooperation and communication between developers and operation experts takes a key role in this situation. Integration in the form of experts of operation activities within development teams and review committees is used to make developers aware about the cost involved in operating their program code.

> *"Now, we do not just do operations, afterwards, when the product is ready, but we are part of the development organization, not a separated IT. And we are organized like this from the beginning of a product's development or when the initial idea is shaped. Our job is to be part of this and review architecture*

drafts to be able to estimate the costs of operation before the first line of code is written." (A-2)

"Right from the beginning, we go for a design-to-cost approach. We know what it is allowed to cost and that's defining the development. It has to be delivered matching these cost targets. We are not talking about development costs but actual resulting operations cost." (A-2)

Operation awareness may also influence a solution's scope and the inclusion of specific features. The knowledge about operations and its costs complements the estimates about development costs to form a clearer picture about the total costs of single features of Software-as-a-Service solutions. Together, this allows for more accurate estimates about the market potential of features.

"I have to consider [the potential of software features]. We, for example, currently do this with different country versions of our solution. What is my potential to sell this? What are the costs of development? What are the costs of provisioning? Then, you have to look at the bottom line whether it is worth it or not. It's not correct that I have to add all sorts of stuff and plenty of it, my perspective is that I have to include the things that will promote sales and make me profitable." (A-2)

By applying effective means of communication and coordination, the development of the software artifact can be guided by its development and operations costs. In addition, a close link between the responsible developers and units operating the development output may further improve the execution quality of the software artifact, as developers not only get access to cost estimates but also realistic performance measures of the system in use.

"We made the experience with our solution that the total cost of ownership aspect was problematic at the beginning. And the learning where the main pitfalls are and where you need to improve is more likely to succeed the closer you are to the actual hosting itself." (A-5)

The *awareness* theme relates to the role of specialization in the context of organizational integration. The cases show that development and operations units may indeed have different goals and are embedded in a different frame of reference. The findings support (Barki & Pinsonneault, 2005) reasoning that specialization increases integration efforts but also indicate that integration can be used to align the goals and frame of references. To be in charge for development and operation calls for integration of these two activities. This integration need is underpinned by the results of Brentani (1989) that reveal an influence of simultaneity on the importance to integrate personnel that is involved in the service delivery into the development process. The customers are purchasing a combination of the end result and the service experience (Brentani, 1989). The adjustments of local goals is also expected by Aulbach et al. (2008) who see a clear priority shift within development from feature enhancement to operational cost reduction. Aspects related to operation such as reusability, scalability, and availability gain emphasis within development (La & Kim, 2009).

Continuity

The second theme is addressing the processes and the synchronization of efforts of stakeholders involved in the innovation process. It describes the avoidance of bottlenecks that are based on problems within the communication and coordination between development and operations' departments.

With the introduction of a service offering, the vendor takes over the operation of the software that was previously done by the customers' IT departments or a third-party provider on behalf of the customer. New activities and responsibilities are added to the value chain of a software vendor. These new activities need to be integrated into the existing processes and structures. The resulting process needs to be streamlined and activities need to be synchronized in order to avoid waste and bottlenecks within the process.

A proper communication and coordination between the development and operations units is required to make sure processes are aligned, given that unaligned processes may result in bottlenecks and the innovation process to come to a halt.

> *"[Software-as-a-Service has an impact] on the development, as we have to deliver new features quite early and quick, and on operations, as these have to be delivered fast. This means that I deploy something new for the customers and ideally they can use it by tomorrow. Developed today and it is available for the customers tomorrow. This is the challenge for operations. How do we get the output from development to the customer very, very quickly? You can see that in-house-operations has a lot of advantages."* (A-3)

Organizationally integrating development and operations within one company may ease potential delays within the flow of a software artifact though the development, deployment and operations process. It reduces the number of involved stakeholders with independent agendas to one company with the shared objective to achieve continuous innovations with low operations costs. Although both activities are executed within one organization, the communication between these two units remains crucial. All involved participants in the process need to align their efforts not to run into bottlenecks. Collaboration and communication between development and operations is required to make sure that the operations departments are ready to implement developed features and the respective developers are able to quickly react to potential problems arising during the update process.

> *"If the development team is creating all the new features and the operations team can't deploy them on time for customers or deploy them in a consistent and reliable way, then they become the bottleneck as well."* (B-1)

The approach applied within the studied companies to achieve the necessary integration varied. While some companies, as discussed within the theme *awareness*, form cross-functional teams from the beginning of development, others re-organize the organizational structure and make the operations unit a sub-division of the development organization.

Company F focuses the integration efforts especially on the crucial phase of software deployment and the update process of the existing live systems by forming a team that consists of developers and operators overlooking the process.

> *"That means, that two developers and two operations' guys sit together and shut down the servers and follow a procedure to deploy it."* (F-1)

An increase in development speed continuously creates new releases that, on the one hand, do not deliver any value without being deployed to the customer and, on the other hand, easily outgrow the operability if old releases are not replaced in the same frequency as new once are developed. The literature suggests that Software-as-a-Service affects the underlying processes of software development and requires adjustments and integration to account for the new software characteristics as well as the new responsibilities (Espadas et al., 2008; Saeed & Jaffar-Ur-Rehmann, 2005; Stuckenberg & Heinzl, 2010). Similar to the discussed aspects within this theme, internal communication gaps between departments are also seen by Brentani (1989) as common reasons that hold back development efforts within service development. Well-planned processes are found to be a solution to reduce communication gaps. The simultaneity characteristic of services is said to disclose a lack of collaboration between producing functions much easier for services than for products (Troy et al., 2008). This is in line with the observation that a lack of collaboration between the pre-product producing function of software development and the consumption enabling production function of solution operations may result in problems and delays within the update process of solutions. These problems likely result in outages or performance drops that are likely to be noticed by customers of the solution.

Increment

The third theme builds on the same basis as the previous theme of *continuity* but focuses on the resulting opportunities for evolvement rather than the related challenge of potential bottlenecks.

Being responsible for development and operations and thus for a considerable portion of the value chain leads to a gain in control of the underlying process. The software artifact does not leave the responsibility and control of the vendor, allowing a reduction of release cycle times and thus an acceleration of the innovation process, provided the prerequisites discussed within *continuity* have been taken care of.

Previously, the software artifact was finalized by the vendor and sent to the customer for installation and operation. Changes to the original software artifact required to publish an official update, the installation of which was left to the customer's discretion. The vendor did not have control of the process after a software artifact had been shipped to the customer. Within the Software-as-a-Service context, the artifact remains within the control of the vendor at all times instead. Thus, the vendor is enabled to make modification to it at any time. The innovation process can be accelerated as new features can be pushed out to the customer base instantly without the need to bundle these innovations into update packages that are easier to manage by the customer.

> *"With Software-as-a-Service, you're able to deliver small functionality faster, but the other thing you're able to do, is that you are also able to fix stuff."* (B-1)

The traditional release approach is challenged, given that software features can be pushed out to the customer on a more continuous basis.

> *"We have smaller iterations and smaller feature packs than it is the case with classic on-premises solutions."* (A-1)

A common characteristic of Software-as-a-Service offerings, especially those of rather new players in the market, is that they start with a small set of core features. Building on these features, the software solution is enhanced over time and at the same time already marketed.

> *"The most concise step was the iterative working with smaller time slices. Software-as-a-Service is more a little piece finger food tactic."* (A-1)

To sum up, the observed aspects in this theme illustrate how the internalization of external activities may lead to opportunities (Barki & Pinsonneault, 2005). Software updates can be reduced in scope and released more continuously, leading to shorter development cycles (Olsen, 2006). A value-chain wide optimization of the solution can be achieved with less effort than in the traditional approach (Luoma & Rönkkö, 2012).

Timing

Turning to the outward-oriented perspective, the forth theme addresses integration challenges with regard to the existence of the external factor, the customer, in the service process.

Although Software-as-a-Service providers are able to deploy new changes of the software to the customers without its involvement from an internal process perspective, challenges remain with regard to the disruption of the customers' business processes. Introducing modifications to existing software components requires a lot of caution.

> *"There are also various legal issues. Even if we are able to [deploy frequent updates] from a software/technical perspective, the customers would say that they currently do not want [an update], for example because they are having an external audit that does not allow them to change anything within the systems."* (A-4)

Next to the disruption of the customers' business and usage of the solution, the flow of new features may also overstrain the customer. New features need to be understood by the end-user. Sometimes additional training sessions may be necessary that require planning in advance.

> *"In principle it is feasible [to deploy new features continuously], however you would outdistance the business. We simply need the flexibility to react to the situation of the customer and that is typically a stream of two to three releases."* (A-4)

> *"We know that we are able to deliver every innovation to the customer instantly, however, our customers are struggling to catch up and use all these new functions."* (D-1)

The described challenges can be reduced with proper means of external integration. In particular, the direct relationship with the end-customer can be used to determine the load and potential rush-hours of the system to decide on a more appropriate timing of updates.

> *"With the hosting operations [...] we can make suggestions with regard to the right timing [of an update]."* (A-4)

The involvement of the external factor within the fulfillment phase of services emphasizes the importance of the customer interface (Brentani, 1989). Changes to this interface, for instance by software updates that alter functionalities, processes or the visual experience, may disrupt the customer in the daily interactions with the Software-as-a-Service solution and eventually the customer's course of business. "Software development is not an isolated practice confined only in technical fields" anymore and needs to consider the environment and the appropriate timing of software releases to the market (Kakihara, 2006, p. 2).

Feedback

While the existence of an external factor implies challenges for software vendors, it may also provide opportunities. In particular, through Software-as-a-Service, providers may obtain access to more precise knowledge about the customer and, as a result, may increase the information quality throughout the whole innovation process.

The responsibility for the operation and control of the infrastructure the software service is relying on, results in a direct relationship with the end-user. While the software vendor previously maintained only limited relationship to end-customers, as a network of partners formed an ecosystem to assist the customer with installation, customization and training, having the customer interact on a vendor's own infrastructure enables a much more direct approach. A potential advantage of a direct relationship is the possibility to observe the customer's interaction with the software service.

> *"I do not just have the customer; instead I have the end-users that I otherwise do not reach."* (D-1)

> *"We operate the system, we can find out what our customers are doing or what they need."* (A-3)

> *"On-premises providers also do not have the transparency, what is actually used, what is actually adopted, what is not accepted. I can't imagine how to actually do this in the on-premises environment. This is just not possible. You have to rely on what you get back verbally."* (D-1)

This feedback channel provides information with regard to the customers' general usage patterns of the software artifact.

> *"We know exactly what is used most, what is not used at all, what is rarely used, and what has a lot of problems."* (A-4)

This inside view into the customers' daily activities with the software provides access to huge amounts of data.

> *"We can see the usage. Not customer data in terms of content, contact data, product descriptions but interactions with the system and the clicks and what is done with the system. We can see the usage and that is the key. We can see the end-user behavior and benchmark it."* (D-1)

This information can be of value to various stakeholders in the development and delivery process and support different activities including requirements engineering, portfolio management, sales, and support. Information may reduce wasted infrastructure capacity as it allows forecasting the demand more accurately within the operations department.

> *"We know when the customers login, in which session, how long they stayed and how often they requested something. This gives us information about the behavior in terms of system load."* (F-1)

The usage patterns can also lead to better estimates about the value of specific features in comparison to the development and delivery cost. Interaction patterns may indicate errors or hard to understand features that result in the customer repeating unnecessary steps or clicks or jumping to the help pages for further information. A better basis of decision-making can be achieved with regard to the scope of a solution and the features included.

> *"I think so, that the development is able to look much more dedicated which features are actually used."* (D-1)

A better basis of decision-making can be achieved with regard to the scope of a solution and the features included.

> *"With regard to the pay-by-usage and provider-operated solutions it is like this: you get totally different data over the lifetime, during the usage time of the product and these data can help to re-adjust your investment or your quality processes."* (A-5)

The analysis of patterns related to requirements engineering is, however, still in its early stages with various unsolved challenges.

> *"To decide whether it is worth it to advance a specific software function based on user behavior data? It is hard to detect which additional functions are required because if the function is not part of the solution it can't be used. I think it is a double-edged sword you need to look at in more detail. To my knowledge, it is not actively used yet but the idea is definitely there. How do I manage to draw conclusions out of it?"* (A-2)

All this information, however, only delivers value if it reaches the right stakeholder within the innovation process. Only if development and operations communicate and cooperate close enough, the information can be facilitated to improve the software service. Development decisions can only be supported if the information and experience form operating the solution is communicated to the developers and solution architects (see *awareness*).

With the end-user involved as the external factor in the service fulfillment phase, software vendors get frequent and immediate feedback of the offered solution's effectiveness. The feedback can help improve the software service (Saeed & Jaffar-Ur-Rehmann, 2005). The analysis of the service usage can provide valuable hints on the reliability of the offering (Banerjee et al., 2010). Existent knowledge and methods from related web-based software used, for instance, in the e-commerce context may guide Software-as-a-Service vendors in realizing such opportunities (Herder, 2009; Hilbert & Redmiles, 1998; Kenett et al., 2008).

5.3.2. Enablers and Inhibitors of Organizational Integration

After the presentation of the five different themes that reflect the organizational integration between development, operations, and the customer, this section highlights three contingency factors that were found to enable or inhibit organizational integration in the context of the five themes. *Service mindset*, *company size* and *technical harmonization* are each described and put into context with the identified integration themes. A factor is considered an enabler when it supports the integration efforts and makes them easier to achieve. Inhibiting factors on the other hand make organizational integration harder to accomplish.

Service Mindset

Service mindset in this study refers to two different but related aspects. First, it describes the attitude of people involved in the development and operations process towards their solution, second, it describes the implementation of this attitude. Service mindset means that involved stakeholders regard the offered Software-as-a-Service solution as a service rather than a software product and also implement the necessary adjustments required when dealing with services.

> *"I think, in the context of Software-as-a-Service you have to develop a service. It is not possible to develop a piece of software and afterwards decide to make*

> *a service out of it. It is not up to the operations unit to transform a piece of software into a service. I think you have to start with this. You have to decide this in advance and afterwards everybody delivers its part."* (A-3)

For instance, the different mindset underlying service development is reflected by the observation that the details running "under the hood" do not need to interest the customer anymore, as long as the promised service can be delivered. The software artifact itself, previously the main output of a software vendor now takes the role of a pre-product within the service process. It is a prerequisite for the service provision and needs to be transformed into executable functions in the moment of service consumption by the customer. The specifics of the software artifact, aside from the ones that define the consumable features or user interface, are less important when it comes to customer acceptance.

> *"As long as we still can manage to provide the services we agreed on with the customer, the customers simply don't need to care about the way we do it."* (A-3)

This leads to an increased flexibility within the development function.

> *"It is a service, we do it today this way and tomorrow we do it differently. How we realize it, to provide the service, always depends on the most cost-efficient option we have."* (A-2)

Services may also lead to an altered understanding of quality. While software quality is typically measured by an indicator such as the number of bugs, delay, or budget overrun, quality in the service context is mainly linked to overall customer satisfaction.

> *"We have role-specific scorecards. Every role has this customer satisfaction aspect included as a metric. You can't neglect this, as it is simply positioned in the middle. It is also feedback for the development and it is precisely measured how the customer satisfaction evolves. [...] We also already break this down to functions to evaluate the impact they have. And there we are back to the topic of a close loop that actually makes all this possible to measure."* (D-1)

In this study's sample, the pure Software-as-a-Service providers tend to have a deeper service mindset compared to vendors with a hybrid approach. To prevent the potentially negative effects of a lack of service mindset, pure Software-as-a-Service vendors go as far as to replace the entire development team.

> *"We started with an entirely new team. We did not take on anyone of our previous employees. We followed a Greenfield strategy with the new company, with new employees, and a new infrastructure, all set up to realize fully-fledged and pure Software-as-a-Service. We did not want legacy, old mindsets or infrastructure to influence the new software but instead built up an unburdened team."* (E-1)

The presence of a service mindset among the people involved in the development and operation process of a Software-as-a-Service solution supports the objectives and goals of all five identified themes. The service mindset increases the awareness of the characteristics of services and the problems and challenges that may be the outcome of these. Stakeholders with a distinct service mindset are expected to be more likely to identify problems that are the result of a service context and thus more likely to find an appropriate solution for them.

Company Size

The company size of a software vendor determines the amount of resources in terms of employees like developers and operators available to participate in the process. Small organizations tend to achieve a higher degree of internal integration, as less people need to get involved with each other. Also the scope of responsibility of one person tends to be bigger as the same variety of development and operation activities need to be spread among a smaller group of people. Less people need to interact with each other increasing the degree of integration to that effect.

In the Software-as-a-Service context, it is more likely that a developer of a small organization is also involved with operation activities or the deployment of the code. Otherwise, the developer may be sharing the same office space with the colleagues responsible for software operation.

In contrast, external integration, for instance in the form of the analysis of usage pattern or direct customer interaction relies on more resources and, therefore, tends to be lower in small organizations. In the Software-as-a-Service context, especially small organizations complained about the increased anonymity of the customer base. As a result of the self-service sign-up for solutions on the providers' website, direct interaction between sales personnel and the customer is not necessary anymore. Vendors do not really know their customers.

> *"There are a lot of customers we haven't had any contact with so far because they subscribed to the software online and then they do not attract any attention."* (E-1)

At the same time, small vendors do not have sufficient resources to implement the analytics required to identify behavior patterns and derive a better customer understanding through these.

> *"At the moment we couldn't manage to do such things as tracking as it is very complex."* (F-1)

Based on this discussion, increasing company size is expected to have a negative effect on internal organizational integration and a rather positive effect on external organizational integration.

Technical Harmonization

Typical Software-as-a-Service solutions share a set of characteristics that aim at a harmonization of the technical capabilities required to provide the offered service. This involves the software and its infrastructure. Solutions have a rather high degree of standardization and implement resource sharing across the customer base. This concept is frequently termed as multi-tenancy. Every customer of a Software-as-a-Service provider is sharing the same software and underlying infrastructure, representing a high level of standardization. Even though customers can only access their own data, the data is stored within the same database. There is only one instance of the software that is shared among all customers (Aulbach et al., 2008). The main advantage of the concept is the decrease in the total cost of ownership and the ease of setting up new accounts for additional customers. Especially in conjunction with the widespread use of free trial periods that aim at reducing the uncertainty of the service offering, these two aspects are very beneficial.

The use of the concept is related to a reduction of the number of co-existing software versions that can also be seen as an indication for the efficiency of the interplay between development and operation. Versions in this case do not stand for the marketing tool of different packages that differ in scope and pricing but for different releases with different source code that are results of the further development of the software. Due to the cost increase related to simultaneously offered releases, the goal of a Software-as-a-Service provider should be to reduce the number of releases to a minimum.

> *"It is a major cost component to have multiple releases running at a time. And a matter of stability because every release is a little different."* (A-2)

Technical harmonization is influencing the integration aspects discussed within the themes. Internal organizational integration is positively influenced by the resource focus that comes with a reduction of versions. The communication and coordination requirements are reduced, easing the process flow.

> *"That is for me the first step within software development that you can concentrate on one release version, on one product. The whole innovation can be put into this [version] and you are much more agile with regard to software development than in the traditional context."* (E-1)

The approaches in terms of the release frequency varied between releases in six months cycles and a continuous flow of features, representing a development methodology without thinking within releases. To handle the increased frequency in development, the mindset of releases for example altered from a scope-base to a time-based approach. Releases are therefore not defined in terms of feature scope to be included but in terms of time available. The scope is then flexible and adjusted with development progress.

The goal to minimize the number of versions may, however, lead to compromises with regard to the ability to align the timing of an update with the customers' activities. With one version, the timing to update is also reduced to only a single timeslot that is used to update the entire customer base to the new version. This makes it more difficult to decide on the most appropriate time that suits all customers and the integration of the customer into this decision is hindered.

> *"Customers cannot make the decision themselves to stick to one release for seven years because they like to do so."* (A-4)

In contrast, integration aspects that relate to the *feedback* theme are likely to take advantage of a reduction of the different versions available to the customer. A harmonization leads to a complexity reduction and makes it easier to interpret the collected data, as it is based on the same software version. The feedback is not blurred by potentially conflicting observations from different implementations within different releases.

The degree of harmonization reflected in the number of simultaneous version varied within the sample. Pure Software-as-a-Service providers follow a clear one-version-approach, whereas hybrid vendors seem to have more problems reducing the number of coexisting releases used by the customer.

> *"Following the Software-as-a-Service spirit, we always have one version only running with our customers."* (E-1)

> *"According to the Software-as-a-Service concept, as we understand it in our company, there is only one version at any given time. And this one version is there for all customers."* (D-1)

The hybrid provider A admitted that reducing the number of versions is a central goal and its achievement linked to an improvement of the coordination and communication within the processes.

> *"Ideally, there is indeed a short time, when we only have one active release. The better we get, the longer this time window gets. But at the moment, we only reach two month having only one active release."* (A-2)

Table 5.2 summarizes the effect of the three described contingency factors on the integration aspects addressed within the five themes and indicate whether the factor can be considered to be an enabler (+) or inhibitor (–) of organizational integration, that is, whether they aggravate or facilitate organizational integration in the context of the respective theme.

Table 5.2.: Enabling and inhibiting factors of integration

	Service mindset	**Company size**	**Technical harmonization**
Awareness	+	–	
Continuity	+	–	+
Increment	+	–	+
Timing	+	+	–
Feedback	+	+	+

5.4. Discussion

Figure 5.4 presents the theoretical model that summarizes the different themes of integration, as well as the different enablers and inhibitors affecting integration in the Software-as-a-Service context. The study's findings address the open questions identified within Figure 5.1. The five themes, *awareness*, *continuity*, *increment*, *timing* and *feedback* provide an in-depth understanding of organizational integration aspects that emerge from applying Software-as-a-Service as a business model. The themes introduce a clearer picture of the relationship between development and operations activities as well as their link to the customers. The three identified enablers and inhibitors of integration provide further insights, as they highlight different contingency factors of these relationships and demonstrate the complexity of the context, while at the same time their impact varies between the different themes.

The findings provide a comprehensive understanding of different internal and external communication and coordination needs in the context of Software-as-a-Service. As such, they illustrate the implications of Software-as-a-Service on software vendors' structures and processes. While the literature review discussed earlier research on such implications, the findings provide a new level of detail. By being embedded in a consistent framework that was deduced from extant literature and supported by relevant theory, the findings increase the understanding of the implications rather than providing a high level list of implications. The three identified enablers and inhibitors further improve the understanding of the context, as they describe surrounding factors that may assist or hinder vendors in their integration efforts. Vendors, for instance, may pro-actively work on establishing a *service mindset* to ease efforts in conjunction with all identified themes of challenges and opportunities. In addition, identifying the potential problems of a not harmonized approach, with regard to software architecture and used technologies, turns the attention to such aspects from early on and thus avoids running into potentially irrevocable issues later in the process of developing and operation Software-as-a-Service. Moreover, the findings show that harmonizing technologies and for instance keeping the number of simultaneously existing software version small is a double-edged sword. While it may save cost and increase the innovation speed, the approach needs to be balanced with the potentially resulting disruption of customers.

The framework that guided this second phase of research has been filled with observations from the case studies and thus has applied the corresponding theory in the Software-as-a-Service context. As suggested by theory, differences in goals and frames of references may hinder integration efforts (Barki & Pinsonneault, 2005). The findings support this and at the same time illustrate potential goal differences and frames of references within the Software-as-a-Service context. For example, while the goal of development may be a feature-rich software solution, the goal of operation, in comparison, may be more focused on cost efficiency of the solution. By linking the framework with constituent characteristics of services, the findings can be put in relation to contributions within the service and Marketing literature.

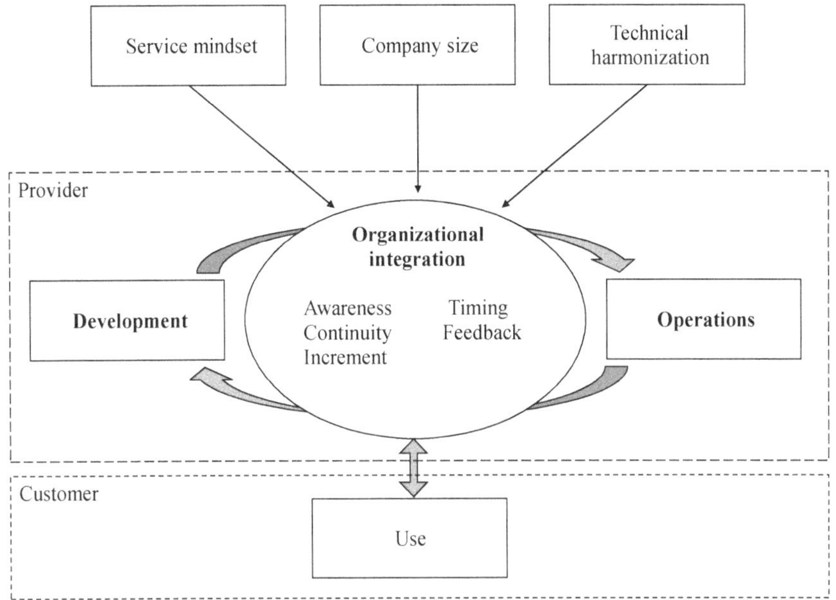

Figure 5.4.: Model of organizational integration in the Software-as-a-Service context

Reflecting the observed findings in the light of the extant literature on organizational integration (Barki & Pinsonneault, 2005; Huang, 2006; Koufteros et al., 2010; Lazonick & West, 1995; Millson & Wilemon, 2002), it is interesting to note that the findings support the common distinction in internal and external integration. In addition to internal integration being considered to require less efforts than external integration (Barki & Pinsonneault, 2005), the Software-as-a-Service context illustrates that internalizing a previously external activity creates additional benefits. Internalizing software operation creates opportunities as described within the themes of *increment* and *feedback*. At the same time, the findings show that it is important to have a certain level of internal organizational integration before being able to take advantage of external organizational integration. For example, taking advantage of observations of the customer behavior, as described within the *feedback* theme, requires an existing link between development and operations to spread and facilitate the information gains. Furthermore, the Software-as-a-Service context illustrates that vertical integration within the value chain may change the boundaries between internal and external organizational integration.

The presented findings inform software vendors about challenges and opportunities that are linked to the Software-as-a-Service concept. As such, software vendors may gain a better understanding of the challenges before deciding to adopt Software-as-a-Service as a business model for delivering and operating their software. The findings provide indications about appropriate means to tackle the challenges. For example, a close integration between development and operation functions is necessary to make sure all stakeholders are aware of the others' activities and a smooth process of developing and operating Software-as-a-Service can be achieved without any bottlenecks. Furthermore, the findings illustrate how integration may result in higher innovativeness and software that matches customer needs. The identified contingency factors inform software vendors about important context variables. The findings illustrate the role of technical harmonization, rendering it crucial to have a consistent strategy with regard to technologies and updates.

The enabler and inhibitor *company size* indicates that small software vendors may have advantages in establishing appropriate means to solve the identified internal integration challenges and facilitate the opportunities, but they need to be aware of their potential competitive disadvantage in terms of external integration. The findings pointed at an increased anonymity of the customer base that relies on automated self-service systems to interact with vendors, instead of personal contacts. Without appropriate countermeasures, small vendors may run into the risk of losing sentiment for their customer base. Large software vendors on the other hand may be required to put much more effort and resources in establishing internal organizational integration.

5.5. Summary

Motivated by the first stage of research that identified changing interdependence between development and operation as well as a changing relationship to customers, the goal of the second stage of research was to provide a better understanding of these implications of Software-as-a-Service on software vendors. In order to reach this goal, a consistent framework was derived by integrating existing literature on the constituent characteristics of services and on organizational integration. This framework guided the second empirical research phase. The findings of the multiple-case study show that Software-as-a-services results in internal and external challenges and opportunities of organizational integration, reflected by the five themes *awareness*, *continuity*, *increment*, *timing*, and *feedback*. The results also show that the salience of these themes is contingent upon *company size*, the *service mindset* among employees, and the degree of *technical harmonization*.

6. Discussion

After the previous presentation of the findings from the two-staged research approach and its two multiple-case studies, the following chapter will consolidate the observations to draw a complete picture of the implications of Software-as-a-Service on software vendors.

Next to a holistic view on the Software-as-a-Service impact, the chapter will discuss the findings and outline their implications for research and practice. The chapter will end with a discussion of the limitations of the study and will outline opportunities for future research.

6.1. A Holistic View on the Impact of Software-as-a-Service

The previous chapters has presented the findings from the two conducted multiple-case studies with an independent discussion of the respective findings of each research phase. However, some aspects have been identified within both phases of research, motivating a joined discussion of the observations from both rounds of case studies. Among these aspects are, for instance, software releases, which have been identified as potential reason for changed dependencies between value chain activities within the first phase of empirical research and as component of a contingency factor within the second study. Furthermore, the findings of both phases of research demonstrate the broad scope of implications for software vendors, who are applying or planning to apply Software-as-a-Service as a software delivery and pricing model.

The two-staged approach has assisted in answering the broad initial research question, as it has allowed to start the research with a broad perspective within the first phase and focus on selected aspects within the second stage. Similar to a funnel, this approach has helped to collect multiple implications and narrow them down to selected implications, which have appeared worthy to investigate in more detail. This approach has demonstrated the disruptive character of Software-as-a-Service for software vendors by providing indications of change in every aspect of a software vendor's business model. Among the observations are various challenges and opportunities, for example, a more complete value proposition, new customer segments, complexity problems of pricing models, automated self-service channels or changing customer and partner relationships. The findings show that software vendors cannot simply introduce a Software-as-a-Service solution as a marketing campaign, but instead need to make significant changes to internal processes and resources.

The findings provide evidence for the concept to especially challenge the internal capabilities of software vendors. Even those rather external-oriented aspects of a business model, like the pricing model or customer communication channels, lead to changes to the internal processes and resources. Self-service systems, for instance, that automate the sales process of Software-as-a-Service solutions and, thus, the interaction with customers, require the internal capabilities to accommodate the automated deployment of additional resources. From an external perspective, pricing models not only advertise variable and flexible cost for Software-as-a-Service customers, but also require the internal capabilities to match with interrelated problems. The findings show that Software-as-a-Service pricing models increase the handling complexity for software vendors and require new knowledge and resources to master the challenge of a high number of small payments.

The combination of the observations of both case studies point at two central aspects, most identified implications are related to. These are, on one hand, concerned with the reorganization of internal processes and capabilities and, on the other hand, related to the changed relationship to the customer. The first aspect is dominated by the responsibility shift of operation activities that need to be integrated into the existing structures. The latter is driven by a customer relationship that can be characterized as more direct and more continuous in the Software-as-a-Service context. Figure 5.1 already indicated these aspects as a result of the initial phase of research. The second round of empirical case studies supported and enriched the previous findings. The five identified themes, for instance, elaborate on the challenges and opportunities linked to the two aspects. At the same time, the themes provide suggestions and increase the awareness of crucial aspects. The themes help to understand the relationship between development and operation, as well as the direct relationship to the customer and thus substantiate the initial observations and reduce the question marks depicted in Figure 5.1.

A holistic view on both conduced case studies points at the special role of software releases within the Software-as-a-Service context. The re-evaluation of the first case study has indicated the goal to reduce the number of simultaneously offered software releases and, thus, the trend towards development without a distinction into releases, to result in different activities of the value chain to move closer together. This interpretation is based on activities, like development and maintenance, to loose their distinctiveness or on the interaction between activities, like development and operation, to require more communication and coordination. As such, the findings point at the dependence between development and operation to become more complex and change from a prevalent sequential to a reciprocal character. In light of a coordination perspective, it has been argued that coordination mechanisms based on mutual adjustment are expected to take a leading role in managing the interdependence between the two activities. Therefore, software releases, or rather the missing of those, have been argued to lead to the requirement to introduce coordination mechanisms that are based on mutual adjustment to cope with the responsibility shift of operation activities and the related internalization of those activities. Within the second empirical study, software releases have again been identified to have an influence. However, instead of a source for the requirement to implement coordination mechanisms of mutual adjustment, it has been identified as an enabler and inhibitor of organizational integration, and thus as a contingency factor of a coordination mechanism of mutual adjustment between stakeholders. Software releases can, therefore, be regarded as a reinforcing element of a transition towards Software-as-a-Service. Developing and operating Software-as-a-Service requires a certain degree of organizational integration, while this integration is again enabled by technical harmonization that is, for instance, reflected by a low number of simultaneously offered releases.

6.2. Implications

As outlined within Section 2.3, previous studies have provided initial indications for potential implications of the Software-as-a-Service concept (Joha & Janssen, 2012; Juell-Skielse & Enquist, 2012; Stuckenberg & Heinzl, 2010). At the same time, vendors appear to underestimate the potential implications and prepare for rather incremental change requisites, resulting from adopting Software-as-a-Service as a delivery and pricing model of their software solutions (Heart et al., 2010). Motivated by this mismatch in the perception of the disruptive character of Software-as-a-Service and the growing importance of the concept as a delivery and pricing model of software (Merz et al., 2011; West et al., 2010), this study has set out to explore the implications of the Software-as-a-Service concept on software vendors and to understand the role of organizational integration for vendors developing and delivering such solutions.

This study is among the first to examine the implications of Software-as-a-Service from a business model perspective and to provide indications for implications of the concept on the entire business model with all its building blocks. Furthermore, by using the explanatory power of related theory, observed phenomena are underpinned with potential explanations. Knowledge from organization literature was used to guide the subsequent analysis and set the focus of following research activities.

In addition, this study is among the first to develop an in-depth understanding of how the adoption of Software-as-a-Service influences the internal organization of software vendors. Rather than simply listing potential implications from case study observations, this study draws on extant theory and incorporates implications into a theoretically deduced framework. In this manner, it links extant knowledge of organizational theory and service research with the Software-as-a-Service concept.

The following sections elaborate on the theoretical, as well as managerial contributions of the study in detail.

6.2.1. Theoretical Implications

This study offers a number of theoretical contributions to the field of IS research, as well as organizational science and service research. Specifically, it explores the implications of the Software-as-a-Service concept on software vendors from different perspectives and highlights selected implications on the business models and value chains of participants of the software industry. In addition, it provides an in-depth understanding of the concept's implications on organizational structures and processes of software vendors. The following sections provide further details with regard to these theoretical contributions.

Explore the impact of Software-as-a-Service on software vendors: This study contributes to the extant literature on Software-as-a-Service by providing a clear definition of the Software-as-a-Service concept and its key characteristics. It adds to previous studies that aimed on forming a comprehensive Software-as-a-Service definition (e.g. Mäkilä et al., 2010; Saaksjarvi et al., 2005) by discussing key characteristics from a product, as well as service perspective. In this manner, it paves the way for a thorough analysis of the implications of the concept on the basis of a clear definition and typically associated characteristics. As such, it allows to link the characteristics with extant theoretical concepts and enables a thorough analysis with existing theoretical lenses. In addition, the study adds to the discussion about the distinctive characteristics of the Software-as-a-Service delivery and pricing model, and enables a clear differentiation to related and preceding concepts (e.g. Cloud Computing). Furthermore, having a clear perception of the concept and its key characteristics at hand enables the comparability of research observations and findings.

This study is among the first to include a traditional service perspective in the analysis of the Software-as-a-Service concept. By drawing on the knowledge of service research with regard to the unique attributes of services (e.g. heterogeneity, intangibility, simultaneity, and the existence of an external factor), the study directs the attention to aspects that go beyond selected technologies and software characteristics.

This study's findings contribute to the literature that is analyzing the implications of the Software-as-a-Service concept (e.g. Heart et al., 2010; Joha & Janssen, 2012; Juell-Skielse & Enquist, 2012; Luoma & Rönkkö, 2012; Saeed & Jaffar-Ur-Rehmann, 2005) by demonstrating the disruptive character of the concept on the entire business model of software vendors. By applying a business model perspective and using a well-established framework, this study adds to the existing literature as it provides a structured and detailed evaluation of Software-as-a-Service and its impact on software vendors. The analysis includes vendor internal as well as external aspects and, thus, allows to observe implications of the Software-as-a-Service concept from different perspectives. While existing studies often limit the evaluation on selected dimensions, e.g. the value proposition (Enquist & Juell-Skielse, 2010), the broader perspective of this study allows to study interrelations between implications on various dimensions. As such, the evaluation, for example, provides indications for the changing pricing model to not only affect the revenue stream of vendors, but also the potential customer segments, required technologies and processes or quality aspects. Furthermore, this study provides empirical observations for potential implications of the delivery and pricing model for every building block of a vendor's business model, enriching previous conceptual studies (e.g. Saeed & Jaffar-Ur-Rehmann, 2005; Stuckenberg & Heinzl, 2010). The findings illustrate the diversity of implications of a switch from an on-premises to a Software-as-a-Service business model.

The findings from the first empirical study show that despite the focus of extant Software-as-a-Service literature on adoption related aspects (e.g. Benlian & Hess, 2010;

Lassila, 2006), a substantial number of challenges reside within the internal structures and processes of software vendors. The findings indicate a lack of research addressing internal capabilities of software vendors that go beyond the discussion of selected technologies. The comparison of the case study observations with extant literature, in addition points at selected gaps within the literature that may offer promising future research opportunities that could not be addressed within this study. One of these is for example the role of self-service systems in communicating with prospective and existing service customers. This study adds to the field of Software-as-a-Service research by providing a thorough review of the extant literature that addresses the impact of Software-as-a-Service on software vendors and by sketching a research agenda for future research.

The use of the business model framework of Osterwalder & Pigneur (2010) as a structural aid within this study adds to the extant literature about business models (e.g. Fielt, 2011). It demonstrates the potential of the framework to analyze the Software-as-a-Service business model and, thus, it is backing the frameworks generality and capability to describe diverse business models. In addition, it shows the possibility to use the framework to highlight and structure change requirements to business models of software vendors. Furthermore, it demonstrates the potential of business model frameworks in general and the framework of Osterwalder & Pigneur (2010) in particular, to analyze the context within an organizational study that applies the theoretical lens of the contingency approach of organizations. The business model analysis as suggested by Osterwalder & Pigneur (2010) already includes various internal and external dimensions (e.g. product mix, technologies, customer structure) that are commonly discussed in research using a contingency approaches (Kieser & Walgenbach, 2003). Due to the broad objective of the business model analysis to describe the way organizations create, delivery, and capture value, the analysis describes organizations and their activities as well as their environment using multiple dimensions. As a result, it allows to develop a thorough understanding of the context of organizations and, thus, enables the identification of dimensions that may influence organizational structures. This study, therefore, suggests a combination of business model research with the research on organizational science (e.g. Donaldson, 2001).

The theory guided funnel like research approach underlying this study illustrates the power of theory to narrow down a rather broad research question and guide research activities. The coordination perspective from organizational science is not only consulted to provide explanation to selected observed phenomena, but is also used to prioritize future research activities. Observing decreasing, as well as increasing complexity of the interdependence between different activities of developing and delivering Software-as-a-Service, led to setting the focus of subsequent research steps on the latter. Extant frameworks and theories, thus, not only assisted in structuring this research, but also in guiding the process of narrowing down the broad scope of observed implications of the Software-as-a-Service concept to those most vital from the selected perspective.

Provide an in-depth understanding of the implications of Software-as-a-Service on organizational structures and processes of software vendors: The findings contribute to the Software-as-a-Service, as well as to the organizational integration literature. Even though extensive implications of Software-as-a-Service have been identified within the Software-as-a-Service literature (Joha & Janssen, 2012; Juell-Skielse & Enquist, 2012; Saeed & Jaffar-Ur-Rehmann, 2005; Stuckenberg et al., 2011), the implications for the structures and processes of software vendors have not been studied in detail yet. This study is among the first to provide a comprehensive understanding of different internal and external communication and coordination needs in the context of Software-as-a-Service. At the same time, these organizational integration requirements are embedded in a consistent framework that is deduced from extant literature. The framework contributes to the literature by providing a clear structure to link the concepts of organizational integration (e.g. Barki & Pinsonneault, 2005) with those of the research on services (e.g. Cloninger, 2004; Troy et al., 2008). Furthermore it offers guidance for the analysis of different communication and coordination patterns within the Software-as-a-Service context.

This study has analyzed the implications of Software-as-a-Service on organizational structures of software vendors by focusing on the coordination dimension of organizational structures. By applying an emphasis on communication and coordination needs, this study has been able to identify initial indications for structural changes within organizations that are a direct or indirect consequence of adopting Software-as-a-Service as a delivery and pricing model of software. The analysis of the interdependencies between value activities in the first empirical study, as well as the thorough evaluation of organizational integration in the second multiple-case study have revealed changing coordination needs between different organizational units. The initial observation that the interdependence between development and operation becomes more complex in the Software-as-a-Service environment has been supported by the detailed observations represented by the five themes of organizational integration. The results show that within the Software-as-a-Service context development and operation cannot be regarded as distinct and independent organizational units anymore. Instead, software vendors need to reconsider existing structures and approaches to account for the changed communication and coordination needs. At the same time, this study challenges the extant software engineering literature that tends to neglect the integration of operation phases within frameworks and process models.

The findings contribute to the field of studies taking a contingency perspective on organizations as the study has identified three contingency factor that appear important in the Software-as-a-Service context. *Service mindset*, *company size* and *technical harmonization* influence the five themes of organizational integration and thus represent three contingency factors that influence the coordination dimension of organizational structures. While *company size* is frequently mentioned as an influencing factor in organizational studies (Kieser & Walgenbach, 2003), the other two are rather novel. The three enablers and inhibitors help to understand the role of surrounding factors related to organizational integration in the Software-as-a-Service context. While company size cannot easily be influenced, the results stress aspects that require special attention by small and large organizations respectively. Service mindset and technological harmonization, by contrast, may be within the control of software vendors. The results of this study indicate that establishing a service mindset among the people involved in the development and operation generally supports organizational integration in the context of Software-as-a-Service solutions. Software-as-a-Service providers, in addition, need to be aware of the potential influence of different software product characteristics and technologies, which are summarized under the term "technical harmonization". While keeping the number of coexisting software versions small is reducing costs and offers potential to increase the innovation capability, it also introduces new challenges that affects customers and may harm their perception of the quality of the solution.

Furthermore, the findings have revealed that the salience of the enablers and inhibitors within the organization varies between firms, both for those which previously offered on-premises software and those that were founded as pure Software-as-a-Service providers. Vendors that have started directly with Software-as-a-Service tend to have a stronger service mindset and to start on a higher level of technological harmonization. Hybrid providers, by contrast, may struggle with changing established structures and processes. Their developers are often still thinking in terms of products instead of services and rely on technologies and architectures form the traditional business model. The number of coexisting versions is a clear indicator in this context. While pure Software-as-a-Service providers tend to apply a one-version-only approach, hybrids are less restrictive, often reflecting the assumption that a larger number of versions would enable them to be more responsive to customer needs.

In addition, this study adds to extant literature on organizational integration (Huang, 2006; Koufteros et al., 2010; Lazonick & West, 1995; Millson & Wilemon, 2002). Specifically, this study contributes to previous research by providing an in-depth understanding of the nature of external and internal organizational integration, as well as different goals and frames of reference in the context of Software-as-a-Service (Barki & Pinsonneault, 2005; Lawrence & Lorsch, 1969). In particular, previous studies suggested that internal organizational integration implies less effort than external integration, and that differences in goals and frames of references across organizational units might hinder organizational integration (Barki & Pinsonneault, 2005). The themes and enablers/inhibitors that emerged from this multiple-case study clarify what these propositions mean in the context of Software-as-a-Service vendors. Moreover, while previous research clearly distinguished between internal and external units, this study shows that changes in an organization's business model (e.g., from on-premises to Software-as-a-Service) may turn formerly external units, such as software operations, into internal ones, resulting in various challenges and opportunities related to organizational integration reflected by the identified themes.

Furthermore, this study conceptually links organizational integration to the constituent characteristics of services, extending the limited research that addresses specific characteristics of services (Brentani, 1989; Cloninger, 2004; Troy et al., 2008). The service characteristic of simultaneity plays a crucial role, as it leads to internalization. The existence of an external factor, as the second characteristic under investigation, emphasizes the customer interface and is thus an important factor in combination with external integration. The findings highlight that the role of organizational integration can be derived from characteristics of the developed artifact. This study is furthermore an example of how concepts from reference disciplines can be fruitfully transferred to IS research and how these may help to fill important knowledge gaps.

The results support Barki & Pinsonneault (2005)'s assertion that the effort to implement organizational integration varies between internal and external units. In particular, the findings show that in the context of Software-as-a-Service, internalizing software operations results in the opportunity to organizationally integrate software development and operations with less effort. This is illustrated by the themes of *increment* and *feedback*. These themes also suggest that "external OI is likely to require that the corresponding internal OI types be implemented first" (Barki & Pinsonneault, 2005, p. 170). For instance, the insights gained from direct customer interaction discussed in the *feedback* theme require a certain level of internal organizational integration in order to create value.

Furthermore, the findings add to previous studies with regard to the differences of integrating primary and secondary activities. Previous literature proposed that organizational integration of secondary activities leads to a higher degree of effectiveness than the integration of primary activities (Barki & Pinsonneault, 2005). The results of this study may suggest the interpretation that the influence of integrating primary and secondary activities on effectiveness is different in the case of Software-as-a-Service. In particular, when developing on-premises software, vendors had to rely on market research or their field organizations in order to obtain knowledge on customer requirements. In contrast, the *feedback* theme shows that the external factor involvement in combination with technological advances may enable software vendors to obtain customer insights that go beyond explicitly expressed customer wishes. For instance, by observing system usage patterns and actual end-user behavior, Software-as-a-Service vendors may be enabled to more effectively gain customer insights. In other words, effectiveness is increased as a direct consequence of the internalization of the primary activity of software operations.

6.2.2. Managerial Implications

The results of this study point at a number of managerial implications for software vendors that have adapted or are planning on introducing Software-as-a-Service as delivery and pricing model of their software solutions. The results help to increase the awareness of small, as well as large software vendors about problems associated with Software-as-a-Service. Also, it informs about problems that may arise during a transition from traditional delivery and pricing models towards offering a Software-as-a-Service. These are especially of interest for hybrid software vendors that offer or plan to offer software applying both models and those that move their entire business towards the service model. Lastly, the results help to understand the special role releases play in developing and delivering Software-as-a-Service. The following section elaborates on these implications for practice in more detail.

Increase the awareness about Software-as-a-Service related challenges and opportunities: For practice, the results point at potential problems that vendors planning to enter the market with a Software-as-a-Service solution may encounter. They therefore create an awareness of potential conflicts and allow vendors to prepare accordingly.

The argument of internal aspects to require more attention within research, as outlined earlier, may also hold true for software vendors offering Software-as-a-Service. It can be speculated that vendors may put too much focus and effort on how to sell the solutions to the customer, rather on obtaining the appropriate capabilities to provide the solutions. This focus bears the risk of not being able to cover the expenses with the smaller but continuous service revenues, once the solution attracts its first customers. The findings highlight multiple implications that concern the internal capabilities of software vendors. Vendors may need to put special emphasis on these challenges in order to be able to develop and operate Software-as-a-Service successfully.

The findings indicate how Software-as-a-Service and associated marketplaces open up the opportunity for small software vendors to gain access to global markets without major investment. Relying on the platform offerings and integrated marketplaces of other vendors, small software vendors can offer their solutions to a large potential customer group. At the same time, using the offerings of other providers to operate the solutions allows an easier match of costs and revenues, as both are directly proportional to the number of subscribed customers and their usage intensity. The findings also show that due to the gain of control over the entire supply chain, software vendors can much easier scale solution in terms of their scope of functions. Vendors can start small and introduce new features on a continuous basis, but at the same time may already collect revenues from the solution. This again allows vendors to get into the business of software much easier and with much lower initial investments. The findings may therefore assist small software vendors in deciding on the right delivery and pricing model for their software solutions.

Decision makers within software vendors, who consider switching to or complementing their existing product portfolio with a Software-as-a-Service deployment model, may learn about challenges that need to be overcome in order to successfully compete in the Software-as-a-Service market. Specifically, managers need to make sure that development and operations functions are integrated, so that members of both divisions are aware of each other's processes and synchronize activities. Moreover, managers have to ensure that update schedules are aligned with customers' business activities. Both, pure and hybrid Software-as-a-Service vendors gain insights into opportunities potentially resulting from the service model. Internal integration efforts may enable vendors to innovate at a higher pace and leverage the customer feedback resulting from direct interaction.

In addition, decision makers are guided as to which factors influence these challenges and opportunities in different circumstances. The findings show that small vendors have to pay particular attention to the anonymity inherent in Software-as-a-Service offerings. In the traditional model, having a close and intimate relationship with customers was considered one of the core assets of small software vendors (Mathiassen & Vainio, 2007). Given that small firms may lack the resources to leverage technology-enabled customer interaction as described in the *feedback* theme, these vendors have to find alternative ways to tailor the offered software to customer needs and to compensate for the potential threat to their previous advantage over larger vendors. Large software vendors, instead, have to be aware of the challenges of internal organizational integration, given that large firms may be more prone to issues related to different goals and frames of reference. The study shows that technical harmonization can be an enabler of organizational integration. This is particularly important for hybrid vendors, given that these firms often tend to stick to legacy technologies and architectures. Embracing Software-as-a-Service concepts, such as multi-tenancy and one-version-only, may enable these firms to seize the opportunities of a transition to Software-as-a-Service. Both, hybrid and pure vendors should be aware of the trade-off implied by technical harmonization. While it helps to overcome challenges of internal integration and take advantage of opportunities, technical harmonization may also hinder responding to customer-specific wishes. Generally, Software-as-a-Service vendors should be aware of the necessity to establish a service mindset.

Highlight the role of releases in developing and delivering Software-as-a- Service: The combined findings of both empirical phases show that the approach to handle releases plays a crucial role in offering Software-as-a-Service. While the motivation to reduce the number of coexisting releases is based on cost saving objectives, implementing release-free approaches implies changes within the interdependence of activities that ask for the adjustment of the necessary coordination mechanism to manage the communication and coordination between those activities. For the crucial value generating activities of development and operation, coordination gets more complex and requires coordination by mutual adjustment. The findings show that organizational integration represents an appropriate coordination mechanisms for this specific situation, but also indicate that release related topics again have an influence. Technical harmonization as a contingency factor of integration eases most of the identified challenges and opportunities, but also adds new constraints by limiting the flexibility to react to individual customer needs. Therefore, the efforts to reduce the number of co-existing releases requires changes that again are being reinforced by accomplishments of achieving this goal and the establishment of an increased technical harmonization. Especially established vendors are likely to be challenged by this within their transformation process of introducing Software-as-a-Service offerings. Newly founded vendors are able to put more emphasis on ensuring technical harmonization right from the beginning, but they still need to tackle the consequences of the associated limitations. Clearly communicating the limited control over the subscribed solution to the customer may increase the awareness about this aspect and make it part of the customer's decision process of sourcing a Software-as-a-Service solution. This may not decrease the vendor's risk of disturbing the customer's processes, but at least renders it a tradeoff between innovation and disruption, which the customer has agreed on when subscribing to a Software-as-a-Service solution.

6.3. Limitations and Outlook

During the two-staged research approach and the discussion of its findings, manifold opportunities for future research endeavors emerged. At the same time, the research design and the study's context have introduced certain limitations that have to be taken into consideration when interpreting the study's findings. This section outlines and discusses such limitations and will indicate research opportunities that may address these constraints in the future.

The extant literature on the implications of Software-as-a-Service was presented in Section 2.3 and in combination with case study findings in Chapter 4. While this approach was considered to allow a better comparison of the empirical observations with focused parts of the literature, the empirical findings may have created a bias on the scope of identified literature. Therefore, the review cannot claim to be complete in covering all relevant extant work. In addition, the continuous inclusion of new articles was considered to be more appropriate within the relatively new research context of Software-as-a-Service than a structured literature review approach. Though this unstructured approach limits the reproducibility of the identification process, it enables to take advantage of the latest contributions and also those published outside of mainstream journals and conferences.

The designs of both multiple-case studies have limitations. The case selection only offers a snap-shot view and is limited to software vendors of complex business applications. This view may be broadened in the future. For instance, the findings indicate that there are differences between Software-as-a-Service vendors with their own platform ecosystems and those that act as complementors on these platforms, the sample however only offered a high level perspective on this relationship. A broader sample may also yield additional results with regard to the transformation process of traditional on-premises vendors towards Software-as-a-Service. Within the first multiple-case study, the data showed the full implications in terms of the different business model elements. This satisfied the objective to identify implications and areas to focus further steps on. Additional interviews and cases with a specific focus on single building blocks may add to a more in-depth understanding of the implications.

This research links organizational integration with constitutive criteria of services and provides indication on how simultaneity and the external factor influence integration. As outlined within the introduction of services in Section 2.1.1, the universal validity of such criteria for service can, however, be questioned. In particular, the criteria imply a focus on the differentiation of services from products and thereby the use of such criteria may limit the perspective on other influential aspects of services (Vargo & Lusch, 2004). Since the novelty of Software-as-a-Service within the market and the associated changes within business models of software vendors, likewise, implied an underlying transformation and comparison perspective, this limitation was deemed rather unproblematic. Future research may, for example, take a Unified Service Theory perspective to investigate whether such a perspective provides additional insights. As this service definition approach highlights the customer input, it may be particular suitable for the analysis of the external integration perspective. Furthermore, Cloninger & Oviatt (2006) argue for variation within the service content of products and services. While it was considered rather unlikely that Software-as-a-Service solution vary in their degree of service characteristics like simultaneity, variance may very likely be observed between the different discussed delivery and pricing models of software discussed in Section 2.1.3. Comparing different extent of service content of business models like on-premises and Software-as-a-Service may add to the results of this study and may be especially relevant in studying a transition from one model to the other.

The external integration perspective considered the customer as the only external unit, neglecting other relationships to external suppliers or partners. The business model perspective on the Software-as-a-Service implications indicates within the *Key Partnership* building block that existing partnership are challenged. While partner organizations were included within the first multiple-case study, the second study neglected the partner perspective to focus on the internal capabilities of software vendors. In settings of multiple vendors working together to deliver a value proposition, the inclusion of partners within the external integration perspective may enrich the findings. Especially, small Software-as-a-Service vendors are not always able to provide the necessary infrastructure to operate their solutions and instead rely on the offerings of Platform-as-a-Service or Infrastructure-as-a-Service providers, rendering them dependent on these vendors. These vendors may also use the platform of other larger software vendors to market their solutions. Therefore, including partners as external units in future research appears promising.

Moreover, a broader perspective on partner networks and the implications of Software-as-a-Service on business models of complementors, like integrators, may extent the view of this study. The study focused on a software vendor in the narrower sense perspective, but the *Key Partnership* discussion indicates different implications for the business models of partners. In extreme situations, the business model of partners becomes obsolete. Further knowledge on the impact of Software-as-a-Service on partner networks or software ecosystems is necessary. Extant research on partner networks identified the respective position of a vendor and its partners on the architectural software stack as an important variable in the coordination of their relationship (Kude et al., 2012). As Software-as-a-Service provider take over the responsibility for the entire software stack, the applied coordination approaches are challenged and require a re-evaluation. Future search on partner networks in the Software-as-a-Service context may yield new insights on how the relationship between vendors and complementors are influenced by the new delivery model and which coordination mechanisms are appropriate for their governance.

Furthermore, the identified contingency factors of organizational integration offer promising opportunities for future research. For instance, future studies may address the question of how service mindsets can be established and of how technical harmonization can be achieved.

Among the implications of the Software-as-a-Service concept, the analysis identified an increased reliance on standardized processes that make use of self-service systems. These are for example used to sell solutions, initiate trial periods, or adjust the scope and scale of solutions in terms of required resources or subscribed users. Self-service systems are common with traditional IT-supported services, but little research could be identified within the literature of their adoption in the Software-as-a-Service context. Since this study highlighted the changed relationship to customers, self-service can be considered a central part in this relationship. Future research may analyze the role self-service systems play and can suggest design guidelines for their appropriate use.

The *continuity* theme highlights the importance of a continuous flow within the innovation process. Software-as-a-Service vendors need to take the appropriate measures to assure such continuous flow. In software development, agile methodologies have led to similar goals. Long release-cycles are abandoned in favor of small sprints that provide a more continued flow of innovation. However, fundamental questions like how flow can be measured and what the right speed of development in different contexts is, remain unanswered. Developing within the Software-as-a-Service context puts additional emphasis on these questions and asks for more research.

The combination of the two identified themes of challenges of organizational integration *awareness* and *increment* indicate that it is not only important to establish appropriate means of information sharing to secure an awareness of everybody's activity, but it is also crucial to assure that information is kept up-to-date continuously. The increased innovation speed leads to the risk of outdated information being shared and, therefore, asks for efficient means of information sharing. While there has been research on how software tools, like micro-blogging, may support the awareness within distributed software development (Klimpke, 2011), future research may analyze their effectiveness in the Software-as-a-Service setting. Research on effective software tools may also support software vendors in increasing the innovation speed. The business model and value chain analysis indicates an increased emphasis on usability and well-designed user-interfaces to reduce education efforts and related support costs. Software tools, which for instance allow easing the process of testing and prototyping different graphical user-interfaces, may assist in such a setting.

As outlined, for instance within the *feedback* theme, the direct relationship to the customer in combination with the control of the service infrastructure and the software artifact opens up the unique opportunity for software vendors to improve the software according to the customer demands and wishes. It enables an improved information quality during the entire innovation process and may open up new insights with regard to the information behavior of the software users. The *timing* theme, however, also indicated potential problems that may emerge. Further research is required to investigate the given opportunity and related problems. The setting allows test-driving software features and conducting experiments with the reaction of a sub-group of the customer base.

An ultimate integration scenario could be small scale experiments that rely on seamless interaction between developers and operators. In this approach, new features could be pushed to a small set of customers to observe their reaction and to identify potential problems that have not been considered yet. The collected feedback could be forwarded to the developers who iteratively adapt the software according to the derived findings. By this means, vendors can study the information behavior of their customers and may ease software usage on this basis. Applying recent research on information behavior (e.g. Hemmer et al., 2012) in the described Software-as-a-Service context can assist vendors in the process. Additionally, research on methods and tools that support this process is required. For example, research with regard to analytical requirements engineering to take advantage of the observable usage pattern of software. Finally, the changed life-span of Software-as-a-Service solutions requires investigating appropriate methods and tools to support the long-term preservation of collected information about customers and conducted experiments, and to make them traceable through-out the entire innovation process.

7. Conclusion

This study has been motivated by the increasing adoption rate of Software-as-a-Service as a delivery and pricing model of software vendors, as well as software customers, and the lack of research investigating the implications of Software-as-a-Service on software vendors. The goal of this study has been to explore the organizational implications of Software-as-a-Service for software vendors and in a second step to understand the role of organizational integration in developing and operating Software-as-a-Service solutions. In order to reach this goal, this study has taken a qualitative approach that comprised out of two multiple-case studies of Software-as-a-Service vendors.

After the introduction and motivation of the study in the first chapter, the second chapter has presented the study's foundations. In particular, the characteristics of software, services and the software industry in general have been presented and the Software-as-a-Service concept has been defined. Then, previous research with regard to the implications of the Software-as-a-Service concept for software vendors has been discussed.

Within Chapter 3, the study's research methodology has been introduced and discussed. The research approach has been based on two explorative case studies. While the first has taken a rather broad approach and explored the implications of Software-as-a-Service from a business model and a value chain perspective, the second case study has been more focused on explaining the role of organizational integration within the Software-as-a-Service context. Chapter 4 and 5 have presented the results of the two rounds of qualitative case studies.

Chapter 6 has given an in-depth discussion of the results of the study. Following the discussion of both empirical studies in a joined manner, the theoretical contribution to the literature, as well as managerial implications for the practice, have been outlined and discussed. Finally, limitations and opportunities for future research have been discussed.

This research study has aimed at answering two underlying research questions. First, the study has posed the research question of how software vendors are influenced by the Software-as-a-Service delivery and pricing model. With the help of two frameworks from extant business model and value chain literature, the study has demonstrated that Software-as-a-Service has an impact on the entire business model of software vendors and multiple activities of the software value chain. The analysis has shown that internal processes and capabilities as well as the relationship to customers are affected in particular. The list of implications for internal activities and resources has been dominated by the requirement to incorporate the previously external activities of operating the software solutions into the existing processes and structures. The observations have pointed at the need of Software-as-a-Service vendors to align and extend processes, and to build up additional knowledge and resources to cope with the operation responsibility of solutions. Furthermore, identified implications have been consequences of the direct and more continuous relationship to customers. The findings have exposed communication channels, like the Internet and self-service systems, to take a leading role in the interaction with customers. In addition, the observations have exposed that offering Software-as-a-Service leads to vendors interacting with software end-users on a continuous basis, rather than just with customer's IT or procurement departments.

The second research question has been addressing the question of how organizational structures and processes need to be adapted in order to develop and operate Software-as-a-Service solutions. Drawing on the literature of coordination and organizational integration, the study has unveiled changing interdependence between software development and operation that are related to reassessing release-based development approaches and let expect increased communication and coordination needs. Based on a consistent framework that has been derived from extant literature and that incorporates constituent characteristics of services, the empirical findings have unveiled internal and external challenges and opportunities of organizational integration. The observations have been reflected by the five themes: *awareness*, *continuity*, *increment*, *timing* and *feedback*. The themes have provided a detailed understanding about the link between development and operation, as well as about the customer relationship in the Software-as-a-Service context. The results have also shown that the salience of these themes is contingent upon *company size*, the *service mindset* among employees, and the degree of *technical harmonization*. These enablers and inhibitors of organizational integration have enriched the understanding of the influence of contextual factors on integration efforts and have substantiated the knowledge about the role software releases play in developing and operating Software-as-a-Service.

Bibliography

Adler, P. S. (1995). Interdepartmental Interdependence and Coordination: The Case of the Design/Manufacturing Interface. *Organization Science*, 6(2), 147–167.

Agarwal, P. (2011). Continuous SCRUM: Agile Management of SaaS Products. In *4th India Software Engineering Conference* (pp. 51–60). Kerala, India: ACM.

Al-Debei, M. M. & Avison, D. (2010). Developing a Unified Framework of the Business Model Concept. *European Journal of Information Systems*, 19(3), 359–376.

Alam, I. (2002). An Exploratory Investigation of User Involvement in New Service Development. *Journal of the Academy of Marketing Science*, 30(3), 250–261.

Anandasivam, A. & Premm, M. (2009). Bid price control and dynamic pricing in clouds. In *European Conference on Information Systems* Verona, Italy.

Anding, M. (2010). SaaS: A Love-Hate Relationship for Enterprise Software Vendors. In A. Benlian, T. Hess, & P. Buxmann (Eds.), *Software-as-a-Service* (pp. 43–56). Wiesbaden: Gabler.

Atteslander, P. & Cromm, J. (2008). *Methoden der Empirischen Sozialforschung*, volume 12. Berlin: Schmidt.

Atuahene-Gima, K. & Evangelista, F. (2000). Cross-Functional Influence in New Product Development: An Exploratory Study of Marketing and R&D Perspectives. *Management Science*, 46(10), 1269–1284.

Aulbach, S., Grust, T., Jacobs, D., Kemper, A., & Rittinger, J. (2008). Multi-tenant databases for software as a service: schema-mapping techniques. In *Proceedings of the 2008 ACM SIGMOD international conference on Management of data* (pp. 1195–1206). Vancouver, Canada: ACM.

Baldwin, C. & Clark, B. (1997). Managing in an age of modularity. *Harvard Business Review*, 75(5), 84–93.

Bandulet, F., Faisst, W., Eggs, H., Otyepka, S., & Wenzel, S. (2010). Software-as-a-Service as Disruptive Innovation in the Enterprise Application Market. In A. Benlian, T. Hess, & P. Buxmann (Eds.), *Software-as-a-Service* (pp. 15–29). Wiesbaden: Gabler.

Banerjee, S., Srikanth, H., & Cukic, B. (2010). Log-Based Reliability Analysis of Software as a Service (SaaS). In *Software Reliability Engineering (ISSRE), 2010 IEEE 21st International Symposium on* (pp. 239–248).

Bansler, J. & Havn, E. (2002). Exploring the role of network effects in IT implementation: The case of knowledge management systems. In *European Conference on Information Systems* (pp. 817–829). Gdansk, Poland.

Barki, H. & Pinsonneault, A. (2005). A model of organizational integration, implementation effort, and performance. *Organization Science*, 16(2), 165–179.

Barki, H., Rivard, S., & Talbot, J. (2001). An integrative contingency model of software project risk management. *Journal of Management Information Systems*, 17(4), 37–69.

Barnes, S. J. (2002). The mobile commerce value chain: analysis and future developments. *International Journal of Information Management*, 22(2), 91–108.

Bauer, M. (2012). Lessons Learned in the Development of a CRM SaaS Solution. In A. Maedche, A. Botzenhardt, & L. Neer (Eds.), *Software for People*, Management for Professionals (pp. 257–274). Springer Berlin Heidelberg.

Benbasat, I., Goldstein, D., & Mead, M. (1987). The Case Research Strategy in Studies of Information Systems. *Management Information Systems Quarterly*, 11(3), 369–386.

Benefield, R. (2009). Agile Deployment: Lean Service Management and Deployment Strategies for the SaaS Enterprise. In R. H. Sprague (Ed.), *42nd Hawaii International Conference on System Sciences* Waikoloa, Hawaii: IEEE.

Benlian, A. & Hess, T. (2009). Welche Treiber lassen SaaS auch in Grossunternehmen zum Erfolg werden? Eine Empirische Analyse der SaaS-Adoption auf Basis der Transaktionskostentheorie. In R. H. Hansen, D. Karagiannis, & H. G. Fill (Eds.), *Wirtschaftsinformatik* (pp. 567–576). Vienna, Austria.

Benlian, A. & Hess, T. (2010). The Risks of Sourcing Software as a Service - An Empirical Analysis of Adoptors and Non-adopters. In T. Alexander, M. Turpin, & J. van Deventer (Eds.), *18th Eurpean Conference on Information Systems* Pretoria, South Africa.

Bennett, K., Layzell, P., Budgen, D., Brereton, P., Macaulay, L., & Munro, M. (2000). Service-based software: The future for flexible software. In F. Titsworth (Ed.), *Seventh Asia-Pacific Software Engineering Conference* (pp. 214–221). Singapore.

Berkovich, M., Esch, S., Leimeister, J. M., & Krcmar, H. (2010). Towards Requirements Engineering for Software as a Service. In *Multikonferenz Wirtschaftsinformatik* Wien, Austria.

Bobrowski, S. (2011). Optimal Multitenant Designs for Cloud Apps. In *Cloud Computing (CLOUD), 2011 IEEE International Conference on* (pp. 654–659).

Bodendorf, F. (1999). *Wirtschaftsinformatik im Dienstleistungsbereich.* Berlin: Springer.

Boell, S. & Cecez-Kecmanovic, D. (2010). Literature reviews and the hermeneutic circle. *Australian Academic and Research Libraries*, 42(2), 129–144.

Boell, S. & Cecez-Kecmanovic, D. (2011). Are Systematic Reviews Better, Less Biased and of Higher Quality? In *European Conference on Information Systems* Helsinki, Finnland.

Bontis, N. & Chung, H. (2000). The evolution of software pricing: from box licenses to application service provider models. *Internet Research*, 10(3), 246–255.

Botzenhardt, A., Meth, H., & Maedche, A. (2011). Cross-Functional Integration of Product Management and Product Design in Application Software Development: Exploration of Success Factors. In *International Conference on Information Systems* Shanghai, China.

Bouwman, H., De Vos, H., & Haaker, T. (2008). *Mobile service innovation and business models*. Heidelberg, Germany: Springer.

Brehm, L., Heinzl, A., & Markus, L. (2001). Tailoring ERP Systems: A Spectrum of Choices and their Implications. In *34. Hawaii International Conference of System Science* Maui, Hawaii, USA.

Brentani, U. (1989). Success and failure in new industrial services. *Journal of Product Innovation Management*, 6(4), 239–258.

Brereton, P., Budgen, D., Bennett, K., Munro, M., Layzell, P., Macaulay, L., Griffiths, D., & Stannett, C. (1999). The future of software. *Communications of the ACM*, 42(12), 78–84.

Brown, A. & Dowling, P. (1998). *Doing Research/Reading Research: A Mode of Interrogation for Education*. Routledge.

Böttcher, M. & Meyer, K. (2004). IT-basierte Dienstleistungen. In K. Fähnrich & C. van Hussen (Eds.), *Entwicklung IT-basierter Dienstleistungen in der Praxis - Kurzstudie zum Co-Desing von Software und Services in deutschen Unternehmen* (pp. 10–20). Stuttgart: Fraunhofer IRB-Verlag.

Büttgen, M. (2002). Kundengerechte Gestaltung von Dienstleistungsprozessen. In M. Bruhn & B. Strauss (Eds.), *Dienstleistungsmangement: Interaktion im Dienstleistungsbereich* (pp. 143–166). Wiesbaden: Gabler.

Buck-Emden, R. & Galimow, J. (1996). *SAP R3 System: A client/server technology*. Boston, MA.: Addison-Wesley Longman.

Bullinger, H. & Schreiner, P. (2006). Service Engineering: Ein Rahmenkonzept für die systematische Entwicklung von Dienstleistungen. In H. Bullinger & A. Scheer (Eds.), *Service Engineering*, volume 2 (pp. 53–84). Berlin, Heidelberg, New York: Springer.

Buxmann, P., Diefenbach, H., & Hess, T. (2008). *Die Softwareindustrie: Ökonomische Prinzipien, Strategien, Perspektiven.* Heidelberg: Springer.

Buxmann, P., Diefenbach, H., & Hess, T. (2013). *The Software Industry - Economic Principles, Strategies, Perspectives.* Berlin: Springer.

Carraro, G. (2006). SaaS Simple Maturity Model. http://blogs.msdn.com/b/ gianpaolo/archive/2006/03/06/544354.aspx.

Cavalcante, S., Kesting, P., & Ulhoi, J. (2011). Business model dynamics and innovation: (re)establishing the missing linkages. *Management Decision*, 49(8), 1327–1342.

Chaisiri, S., Bu-Sung, L., & Niyato, D. (2012). Optimization of Resource Provisioning Cost in Cloud Computing. *Services Computing, IEEE Transactions on*, 5(2), 164–177.

Chalmers, A. (1999). *What is this thing called Science?*, volume 3rd. Berkshire, UK: Open University Press.

Chard, K. & Bubendorfer, K. (2013). High Performance Resource Allocation Strategies for Computational Economies. *Parallel and Distributed Systems, IEEE Transactions on*, 24(1), 72–84.

Chellappa, R. K. & Saraf, N. (2010). Alliances, Rivalry, and Firm Performance in Enterprise Systems Software Markets: A Social Network Approach. *Information Systems Research*, 21(4), 849–871.

Chen, W. & Hirschheim, R. (2004). A paradigmatic and methodological examination of information systems research from 1991 to 2001. *Information Systems Journal*, 14(3), 197–235.

Chesbrough, H. (2006). *Open business models: How to thrive in the new innovation landscape.* Boston, MA: Harvard Business School Press.

Chesbrough, H. (2010). Business Model Innovation: Opportunities and Barriers. *Long Range Planning*, 43(2-3), 354–363.

Chesbrough, H. & Rosenbloom, R. (2002). The role of the business model in capturing value from innovation: Evidence from Xerox Corporation's technology spin-off companies. *Industrial and Corporate Change*, 11(3), 529–555.

Choudhary, V. (2007a). Comparison of Software Quality Under Perpetual Licensing and Software-as-a-Service. *Journal of Management Information Systems*, 24(2), 141–165.

Choudhary, V. (2007b). Software as a Service: Implications for Investment in Software Development. In R. H. Sprague (Ed.), *40th Hawaii International Conference on System Sciences* Waikoloa, Hawaii: IEEE.

Christensen, C. (1997). *The Innovator's Dilemma.* Boston, USA: Harper Paperbacks.

Clark, T., Rajaratnam, D., & Smith, T. (1996). Toward a Theory of International Services: Marketing Intangibles in a World of Nations. *Journal of International Marketing*, 4(2), 9–28.

Cloninger, P. A. (2004). The Influence of Service Content on the International Market Entry Mode: Theory and Empirical Test. *Journal of International Business and Exonomics*, 2(1), 72–88.

Cloninger, P. A. & Oviatt, B. (2006). Measuring service content: A scale development. *Thunderbird International Business Review*, 48(5), 643–643.

Conte, T., Blau, B., & Xu, Y. (2010). Competition of Service Marketplaces: Designing Growth in Service Networks. In *European Conference on Information Systems* Pretoria, South Africa.

Cordon-Pozo, E., Garcia-Morales, J., & Aragon-Correa, J. (2006). Inter-departmental collaboration and new product development success: a study on the collaboration between marketing and R&D in Spanish high-technology firms. *International Journal of Technology Management*, 35(1), 52–73.

Correia, J., Eschinger, C., Dharmasthira, Y., & Roster, J. (2012). Survey Analysis: Buyers Tell Us About SaaS and Cloud Adoption Through 2014.

Corsten, H. (2001). *Dienstleistungsmanagement*, volume 4. München, Wien: Oldenbourg.

Crowston, K. (1997). A Coordination Theory Approach to Organizational Process Design. *Organization Science*, 8(2), 157–175.

Crowston, K., Rubleske, J., & Howison, J. (2006). Coordination theory and its application in HCI. In P. Zhang & D. Galletta (Eds.), *Human-Computer Interaction in Management Information Systems*. M. E. Sharpe.

Curtis, B. (1989). Modeling coordination from field experiments. In *Organizational Computing, Coordination and Collaboration: Theories and Technologies for Computer-Supported Work*. Austin, TX.

Cusumano, M. A. (2008). The Changing Software Business: Moving from Products to Services. *Computer*, 41(1), 20–27.

Dibbern, J., Goles, T., Hirschheim, R., & Jayatilaka, B. (2004). Information systems outsourcing: a survey and analysis of the literature. *SIGMIS Database*, 35(4), 6–102.

Dibbern, J., Winkler, J., & Heinzl, A. (2008). Explaining Variations in Client Extra Costs between Software Projects Offshored to India. *MIS Quarterly*, 32(2), 333–366.

Dimitrakos, T., Randal, M., Yuan, F., Geata, M., Laria, G., Ritrovato, P., Serham, B., Wesner, S., & Wulf, K. (2003). An emerging architecture enabling grid based application service provision. In *Seventh IEEE International Enterprise Distributed Object Computing Conference* (pp. 240–251).

Dobson, P., Myles, J., & Jackson, P. (2007). Making the Case for Critical Realism: Examining the Implementation of Automated Performance Management Systems. *Information Resources Management Journal*, 20(2), 138–152.

Donaldson, L. (2001). *The Contingency Theory of Organizations*. Foundations For Organizational Science. Thousand Oaks, CA: Sage Publications.

Dubé, L. & Paré, G. (2003). Rigor in Information Systems Positivist Case Research: Current Practices, Trends, and Recommendations. *MIS Quarterly*, 27(4), 597–636.

Eisenhardt, K. M. (1989). Building theories form case study research. *Academy of Management Review*, 14(4), 532–550.

Engelhardt, S. (2008). The Economic Properties of Software. In *Jena economic research papers*, number 2008-045. Max-Planck-Institute of Economics.

Enquist, H. & Juell-Skielse, G. (2010). Value Propositions in Service Oriented Business Models for ERP: Case Studies. In W. Abramowicz & R. Tolksdorf (Eds.), *Business Information Systems*, Lexture Notes in Business Information Processing Berlin, Germany: Springer.

Erramilli, M. K. & Rao, C. P. (1993). Service Firms' International Entry-Mode Choice: A Modified Transaction-Cost Analysis Approach. *Journal of Marketing*, 57(3), 19–38.

Espadas, J., Concha, D., & Arturo, M. (2008). Application Development over Software-as-a-Service Platforms. In H. Mannaert, T. Ohta, C. Dini, & R. Pellerin (Eds.), *The Third International Conference on Software Engineering Advances* (pp. 97–104). Sliema, Malta.

Ettlie, J. E. & Reza, E. M. (1992). Organizational Integration and Process Innovation. *Academy of Management Journal*, 35(4), 795–827.

Eurich, M., Giessmann, A., Mettler, T., & Stanoevska-Slabeva, K. (2011). Revenue Streams of Cloud-based Platforms: Current State and Future Directions. In *Americas Conference on Information Systems* Detroit, USA.

Evans, D., Hangiu, A., & Schmalensee, R. (2006). *Invisible engines: How software platforms drive innovation and transform industries*. Cambridge, MA: The MIT Press.

Fan, M., Kumar, S., & Whinston, A. B. (2009). Short-term and long-term competition between providers of shrink-wrap software and software as a service. *European Journal of Operational Research*, 196(2), 661 – 671.

Faraj, S. & Xiao, Y. (2006). Coordination in fast-response organizations. *Management Science*, 52(115-1189).

Fehling, C., Leymann, F., & Mietzner, R. (2010). A Framework for Optimized Distribution of Tenants in Cloud Applications. In *Cloud Computing (CLOUD), 2010 IEEE 3rd International Conference on* (pp. 252–259).

Ferrante, D. (2006). Software Licensing Models: What's Out There? *IT Professional*, 8(6), 24–29.

Fielt, E. (2011). Understanding business models. In *Working Paper Series*. Eveleigh, NSW: Smart Services CRC.

Fitzsimmons, J. & Fitzsimmons, M. (2011). *Service Management: Operations, Strategy, Information Technology*, volume 7th edition. New York: McGraw Hill.

Froehle, C. M., Roth, A. V., Chase, R. B., & Voss, C. A. (2000). Antecedents of New Service Development Effectiveness. *Journal of Service Research*, 3(1), 3–17.

García, N., Sanzo, M. J., & Trespalacios, J. A. (2008). New product internal performance and market performance: Evidence from Spanish firms regarding the role of trust, interfunctional integration, and innovation type. *Technovation*, 28(11), 713–725.

Gartner (2009). *Fact Checking: The Five Most-Common SaaS Assumptions*. Gartner.

Gattiker, T. F. & Goodhue, D. L. (2005). What Happens after ERP Implementation: Understanding the Impact of Interdependence and Differentiation on Plant-Level Outcomes. *MIS Quarterly*, 29(3), 559–585.

Ge, C. & Huang, K. (2011a). Productivity Differences and Catch-Up Effects among Software as a Service Firms: A Stochastic Frontier Approach. In *International Conference on Information Systems* Shanghai, China.

Ge, C. & Huang, K. (2011b). R&D And Catch-Up Effect Among Software-As-A-Service Firms: A Stochastic Frontier Approach. In *Pacific Asia Conference on Information Systems* Brisbane, Australia.

Ghaziani, A. & Ventresca, M. (2005). Keywords and cultural change: Frame analysis of Business Model public talk, 1975–2000. *Sociological Forum*, 20(4), 523–559.

Goodhue, D. L., Wybo, M. D., & Kirsch, L. J. (1992). The Impact of Data Integration on the Costs and Benefits of Information Systems. *MIS Quarterly*, 16(3), 293–311.

Gordijn, J. (2002). *Value based requirements engineering: Exploring innovative e-commerce ideas*. PhD thesis.

Gordijn, J., Osterwalder, A., & Pigneur, Y. (2005). Comparing two business model ontologies for designing e-business models and value constellations. In D. R. Vogel, P. Walden, J. Gricar, & G. Lenart (Eds.), *Proceedings of the 18th Bled Electronic Commerce Conference*. Bled, Slovenija: University of Maribor.

Gregor, S. (2006). The Nature of Theory in Information Systems. *MIS Quarterly*, 30(3), 611–642.

Grohmann, W. (2009). *Von der Software zum Service: ASP-Software on Demand - Software-as-a-Service - Neue Formen der Software-Nutzung*. H.K.P. Conculting.

Grohmann, W. (2011). SaaS-Forum Lösungskatalog. http://www.saas-forum.net/anwendungen.html.

Grove, A. (1996). *Only the Paranoid Survive*. New York, Toronto: Currency Doubleday.

Guo, W. & Wang, Y. (2009). An Incident Management Model for SaaS Application in the IT Organization. In *International Conference on Research Challenges in Computer Science*: IEEE.

Gupta, A. & Herath, S. (2005). Latest trends and issues in the ASP service market. *International Management & Data Systems*, 105(1), 19–25.

Gupta, A. K., Raj, S. P., & Wilemon, D. (1986). A Model for Studying Resarch-and-Development - Marketing Interface in the Product Innovation Process. *Journal of Marketing*, 50(2), 7–17.

Guptill, B. (2012). RESEARCH ALERT: Saugatuck 2012 SaaS Survey Indicates More User Focus on Business Improvement, With Big Changes Coming Soon.

Hacking, I. (1996). *Einführung in die Philosophie der Naturwissenschaften*. Stuttgart: Reclam.

Haines, M. N. (2007). The Impact of Service-Oriented Application Development on Software Development Methodology. In *40th Annual Hawaii International Conference on System Sciences*.

Hansen, H. & Neumann, G. (2007). *Wirtschaftsinformatik*, volume 7. Stuttgart: Lucius & Lucius.

Hao, Y., Juell-Skielse, G., & Uppström, E. (2012). Cloud ERP development process model from the perspective of user organizations. In C. Moller & S. Chaudhry (Eds.), *Advances in Enterprise Information Systems II*, Business & Economics (pp. 407). London, UK: Taylor & Francis Group.

Hartman, D. & Lindgren, J. (1993). Consumer evaluations of goods and services: implications for services marketing. *Journal of Services Marketing*, 7(2), 4–15.

Heart, T., Tsur, N. S., & Pliskin, N. (2010). Software-as-a-Service Vendors: Are They Ready to Successfully Deliver? In I. Oshri & J. Kotlarsky (Eds.), *Global Sourcing of Information Technology and Business Processes*, volume 55 of *Lecture Notes in Business Information Processing* (pp. 151–184). Berlin, Heidelberg: Springer.

Hedman, J. & Kalling, T. (2003). The business model concept: Theoretical underpinnings and empirical illustrations. *European Journal of Information Systems*, 12(1), 49–59.

Heinrich, L., Heinzl, A., & Riedl, R. (2011). *Wirtschaftinformatik – Einführung und Grundlegung*, volume 4. Berlin, Heidelberg: Springer.

Heinrich, L., Heinzl, A., & Roithmayr, F. (2004). *Wirtschaftsinformatik-Lexikon*, volume 7. Auflage. München, Wien: Oldenbourg.

Hemmer, E., Heinzl, A., & Leidner, D. (2012). The 'I' in 'IS': Understanding Human Computer-Based Information Behavior. In *European Conference on Information Systems* Barcelona, Spain.

Herder, E. (2009). *Forward, Back and Home Again - Analyzing User Behavior on the Web*. Saarbrücken: Vdm Verlag Dr. Müller.

Herriott, R. & Firestone, W. (1983). Multisite qualitative policy research: Optimizing description and generalizability. *Educational Researcher*, 12, 14–19.

Hilbert, D. & Redmiles, D. (1998). An approach to large-scale collection of application usage data over the Internet. In *International Conference on Software Engineering* (pp. 136–145). Kyoto, Japan: IEEE Computer Society.

Hilkert, D., Wolf, C. M., Benlian, A., & Hess, T. (2010). The "as-a-Service"-Paradigm and its Implications for the Software Industry – Insights from a Comparative Case Study in CRM Software Ecosystems. In *First International Conference on Software Business (ICSOB 2010)* Jyväskylä, Finland.

Hirsch, S. (1993). The globalization of services and service-intensive goods industries. In Y. Aharoni (Ed.), *Coalitions and competions: THe globalization of professional services* (pp. 66.78). London: Routledge.

Hirschheim, R. (1992). Information Systems Epistemology: An Historical Perspective. In R. Galliers (Ed.), *Information Systems Research: Issues, Methods and Practical Guidelines* (pp. 28–60). Oxford: Blackwell Scientific Publications.

Huang, J. (2006). IT Organizational Integration : Innovation for E-Business. In *Service Operations and Logistics, and Informatics, 2006. SOLI '06. IEEE International Conference on* (pp. 902–907).

Huang, K. & Wang, M. (2009). Firm-Level Productivity Analysis for Software as a Service Companies. In *International Conference on Information Systems* Phoenix, USA.

Ivari, J., Hirschheim, R., & Klein, H. (2001). Towards More Professional Information Systems Development: ISD as Knowledge Work. In *European Conference on Information Systems* Bled, Slovenia.

Jaw, C., Lo, J.-Y., & Lin, Y.-H. (2010). The determinants of new service development: Service characteristics, market orientation, and actualizing innovation effort. *Technovation*, 30(4), 265–277.

Joha, A. & Janssen, M. (2012). Design Choices Underlying the Software-as-a-Service Business Model from the User Perspektive: Exploring the Fourth Wave of Outsourcing. *Journal of Universal Computer Science*, 18(11), 1501–1522.

Johnson, M. (2010). *Seizing the white space: Business model innovation for growth and renewal.* Boston, MA: Harvard Business Press.

Johnson, M., Christensen, C., & Kagermann, H. (2008). Reinventing your business model. *Harvard Business Review*, 86(12), 50–59.

Juell-Skielse, G. & Enquist, H. (2012). Implications of ERP-as-Service. In C. Møller & S. Chaudhry (Eds.), *Re-conceptualizing Enterprise Information Systems*, volume 105 of *Lecture Notes in Business Information Processing* (pp. 129–151). Berlin, Heidelberg: Springer.

Kahn, K. B. (1996). Interdepartmental integration: A definition with implications for product development performance. *Journal of Product Innovation Management*, 13(2), 137–151.

Kakihara, M. (2006). Developing Software-as-a-Service in the Rapidly Changing Environment. *International Review of Business*, (8), 1–17.

Kapuruge, M., Colman, A., & Jun, H. (2011). Defining Customizable Business Processes without Compromising the Maintainability in Multi-tenant SaaS Applications. In *Cloud Computing (CLOUD), 2011 IEEE International Conference on* (pp. 748–749).

Keil, M. & Carmel, E. (1995). Customer-developer links in software development. *Commun. ACM*, 38(5), 33–44.

Kenett, R., Harel, A., & Ruggeri, F. (2008). Controlling the Usability of Web Services. *International Journal of Software Engineering and Knowledge Engineering.*

Kerlinger, F. N. & Lee, H. B. (2000). *Foundations of Behavioral Research.* Fort Worth, TX: Harcourt College Publishers.

Khazaei, H., Misic, J., & Misic, V. B. (2012). Performance Analysis of Cloud Computing Centers Using M/G/m/m+r Queuing Systems. *Parallel and Distributed Systems, IEEE Transactions on*, 23(5), 936–943.

Kieser, A. (2006). *Organisationstheorien*, volume 6. Stuttgart: Kohlhammer.

Kieser, A. & Walgenbach, P. (2003). *Organisation*, volume 4. Stuttgart: Schaffer-Poeschel Verlag.

Kitchenham, B. (2004). *Procedures for performing systematic reviews.* Technical report, Keele University and NICTA.

Klimpke, L. (2011). Microblogging in Global Software Development. In C. Boldyreff, S. Islam, M. Leonard, & B. Thalheim (Eds.), *CAiSE* London, UK.

Koufteros, X. A., Rawski, G. E., & Rupak, R. (2010). Organizational Integration for Product Development: The Effects on Glitches, On-Time Execution of Engineering Change Orders, and Market Success. *Decision Sciences*, 41(1), 49–80.

Kraut, R. & Streeter, L. (1995). Coordination in software development. *Communication of the ACM*, 38(3), 69–81.

Kude, T., Dibbern, J., & Heinzl, A. (2012). Why Do Complementors Participate? An Analysis of Partnership Networks in the Enterprise Software Industry. *IEEE Transactions on Engineering Management*, 59(2), 250–265.

Kujala, S. (2003). User involvement: a review of the benefits and challenges. *Behaviour & Information Technology*, 22(1), 1–16.

La, H. & Kim, S. (2009). A Systematic Process for Developing High Quality SaaS Cloud Services. In M. Jaatun, G. Zhao, & C. Rong (Eds.), *Cloud Computing*, Lecture Notes in Computer Science (pp. 278–289). Berlin, Heidelberg: Springer.

Lassila, A. (2006). Offering software as a service: case study of system integrators. In *European Conference on Information Systems* Göteborg, Sweden.

Lawrence, P. & Lorsch, J. (1969). *Organization and Environment.* Boston, MA: Harvard Business School Press.

Lazic, M. (2011). IT Governance and Business Performance - A Resource Based Analysis. In *Pacific Asia Conference on Information Systems* Brisbane, Australia.

Lazonick, W. & West, J. (1995). Organizational Integration and Competitive Advantage: Explaining Strategy and Performance in American Industry. *Industrial and Corporate Change*, 4(1), 229–270.

Lee, A. S. (1989). A Scientific Methodology for MIS Case Studies. *MIS Quarterly*, 13(1), 33–50.

Lee, A. S. (1991). Integrating Positivist and Interpretive Approaches to Organizational Research. *Organization Science*, 2(4), 342–365.

Lehmann, S. & Buxmann, P. (2009). Preisstrategien von Softwareanbietern. *Wirtschaftsinformatik*, 51, 519–529.

Leimeister, S., Böhm, M., Riedl, C., & Krcmar, H. (2010). The Business Perspective of Cloud Computing: Actors, Roles and Value Networks. In *European Conference on Information Systems* Pretoria, South Africa.

Li, F. & Whalley, J. (2002). Deconstruction of the telecommunications industry: from value chains to value networks. *Telecommunications Policy*, 26(9–10), 451–472.

Liang-Jie, Z. & Jia, Z. (2009). Architecture-Driven Variation Analysis for Designing Cloud Applications. In *Cloud Computing, 2009. CLOUD '09. IEEE International Conference on* (pp. 125–134).

Lovelock, C. & Grummesson, E. (2004). Whither services marketing? In search of a new paradigm and fresh perspectives. *Journal of Service Research*, 7(1), 20–41.

Lundkvist, A. & Yakhlef, A. (2004). Customer involvement in new service development: a conversational approach. *Managing Service Quality*, 14(2/3), 249–257.

Luoma, E. & Rönkkö, M. (2012). Software-as-a-Service Business Models. *Communications of Cloud Software*, 1(1).

Ma, D. (2007). The Business Model of "Software-As-A-Service". In *Services Computing, 2007. SCC 2007. IEEE International Conference on* (pp. 701–702).

Ma, D. & Seidmann, A. (2008). The Pricing Strategy Analysis for the "Software-as-a-Service" Business Model. In J. Altmann, D. Neumann, & T. Fahringer (Eds.), *Grid Economics and Business Models*, Lecture Notes in Computer Science (pp. 103–112). Berlin, Heidelberg: Springer.

Magnusson, P. (2003). Benefits of involving users in service innovation. *European Journal of Innovation Management*, 6(4), 228–238.

Malone, T. W. (1988). *What is coordination theory?* MIT Sloan School of Management.

Malone, T. W. & Crowston, K. (1990). What is coordination theory and how can it help design cooperative work systems?

Malone, T. W. & Crowston, K. (1994). The Interdisciplinary Study of Coordination. *Computing Surveys*, 26(1), 87–119.

Manford, C. (2008). The Impact of SaaS model of Software Delivery. In *21st Annual Conference of the Natgional Advisory Committee on Computing Qualifications* (pp. 283–286). Auckland, New Zealand.

March, J. & Simon, H. (1958). *Organizations.* New York: John Wiley and Sons, Inc.

Markus, M. L. & Tanis, C. (2000). The enterprise systems experience-from adoption to success. In R. W. Zmud (Ed.), *Framing the Domains of IT Management: Projecting the Future Through the Past* (pp. 173–207). Pinnaflex Education Resources, Inc.

Mathiassen, L. & Vainio, A. M. (2007). Dynamic Capabilities in Small Software Firms: A Sense-and-Respond Approach. *Engineering Management, IEEE Transactions on*, 54(3), 522–538.

Mazzucco, M. & Dumas, M. (2011). Reserved or On-Demand Instances? A Revenue Maximization Model for Cloud Providers. In *Cloud Computing (CLOUD), 2011 IEEE International Conference on* (pp. 428–435).

Mazzucco, M., Dyachuk, D., & Deters, R. (2010). Maximizing cloud providers' revenues via energy aware allocation policies. In *Cloud Computing (CLOUD), 2010 IEEE 3rd International Conference on* (pp. 131–138).: IEEE.

Mertens, P. (2001). *Lexikon der Wirtschaftsinformatik*, volume 4. Berlin: Springer.

Mertens, P. (2007). *Integrierte Informationsverarbeitung 1 - Operative Systeme in der Industrie*, volume 16. Wiesbaden: Gabler.

Mertz, S., Eschinger, C., Eid, T., Pang, C., Swinehart, H., Dharmasthira, Y., Wurster, L., Ebina, T., & Nakao, A. (2012). Forecast: Software as a Service, All Regions, 2010-2015, 1H12 Update.

Merz, S., Eschinger, C., Eid, T., Pang, C., & Wurster, L. (2011). *Forecast: Software as a Service, Worldwide, 2010-2015, 1H11 Update*. Technical report, Gartner Research.

Messerschmitt, D. & Szyperski, C. (2003). *Software Ecosystem*. Cambridge: The MIT Press.

Meyer, K. & Van Hussen, C. (2008). Die ServCASE-Methode im Überblick. In K. Fähnrich & C. van Hussen (Eds.), *Entwicklung IT-basierter Dienstleistungen* (pp. 11–25). Heidelberg: Physica-Verlag.

Miles, M. & Hubermann, A. (1994). *Qualitative Data Analysis: An Expanded Sourcebook*, volume 2nd edition. Thousand Oaks, CA: Sage Publications.

Milliken, F. J. & Martins, L. L. (1996). Searching for Common Threads: Understanding the Multiple Effects of Diversity in Organizational Groups. *The Academy of Management Review*, 21(2), 402–433.

Millson, M. R. & Wilemon, D. (2002). The impact of organizational integration and product development proficiency on market success. *Industrial Marketing Management*, 31(1), 1–23.

Mingers, J. (2004). Real-izing Information Systems: Critical Realism as an Underpinning Philosophy for Information Systems. *Information & Organization*, 14(2), 87–103.

Mingers, J., Mutch, A., & Willcocks, L. (2011). Call for Papers, MIS Quarterly Special Issue on Critical Realism in Information Systems Research.

Mintzberg, H. (1983). *Structure in Fives: Designing Effective Organizations*. Englewood Cliffs, NJ: Prentice-Hall.

Mäkilä, T., Järvi, A., Rönkkö, M., & Nissilä, J. (2010). How to Define Software-as-a-Service – An Empirical Study of Finnish SaaS Providers. In P. Tyrväinen, S. Jansen, & M. A. Cusumano (Eds.), *Software Business*, Lecture Notes in Business Information Processing (pp. 115–124). Berlin, Heidelberg: Springer.

Mohammed, A. B., Altmann, J., & Hwang, J. (2010). Cloud Computing Value Chains: Understanding Businesses and Value Creation in the Cloud. In D. Neumann, M. Baker, J. Altmann, & O. Rana (Eds.), *Economic Models and Algorithms for Distributed Systems*, Autonomic Systems (pp. 187–208). Basel: Birkhäuser.

Morris, M., Schindehutte, M., & Allen, J. (2005). The entrepreneur's business model: Toward a unified perspective. *Journal of Business Research*, 58(6), 726–735.

Myers, M. (1997). Qualitative Research in Information Systems. *MIS Quarterly*, 21(2), 241–242.

Myers, M. (2009). *Qualitative Research in Business & Management*. London: Sage Publications.

Nambisan, S. & Wilemon, D. (2000). Software development and new product development: potentials for cross-domain knowledge sharing. *Engineering Management, IEEE Transactions on*, 47(2), 211–220.

National Institute of Standards a. Technology (2011). The NIST Definition of Cloud Computing.

NSF-IRIS (1989). *A report by the NSF-IRIS Review Panel for Research on Coordination Theory and Technology*. Technical report.

Ojala, A. & Tyrväinen, P. (2011). Value networks in cloud computing. *Journal of Business Strategy*, 32(6), 40–49.

Ojala, A. & Tyrväinen, P. (2012). Revenue models in cloud computing. In *Proceedings of 5th Computer Games, Multimedia & Allied Technology Conference (CGAT 2012)*: GSTF.

Okhuysen, G. & Bechky, B. (2009). Coordination in Organizations: An Integrated Perspective. *The Academy of Management Annals*, 3(1), 463–502.

Olsen, R. (2006). Transitioning to Software as a Service: Realigning software engineering practices with the new business model. In *IEEE International Conference on Service Operations and Logistics, and Informatics* (pp. 266–271). Shanghai, China: IEEE.

Orlikowski, W. J. & Baroudi, J. J. (1991). Studying Information Technology in Organizations: Research Approaches and Assumptions. *Information Systems Research*, 2(1), 1–28.

Osterwalder, A. (2004). *The Business Model Ontology: A proposition in a design science approach*. PhD thesis, Faculty of Business and Economics.

Osterwalder, A. & Pigneur, Y. (2010). *Business model generation: A handbook for visionaries, game changers, and challengers*. (self-published).

Osterwalder, A., Pigneur, Y., & Tucci, C. L. (2005). Clarifying business models: Origins, present, and future of the concept. *Communications of AIS*, 16(1), 1–25.

Pateli, A. G. & Giaglis, G. M. (2004). A research framework for analysing eBusiness models. *European Journal of Information Systems*, 13(4), 302–314.

Picot, A., Dietl, H., & Frank, E. (2002). *Organisation*, volume 3. Stuttgart: Schaffer -Poeschel Verlag.

Pinto, M. B. & Pinto, J. K. (1990). Project Team Communication and Cross-Functional Cooperation in New Program Development. *Journal of Product Innovation Management*, 7(3), 200–212.

Porter, M. (1985). *Competitive Advantage*. London: The Free Press.

Pueschel, T., Putzke, F., & Neumann, D. (2012). Revenue Management for Cloud Providers–A Policy-Based Approach under Stochastic Demand. In *System Science (HICSS), 2012 45th Hawaii International Conference on* (pp. 1583–1592).

Pugh, D. S., Hickson, D. J., Hinings, C. R., & Turner, C. (1968). Dimensions of Organization Structure. *Administrative Science Quarterly*, 13(1), 65–105.

Pussep, A., Schief, M., & Widjaja, T. (2012). The Software Value Chain: Methods for Construction and their Application. In *European Conference on Information Systems* Barcelona, Spain.

Pussep, A., Schief, M., Widjaja, T., Buxmann, P., & Wolf, C. M. (2011). The Software Value Chain as an Analytical Framework for the Software Industry and Its Exemplary Application for Vertical Integration Measurement. In *Americas Conference on Information Systems (AMCIS)* Detroit.

Ramaswamy, R. (1994). *Design and management of service processes: Leeping customers for Life*. Reading, MA, USA: AddisonWesley.

Ravishankar, M., Pan, S., & Leidner, D. (2011). Examining the Strategic Alignment and Implementation Success of a Kms: A Subculture-Based Multilevel Analysis. *Information Systems Research*, 22(1), 39–59.

Reavis Conner, K. & Rumelt, R. P. (1991). Software Piracy: An Analysis of Protection Strategies. *Management Science*, 37(2), 125–139.

Riedl, R. (2005). *Application Service Providing: Entwicklung eines Modells zur Qualitätsmessung*. Wiesbaden: Deutscher Universitäts-Verlag.

Ruhe, G. & Saliu, M. O. (2005). The art and science of software release planning. *Software, IEEE*, 22(6), 47–53.

Saaksjarvi, M., Lassila, A., & Nordstrom, H. (2005). Evaluating the software as a service business model: From CPU time-sharing to online innovation sharing. In P. K. Petro Isaisas & M. Mc-Pherson (Eds.), *IADIS International Conference e-Society 2005* (pp. 177–186). Qawra, Malta.

Saeed, M. & Jaffar-Ur-Rehmann, M. (2005). Enhancement of software engineering by shifting from software product to software service. In W. Khan & F. Ahmed (Eds.), *First International Conference on Information and Communication Technologies (ICICT)* (pp. 302–308). Karachi, Pakistan.

Sampson, S. (2001). *Understanding service businesses: Applying principles of the unified service theory*, volume 2. New York: John Wiley & Sons.

Sampson, S. & Froehle, C. M. (2006). Foundations and Implications of a Proposed Unified Service Theory. *Production and Operations Management*, 15(2), 329–343.

Sarker, S., Sarker, S., & Sahaym, A. (2012a). Exploring Value Co-creation in Relationships between an ERP Vendor and its Partners: A Revelatory Case Study. *MIS Quarterly*, 36(1), 317–338.

Sarker, S., Xiao, X., & Beaulieu, T. (2012b). Towards an Anatomy of "Successful" Qualitative Research Manuscripts in IS: A Critical Review and Some Recommendations. In *International Conference on Information Systems* Orlando, Florida.

Scandura, T. A. & Williams, E. A. (2000). Research Methodology in Management: Current Practices, Trends, and Implications for Future Research. *The Academy of Management Journal*, 43(6), 1248–1264.

Schilling, M. A. & Hill, C. W. L. (1998). Managing the New Product Development Process: Strategic Imperatives. *The Academy of Management Executive (1993-2005)*, 12(3), 67–81.

Sewook, W. (2011). Debunking Real-Time Pricing in Cloud Computing. In *Cluster, Cloud and Grid Computing (CCGrid), 2011 11th IEEE/ACM International Symposium on* (pp. 585–590).

Shafer, S. M., Smith, H. J., & Linder, J. C. (2005). The power of business models. *Business Horizons*, 48(3), 199–207.

Shapiro, C. & Varian, H. (1998). *Information rules: A strategic guide to the network economy*. Boston: Harvard Business School Press.

Simon, H. (1945). *Administrative behavior: A study of decision-making processes in administrative organizations*. Thousand Oaks, CA: Free Press.

Singh, M. (2008). U-SCRUM: An Agile Methodology For Promoting Usability. In *Agile 2008* (pp. 555–560).: IEEE.

Smith, M. (2006). Overcoming Theory-Practice Inconsistencies: Critical Realism and Information Systems Research. *Information & Organization*, 16(3), 191–211.

Sommerville, I. (2011). *Software Engineering*, volume 9. edition. Bosten, Munich: Pearson.

Song, M. & Montoya-Weiss, M. M. (2001). The Effect of Perceived Technological Uncertainty on Japanese New Product Development. *The Academy of Management Journal*, 44(1), 61–80.

Song, X. M., Montoya-Weiss, M. M., & Schmidt, J. B. (1997). Antecedents and Consequences of Cross-Functional Cooperation: A Comparison of R&D, Manufacturing, and Marketing Perspectives. *Journal of Product Innovation Management*, 14(1), 35–47.

Song, X. M., Neeley, S. M., & Zhao, Y. Z. (1996). Managing R&D - Marketing integration in the new product development process. *Industrial Marketing Management*, 25(6), 545–553.

Song, X. M., Xie, J., & Dyer, B. (2000). Antecedents and Consequences of Marketing Managers' Conflict-Handling Behaviors. *The Journal of Marketing*, 64(1), 50–66.

Stabell, C. B. & Fjeldstad, y. D. (1998). Configuring value for competitive advantage: on chains, shops, and networks. *Strategic Management Journal*, 19(5), 413–437.

Staudenmayer, N. (1997). *Interdependency: Conceptual, empirical, & practical issues.* Technical report, International Center for Research on Management of Technology, Sloan School of Management, Messachusetts Institute of Technology.

Stelzer, D. (2004). Production digitaler Güter. In A. Braßler & H. Corsten (Eds.), *Entwicklungen im Produktionsprozessmanagement* (pp. 233–250). München: Vahlen.

Stickel, E. (1997). *Gabler-Wirtschaftsinformatik-Lexikon.* Wiesbaden: Gabler.

Stone, E. (1978). *Research Methods in Organizational Behavior.* Santa Monica, CA: Goodyear Publishing Company Inc.

Straub, D., Boudreau, M., & Gefen, D. (2004). Validation guidelines for IS positivist research. *Communications of the Association for Information Systems*, 13(24), 380–427.

Strode, D., Huff, S., Hope, B., & Link, S. (2012). Coordination in co-located agile software development projects. *The Journal of Systems and Software*, 85(6), 1222–1238.

Stuckenberg, S. & Beiermeister, S. (2012). Software-as-a-Service Developement: Driving Forces of Process Change. In *Pacific Asia Conference on Information Systems* Ho Chi Minh City, Vietnam.

Stuckenberg, S., Fielt, E., & Loser, T. (2011). The Impact of Software-as-a-Service on Business Models of Leading Software Vendors: Experiences from three Explorative Case Studies. In *Pacific Asia Conference on Information Systems* Brisbane, Australia.

Stuckenberg, S. & Heinzl, A. (2010). The Impact of the Software-as-a-Service Concept on the Underlying Software and Service Development Processes. In *14th Pacific Asia Conference on Information Systems* (pp. 1297–1308). Taipei, Taiwan.

Stuckenberg, S., Kude, T., & Heinzl, A. (2014). Understanding the role of organizational integration in developing and operating Software-as-a-Service. *Journal of Business Economics*. Forthcoming.

Sun, W., Zhang, K., Chen, S.-K., Zhang, X., & Liang, H. (2007). Software as a Service: An Integration Perspective. In B. Krämer, K.-J. Lin, & P. Narasimhan (Eds.), *Service-Oriented Computing – ICSOC 2007*, volume 4749 of *Lecture Notes in Computer Science* (pp. 558–569). Berlin, Heidelberg: Springer.

Susarla, A., Barua, A., & Whinston, A. (2009). A transaction cost perspective of the "software as a service" business model. *Journal of Management Information Systems*, 26(2), 205–240.

Tamm, G. & Günther, O. (2005). *Webbasierte Dienste: Technologien, Märkte und Geschäftsmodelle*. Heidelberg: Physica-Verlag.

Teece, D. J. (2010). Business Models, Business Strategy and Innovation. *Long Range Planning*, 43(2-3), 172–194.

Thompson, J. (1967). *Organizations in Action*. New York: Mc Graw-Hill.

Tiwana, A. (2004). An empirical study of the effect of knowledge integration on software development performance. *Information and Software Technology*, 46(13), 899–906.

Troy, L., Hirunyawipada, T., & Paswan, A. (2008). Cross-Functional Integration and New Product Success: An Empirical Investigation of the Findings. *Journal of Marketing*, 72(6), 132–146.

Turner, M., Budgen, D., & Brereton, P. (2003). Turning software into a service. *Computer*, 36(10), 38–44.

Tyrväinen, P. & Selin, J. (2011). How to Sell SaaS: A Model for Main Factors of Marketing and Selling Software-as-a-Service. In B. Regnell, I. Weerd, & O. Troye (Eds.), *Software Business (ICSOB 2011)*, volume 80 of *Lecture Notes in Business Information Processing* (pp. 2–16). Brussels, Belgium: Springer-Verlag.

Urwick, L. (1963). Organization and coordination: Principles. In J. Litterer (Ed.), *Organizations. Structure and Behavior* (pp. 64–75). New York: Wiley.

Van de Ven, A., Delbecq, A., & Koenig, R. (1976). Determinants of coordination modes within organizations. *American Sociological Review*, 41, 322–338.

Vargo, S. L. & Lusch, R. F. (2004). The four service marketing myths: Remnants of a goods-based manufacturing model. *Journal of Service Research*, 6(4), 324.

Walsham, G. (1993). *Interpreting Information Systems in Organizations*. Chichester: Wiley.

Walsham, G. (1995). Interpretive case studies in IS research: nature and method. *European Journal of Information Systems*, 4, 74–81.

Walz, D., Elam, J., & Curtis, B. (1993). Inside a Software Design Team: Knowledge Acquisition, Sharing, and Integration. *Communication of the ACM*, 36(10), 63–77.

Weber, R. (2003). Editor's Comment: The Rhetoric of Positivism Versus Interpretivism: A Personal View. *MIS Quarterly*, 28(1), iii–xii.

Webster, J. & Watson, R. (2002). Analyzing the Past to Prepare for the Future: Writing a Literature Review. *MIS Quarterly*, 26(2), xiii–xxiii.

Weill, P. & Vitale, M. R. (2001). *Place to space: Migrating to eBusiness models*. Boston, MA: Harvard Business School Press.

Weinhardt, C., Anandasivam, A., Blau, B., Borissov, N., Meinl, T., Michalk, W., & Stößer, J. (2009). Cloud Computing – A Classification, Business Models, and Research Directions. *Business & Information Systems Engineering*, 1(5), 391–399.

Wemmerlöv, U. (1990). A taxonomy for service processes and its implications for system design. *International Journal of Service Industry Management*, 1(3), 13–27.

West, M., McNee, B., Geisehecker, L., Guptill, B., McNeill, R., & Burns, C. (2010). Key SaaS, PaaS and IaaS Trends Through 2015: Business Transformation via the Cloud.

Wu, W.-W., Lan, L. W., & Lee, Y.-T. (2011). Exploring decisive factors affecting an organization's SaaS adoption: A case study. *International Journal of Information Management*, 31(6), 556–563.

Wynn, D. & Williams, C. (2012). Principles for Conducting Critical Realist Case Study Research in Information Systems. *MIS Quarterly*, 36(3), 787–810.

Xin, M. & Levina, N. (2008). Software-as-a Service Model: Elaborating Client-Side Adoption Factors. In R. Boland, M. Limayem, & B. Pentland (Eds.), *29th International Conference on Information Systems* Paris, France.

Yang, H. & Tate, M. (2012). A Descriptive Literature Review and Classification of Cloud Computing Research. *Communications of the Association for Information Systems*, 31(2).

Yin, R. K. (2009). *Case Study Research - Design and Methods*. Thousand Oaks: Sage Publications.

Zeithaml, V. A., Parasuraman, A., & Berry, L. L. (1985). Problems and Strategies in Services Marketing. *The Journal of Marketing*, 49(2), 33–46.

Zheng, Z., Zhou, T. C., Lyu, M. R., & King, I. (2012). Component Ranking for Fault-Tolerant Cloud Applications. *Services Computing, IEEE Transactions on*, 5(4), 540–550.

Appendix

A. Interview guidelines

A.1. High Level Interview Guidelines of the First Phase

A Information regarding company and interview partner

1. Interviewee's position within organization, role regarding Software-as-a-Service development and operation, interviewee's experience

B Business models and value chain

1. **Value Proposition**: Which products and services does you company offer? Describe their value for your customers. How will Software-as-a-Service change the software industry?
2. **Customer Segments**: Who are your target customers (Company size, industry, IT department vs. business unit)?
3. **Channels**: How do you reach your customers? How do you generate leads?
4. **Customer Relationship**: How do you maintain your customer relationship? How do you build up these relationships?
5. **Revenue Stream**: How do you generate revenues?
6. **Key Activities / Resources**: What are your core competencies? Describe the value chain of your company and its activities?
7. **Key Partnerships**: Describe your companies relationship with partners. What is your task in the partner network? What are your targets? How does Software-as-a-Service change the partner network and its key stakeholders? What is the role of marketplaces in the Software-as-a-Service context?

A.2. High Level Interview Guidelines of the Second Phase

A Information regarding company and interview partner

1. Interviewee's position within organization, role regarding Software-as-a-Service development and operation, interviewee's experience

B Internal integration

1. Describe the development and operation processes of your Software-as-a-Service solution.
2. Are development and operations separated or integrated processes within your organization? What interfaces exist between the two areas?
3. Does Software-as-a-Service require special technologies? Do these technologies have an impact on the development and operation processes?

C External integration

1. Does Software-as-a-Service change the way customers are integrated / involved in the development and processes in general?
2. Does your organization create an advantage out of the direct customer relationship?
3. Does the changed customer relationship have implications on a process level?

ENTSCHEIDUNGSUNTERSTÜTZUNG FÜR ÖKONOMISCHE PROBLEME

Herausgegeben von Christian Becker, Wolfgang Gaul, Armin Heinzl, Alexander Mädche und Martin Schader

Band 1 Ingo Böckenholt: Mehrdimensionale Skalierung qualitativer Daten. Ein Instrument zur Unterstützung von Marketingentscheidungen. 1989.

Band 2 Jürgen Joseph: Arbeitswissenschaftliche Aspekte der betrieblichen Einführung neuer Technologien am Beispiel von Computer Aided Design (CAD). Felduntersuchung zur Ermittlung arbeitswissenschaftlicher Empfehlungen für die Einführung neuer Technologien. 1990.

Band 3 Eva Schönfelder: Entwicklung eines Verfahrens zur Bewertung von Schichtsystemen nach arbeitswissenschaftlichen Kriterien. 1992.

Band 4 Michael Bargl: Akzeptanz und Effizienz computergestützter Dispositionssysteme in der Transportwirtschaft. Empirische Studien zur Implementierungsforschung von Entscheidungsunterstützungssystemen am Beispiel computergestützter Tourenplanungssysteme. 1994.

Band 5 Reinhold Decker: Analyse und Simulation des Kaufverhaltens auf Konsumgütermärkten. Konzeption eines modell- und wissensorientierten Systems zur Auswertung von Paneldaten. 1994.

Band 6 Wolfgang Gaul / Martin Schader (Hrsg.): Wissensbasierte Marketing-Datenanalyse. Das WIMDAS-Projekt. 1994.

Band 7 Daniel Baier: Konzipierung und Realisierung einer Unterstützung des kombinierten Einsatzes von Methoden bei der Positionierungsanalyse. 1994.

Band 8 Ulrich Lutz: Preispolitik im internationalen Marketing und westeuropäische Integration. 1994.

Band 9 Kirsten Petersen: Design eines Courseware-Entwicklungssystems für den computerunterstützten universitären Unterricht. CULLIS-Teilprojekt I. 1996.

Band 10 Stefan Neumann: Einsatz von Interactive Video im computerunterstützten universitären Unterricht. CULLIS Teilprojekt II. 1996.

Band 11 Eberhard Aust: Simultane Conjointanalyse, Benefitsegmentierung, Produktlinien- und Preisgestaltung. 1996.

Band 12 Peter Heydebreck: Technologische Verflechtung. Ein Instrument zum Erreichen von Produkt- und Prozeßinnovationserfolg. 1996.

Band 13 Michael Pesch: Effiziente Verkaufsplanung im Investitionsgütermarketing. 1997.

Band 14 Frank Wartenberg: Entscheidungsunterstützung im persönlichen Verkauf. 1997.

Band 15 Thomas Lechler: Erfolgsfaktoren des Projektmanagements. 1997.

Band 16 Alexandre Saad: Anbahnung und Erfolg von europäischen kooperativen F&E-Projekten. Eine empirische Analyse anhand von ESPRIT-Projekten. 1998.

Band 17 Michael Löffler: Integrierte Preisoptimierung. 1999.

Band 18 Frank Säuberlich: KDD und Data Mining als Hilfsmittel zur Entscheidungsunterstützung. 2000.

INFORMATIONSTECHNOLOGIE UND ÖKONOMIE

(Neuer Reihentitel ab Band 19)

Band 19 Rainer Kiel: Dialog-gesteuerte Regelsysteme. Definition, Eigenschaften und Anwendungen. 2001.

Band 20 Axel Korthaus: Komponentenbasierte Entwicklung computergestützter betrieblicher Informationssysteme. 2001.

Band 21 Markus Aleksy: Entwicklung einer komponentenbasierten Architektur zur Implementierung paralleler Anwendungen mittels CORBA. Mit Beispielen aus den Wirtschaftswissenschaften. 2003.

Band 22 Michael Zapf: Flexible Kundeninteraktionsprozesse im Communication Center. 2003.

Band 23 Yvonne Staack: Kundenbindung im eBusiness. Eine kausalanalytische Untersuchung der Determinanten, Dimensionen und Verhaltenskonsequenzen der Kundenbindung im Online-Shopping und Online-Brokerage. 2004.

Band 24 Lars Schmidt-Thieme: Assoziationsregel-Algorithmen für Daten mit komplexer Struktur. Mit Anwendungen im Web Mining. 2003.

Band 25 Stefan Hocke: Flexibilitätsmanagement in der Logistik. Systemtheoretische Fundierung und Simulation logistischer Gestaltungsparameter. 2004.

Band 26 Viktor Jung: Markteintrittsgestaltung neugegründeter Unternehmen. Situationsspezifische und erfolgsbezogene Analyse. 2004.

Band 27 Lars Brehm: Postimplementierungsphase von ERP-Systemen in Unternehmen. Organisatorische Gestaltung und kritische Erfolgsfaktoren. 2004.

Band 28 Ralf Gitzel: Model-Driven Software Development Using a Metamodel-Based Extension Mechanism for UML. 2006.

Band 29 Bernd Stauß: Optimale Gestaltung von Auswahlmenüs und deren Verwendung im Variantenmanagement. 2006.

Band 30 Nils Schumacher: EDI via XML. Potentiale und Strategien für global orientierte kleine und mittlere Unternehmen. 2007.

Band 31 Christian Cuske: Quantifizierung operationeller Technologierisiken bei Kreditinstituten. Eine Ontologie-zentrierte Vorgehensweise im Spannungsfeld bankinterner und aufsichtsrechtlicher Sichtweise. 2007.

Band 32 Matthias Merz: Konzeptioneller Entwurf und prototypische Implementierung einer Sicherheitsarchitektur für die Java Data Objects-Spezifikation. 2008.

Band 33 Tobias Hildenbrand: Improving Traceability in Distributed Collaborative Software Development. A Design Science Approach. 2008.

Band 34 Karen H. L. Tso-Sutter: Towards Metadata-Aware Algorithms for Recommender Systems. 2010.

Band 35 Thomas Schoberth: Eine Längsschnittstudie der Kommunikationsaktivität in virtuellen Gemeinschaften. 2010.

Band 36 Nima Mazloumi: Entwurf eines Referenzmodells und Frameworks zur Erstellung hybrider Lehr- und Lernszenarien. Mit Fallbeispielen aus der Betriebswirtschaftslehre und der Wirtschaftsinformatik. 2010.

Band 37 Anja Zöller: Effizienzanalyse grundlegender Gestaltungsgrößen der OP-Organisation. 2010.

Band 38 Jessica Katharina Winkler: International Entry Mode Choices of Software Firms. An Analysis of Product-Specific Determinants. 2009.

Band 39 Martin J. Lafleur: *Loyalty Profiling*. Erfolgsdimensionen und Modellansätze eines effizienten und effektiven Customer Relationship Management. 2010.

Band 40 Ingo Ott: Effizientes Prozessmanagement im öffentlichen Dienst. 2010.

Band 41 Stefan Seedorf: Ontologie-gestützte Entwicklung komponentenbasierter Anwendungssysteme. Ein wissensbasiertes Informationssystem zur Unterstützung der Entwicklung und Wartung von Geschäftskomponenten (KompIS). 2010.

Band 42 Dominic Gastes: Erhebungsprozesse und Konsistenzanforderungen im Analytic Hierarchy Process (AHP). 2011.

Band 43 *erscheint in Kürze*

Band 44 Olaf Thiele: Informationsvisualisierungen auf mobilen Endgeräten zur Unterstützung des betrieblichen Datenmanagements. 2011.

Band 45 Krisztian Antal Buza: Fusion Methods for Time-Series Classification. 2011.

Band 46 Thomas Kude: The Coordination of Inter-Organizational Networks in the Enterprise Software Industry. The Perspective of Complementors. 2012.

Band 47 Alexandra Rebecca Klages: Clusteranalyse für Netzwerke. 2012.

Band 48 Christian Thum: Enabling Lightweight Real-time Collaboration. 2012.

Band 49 Miroslav Lazic: The Impact of Information Technology Governance on Business Performance. 2013.

Band 50 Verena Elisabeth Majuntke: Application Coordination in Pervasive Systems. 2013.

Band 51 Lars Klimpke: Konzeption und Realisierung eines integrierten Mikroblog-basierten Kommunikationsansatzes für die verteilte Softwareentwicklung. 2013.

Band 52 Erik Hemmer: Information Seeking Stopping Behavior in Online Scenarios. The Impact of Task, Technology and Individual Characteristics. 2013.

Band 53 Christoph Winkler: Optimierung im Airline Revenue Management. 2013.

Band 54 Sven Scheibmayr: Graphical User Interface Prototyping for Distributed Requirements Engineering. 2014.

Band 55 Sebastian Stuckenberg: Exploring the Organizational Impact of Software-as-a-Service on Software Vendors. The Role of Organizational Integration in Software-as-a-Service Development and Operation. 2014.

www.peterlang.com

Zeitfracht Medien GmbH
Ferdinand-Jühlke-Straße 7
99095 Erfurt, Deutschland
produktsicherheit@kolibri360.de